Power and Education

Power and Education

Contexts of Oppression and Opportunity

Edited by

Antonia Kupfer

First published 2015 by
PALGRAVE MACMILLAN.

Palgrave Macmillan in the UK is an imprint of Macmillan Publishers Limited,
registered in England, company number 785998, of Houndmills, Basingstoke,
Hampshire RG21 6XS.

Palgrave Macmillan in the US is a division of St Martin's Press LLC,
175 Fifth Avenue, New York, NY 10010.

Palgrave Macmillan is the global academic imprint of the above companies
and has companies and representatives throughout the world.

Palgrave® and Macmillan® are registered trademarks in the United States,
the United Kingdom, Europe and other countries.

ISBN: 978–1–137–41534–9

This book is printed on paper suitable for recycling and made from fully
managed and sustained forest sources. Logging, pulping and manufacturing
processes are expected to conform to the environmental regulations
of the country of origin.

A catalogue record for this book is available from the British Library.

Library of Congress Cataloging-in-Publication Data
    Power and education : contexts of oppression and opportunity / edited by
Antonia Kupfer, Professor of Macrosociology, Technical University of Dresden,
Germany.
        pages cm
    Includes bibliographical references.
    ISBN 978–1–137–41534–9
    1. Educational sociology. 2. Power (Social sciences) 3. Knowledge, Theory of.
I. Kupfer, Antonia, editor of compilation.
LC191.P658 2015
306.43—dc23   2015021448

Contents

Notes on Contributors   vii

Introduction   1
Antonia Kupfer

Part I   Theories

1   Arendt, Power and Education   13
    Wayne Veck

2   Symbolic Violence: Education as Concealed Power   26
    Antonia Kupfer

3   Gramsci, Education and Power   41
    Peter Mayo

Part II   Knowledge

4   Programming Power: Policy Networks and the Pedagogies
    of 'Learning to Code'   61
    Ben Williamson

5   Researching Power and the Power in Research   88
    Naomi Hodgson

Part III   Social Inequality

6   Gender, Power and Education   111
    Gabrielle Ivinson

7   UK Secondary Schools Under Surveillance: What are the
    Implications for Race? A Critical Race and Butlerian
    Analysis   128
    Charlotte Chadderton

8   Naming and Blaming Early School Leavers: An Analysis of
    Education Policies, Discourses and Practices in Spain   146
    Aina Tarabini

Part IV   Empowerment

9   21st Century Emancipation: Pedagogies in and from
    the Margins   169
    Sara C. Motta

10 Power and Education in the Bolivarian Republic of
    Venezuela   194
    Mike Cole

Index   215

Notes on Contributors

Charlotte Chadderton is Senior Research Fellow at the Cass School of Education and Communities, University of East London, UK. Chadderton's main area of expertise is social justice and inequalities in education, with a particular focus on race equality. She also investigates poststructural theories in education, public pedagogies and securitisation and militarisation of education.

Mike Cole is Professor of Education at the University of East London and Emeritus Research Professor of Education and Equality at Bishop Grosseteste University, UK. His research priority is the relationship between critical race theory and Marxism within educational theory.

Naomi Hodgson is Visiting Research Fellow at the Centre for Philosophy, Institute of Education, University College London, UK and the Laboratory for Education and Society, KU Leuven, Belgium. Her research focus is on education, political philosophy and higher education. Hodgson supervises MA students as Visiting Lecturer in Education at Leeds Trinity University, UK.

Gabrielle Ivinson is Professor of Education at the University of Aberdeen, UK. Her special interest is in how children and young people learn in and outside schools. Inspired by Basil Bernstein, she works in the sociology of pedagogy. Ivinson is co-editor of *Gender and Education*.

Antonia Kupfer is Professor of Macrosociology at the Technical University of Dresden, Germany. Her research focuses on globalisation and changes in labour and education out of a perspective of inequality and on low wage workers in a comparative perspective.

Peter Mayo is Professor of Education Studies at the University of Malta. He is a member of the Collegio Docenti for the doctoral research programme in Educational Sciences and Continuing Education at the Università degli Studi di Verona, Italy. He researches issues of educational sociology, adult education and comparative education, as well as social theory, critical pedagogy and cultural studies.

Sara C. Motta is Senior Lecturer in Politics at Newcastle Business School, Australia. Her scholarly practice transgresses borders – epistemological, social and spatial – as a means to co-construct with communities in struggle a critical political science practice for and of the subaltern. She has published widely in international journals including *Political Studies* and *Latin American Perspectives,* and produced a number of books including (co-edited with Mike Cole, forthcoming) *Education and Social Change in Latin America* (Palgrave Macmillan).

Aina Tarabini is Senior Lecturer at the University of Barcelona, Spain. She analyses the impact of globalisation on the political and educational system, researching the processes of re-contextualisation of global agendas and national policies at the school level. She investigates the relationship between education policies and poverty.

Wayne Veck is Senior Lecturer in Education at the University of Winchester, UK with the focus on education, health and social care. His research explores inclusive education, disability studies, values in education and research and the philosophy of education.

Ben Williamson is Lecturer in the Initial Teacher Education Programme at the University of Stirling, UK. His research examines education policy and curriculum change. Previously, he has been a researcher at Futurelab, a nonprofit educational organisation which explored the role of digital media and technology in education.

Introduction

Antonia Kupfer

Power has numerous, diverse, even opposing meanings. Classical approaches, such as Max Weber's, define it as coercion; that is, the imposition of one person's will over another's. In contrast, Hannah Arendt saw power as the ability to act. The meaning of education is similarly contested, comprehending knowledge acquisition, emancipation and liberation on the one hand and estrangement, obedience and suppression on the other. As a consequence, the study of the interrelationships between these processes must draw on different accounts of, and perspectives on, a variety of concepts and analyses. Nevertheless, all the analyses of concepts of power in this volume try to avoid the simple, uncritical notion of legitimate leadership directed toward 'best practices'. The authors propose a counterweight to mainstream education studies on school effectiveness, comparisons of attainment and performance, and institutional leadership. They cover both the broad critical spectrum and the contradictory empirical findings to start a debate on how power over education and power in education affect today's societies.

This introduction provides first an overview of the research literature on power and education followed by an outline of the new research presented in this anthology.

Earlier studies on power and education

Studies explicitly analysing power in relation to education can be classified under four themes: knowledge, social inequality, empowerment, and policy. More generally, in the classic *Schooling in Capitalist America* (1976), Bowles and Gintis assert a correspondence between the economic system and the way schools are organised and hierarchised to serve as feeders for the labour market. Another classical work at the opposite pole from this Marxist view is Freire's *Pedagogy of the Oppressed* (1973), which conceives education as a possibility for liberation. It criticises 'banking' forms of education as oppressive in providing fixed content, and suggests replacing them with dialogues through which learners can decide what and how to learn. This volume presents and discusses three other classic theoretical works on the relationship between power and education by 1) Bourdieu/Passeron, 2) Gramsci and 3) Foucault (see Ball [2013] for an introduction to Foucault's work on power and education).

In the area of knowledge, Young's anthology *Knowledge and Control* (1971) initiated a major debate on 'what counts as educational knowledge' and how it is created, shifting the focus of analysis towards the social organisation of knowledge. Young aimed to establish a new sociology of education that would explore how and why teachers and pupils' statements persistently reflect dominant categories, and how those categories might be connected to the interests of influential groups, such as professional associations. Later, he began to enquire how knowledge could be differentiated as weak or powerful in terms of enabling people to participate in society, which he considers crucial for social justice. The way knowledge is created remains the determining factor, and he suggests that knowledge created within disciplines and by experts is more reliable, hence powerful, than other knowledge (Young 2008, 2014).

The anthology *Power and Ideology in Education* (1977) edited by Karabel and Halsey contains a contribution to the new sociological debate on knowledge transmission as cultural reproduction and as the mainstay of social hierarchies. Bernstein and Bourdieu address the power structures of societies and define the processes that affect what counts as knowledge, as well as who has access to it and how it is measured and certified.

In *Education and Power* (1982) Apple emphasises contradictions in the relationship. He examines the curriculum and the increasingly right-wing state influence that enforces a policy of commodification in education. Despite deteriorating economic and political conditions, however, he conceives education as an area of liberation, and stresses that neither the concept nor its actors are purely subordinate to any powerful structures or agents.

Shrinking social policies, declining wages and worsening employment conditions have characterised many northwestern countries since the 1980s. Neoliberal discourses came to dominate the universities and changed the subjects and conditions of research, which probably explains why, for a rather long time, the link between power and education has been exempt from critical analysis. Only in 2012 did Moore et al.'s anthology *Knowledge, Power and Educational Reform* pick up the discussion of the 1970s, focusing on Bernstein applying his view to analyse knowledge structures, knowledge, identity and voice, and pedagogy.

The second major area of research on the relationship between power and education focuses on social inequality, which is the major focus of the sociology of education. What is the relationship between social inequality and power? If power is seen as an instrument to secure privileges, and privileges are inextricably bound to inequitable contexts, then power and social inequality go hand-in-hand. Power is used to maintain social inequality, and socially unequal people have unequal range of, and access to power. Without going into the vast literature on social inequality and education, I will focus on studies that explicitly include power in their analysis. In *Culture and Power in the Classroom* (1991) Darder analyses the content of teaching that further marginalises social groups, such as Blacks and Latinos, who are already discriminated against, and the impact of this teaching content on the dominant culture. Focusing on bicultural education from a Freirean perspective, Darder proposes ways for teachers to act as 'transformative intellectuals' rather than imposing knowledge on pupils. Rosen and Farrokhzad pick up on this idea in their 2008 anthology on power, culture and education, applying a predominantly educationalist perspective, and focusing on pedagogy rather than sociology, to demonstrate how non-German citizens experience oppression in educational settings.

In the third area, empowerment, Bishop and Glynn demonstrate in *Culture Counts* (1999) that education *can* offer indigenous people possibilities. Their assertion is based on an analysis of Maoris' responses to dominant educational discourses in New Zealand. In the anthology *Popular Education, Power and Democracy* (2013), Laginder et al. see popular education as the achievement of social movements that work to create a form of education that is not only widely accessible but also serves the needs and interests of the people; both factors in promoting democracy and power sharing. The authors also analyse the power structures within popular education.

Closely related to empowerment is critical pedagogy, which can be seen as a form of resistance. In *Power, Crisis, and Education for Liberation* (2008), De Lissovoy builds on Freire and Fanon to propose new, oppositional subjects in education and society and outlines a concept of cultural hybridity organised against capital as an encompassing global logic.

Studies on policies also address power in relation to education. In *Power and Politics. Federal Higher Education Policy Making in the 1990s* (1997), Parsons looks at the power wielded by actors in US federal higher education policy in addressing problems based on societal structures and institutions. The analysis includes personal and social relationships in communities and the beliefs and values that guide policy actors' decisions.

Teacher education is closely connected to state-education policies. Popkewitz edited *Changing Patterns of Power: Social Regulation and Teacher Education Reform* (1993), which compares teacher education policies in eight countries. A study by Youdell (2009) examines school policies, and in the anthology edited by Stensaker and Harvey (2011), the authors focus on the massive recent changes in higher education, including increased accountability due to decreased public funding, which has forced universities to seek support elsewhere.

Last, but not least, power plays a huge role in the policies of the World Trade Organisation, and on the General Agreement on Trade in Services (GATS), which views education as a service. Robertson et al. (2002) note that as clearly identifiable actors with an increasingly globalised outlook created GATS policy, this might move education to the forefront of national political battles. Venger (2007) aims to shed light on some of the mechanisms of what he calls a black box: the process of establishing a global trade regime in education. Cossa (2008) focuses on the power dynamics in GATS negotiations between international regimes and local governments in southern Africa.

In concluding this brief overview of previous studies of power and education, I want to raise questions about the research gaps to which the studies in this anthology, to some degree, respond. Prior accounts of knowledge in relation to power started from the revelations that knowledge is socially constructed, and powerful people use it to influence others. Current studies hold that different types of knowledge are valuable in different contexts. However, the status of criteria to judge the quality of knowledge will always be disputed. Nevertheless, we can not avoid making judgements to the knowledge to be passed on to the next generation.

In the area of social inequality and power, studies so far have not drawn a clear distinction between the two. The socially privileged and the powerful are closely linked, but social inequality depends on power structures, which suggests that they differ. Here, Bourdieu and Passeron's account of symbolic violence as a hidden power that acts and influences through education, which is explained in the second chapter, is illuminating.

Earlier studies on empowerment showed that education could lead to emancipation and was not simply a means or a vehicle of oppression. However, they did not discuss how far that empowerment could go and how sustainable it might be. Does education enable only moments of realisation or a long-standing transformation? In this volume Cole's outline of the Bolivarian Revolution in Venezuela, which put educational change at the forefront, offers an insight into a societal change that goes beyond individual moments of empowerment.

Another question is prompted by the policy debate on the extent to which the state control of education is limited by emerging international organisations: Should education be subject to policy at all, or should it function autonomously according to its own intrinsic, logic? This debate often takes place in the context of creating universities, and Hodgson demonstrates in her chapter how current policies scale down researchers' autonomy, increasingly changing knowledge into a commodity.

The current chapters

The first part of the volume comprises three chapters on theory. The first two mark the range of discourse on the relationship between power and education. At one pole stands Hannah Arendt's enthusiastic view of education as a second 'birth' urging people to appear, to relate to each other and to become powerful. At the other pole Bourdieu and Passeron argue that education is a concealed power that dominates people and maintains social hierarchies. The third chapter offers an intermediate view: Gramsci's conceptualisation of education as both a part of state hegemony and a possibility for social transformation, if workers and intellectuals become conscious and develop counter discourses.

In the first chapter, Wayne Veck offers insights into Hannah Arendt's little-known work in the area of education. Her famous distinction between power and violence informs her positive view. According to Arendt, power should not be mistaken for the violence that leads to suppression but stems from a union that enables people to act. Education leads to empowerment by preparing people to see the potential of human power. What makes Arendt's account so attractive and cheerful, alongside her optimistic view on education, is her poetic language: by *natality* she means that each child's birth brings potential renewal, or an actualisation of power to sustain a plural world.

In the second chapter, the tone changes completely, and the relationship between power and education weighs heavily. Antonia Kupfer reconstructs an early text on symbolic violence by Pierre Bourdieu and Jean-Claude Passeron, the seed of Bourdieu's examination and theorisation of power as concealed domination. He sees education as *the* social arena in which content is transmitted in a way that conceals its proximity to the privileged, the upper classes; the universal tacit acceptance of both form and content serving to maintain social hierarchies.

In the third chapter, Peter Mayo demonstrates that education can be both oppressive and empowering. He explains the two sides of Antonio Gramsci's concept of power: force and consent. Further, in Gramsci's concept of hegemony, the two always go together; no apparatus is *completely* repressive or *completely* ideological. Hegemony is seen as a dynamic process, with a force that is conditional rather than determined. Gramsci does not limit education to schools; he sees factory councils as educational agencies and explains how education can transform societies through workers' broader knowledge of production processes.

The second part of this volume explores knowledge in relation to power. Ben Williamson's chapter discusses the power of the software being used in schools as part of the newly introduced subject *learning to code* in the UK National Curriculum. He reveals how its pedagogies convey to young people a certain way of seeing, thinking and acting, using specific, not neutral content. In a short period, this new subject made its way from a grass-roots initiative into curricular policy, although Williamson illustrates how its original supporters have not formed a stable, coherent network; on the contrary, as learning to code is the product of a messy hybrid of intentions, ambitions and interests.

The fifth chapter by Naomi Hodgson focuses on research, the key to production of new knowledge. By applying the view of Michel Foucault, Hodgson shifts the perspective from conceptualising power as domination and suppression or liberation to understanding how it works and what it produces. In the so-called knowledge economy created by national and European policymakers, knowledge is constructed as a vital resource for competition, and research responds and adapts to present needs, producing short-term, measurable outputs. Hodgson's analysis demonstrates that the processes of power, or what Foucault calls *governmentality,* prevent education in the sense of *educere,* to draw out knowledge, an indeterminate, critical and potentially transformative process, but instead to education as imparting expertise to deliver fixed results.

The chapters in the third part of the anthology deal with power and education in relation to social inequality. Gabrielle Ivinson focuses on gender by illustrating, with examples from her own empirical research, how schools perpetuate a hierarchical valuing of men and women despite the abolition of formal barriers for women after long, hard political fights. Ivinson detects a 'ghosting of gender' in such educational institutions as science labs and theorises power with the help of Deleuze and Guattari's notion of territorialisation by invisible forces. Boys and girls are still treated differently in classrooms according to their prescribed gender roles, and how power in schools conveys and maintains social gender hierarchies becomes quite clear.

In the seventh chapter, Charlotte Chadderton analyses the effects of school surveillance mainly through CCTV cameras on pupils of different ethnic backgrounds. Since the 'war on terrorism', schools have invested huge sums in new surveillance technologies. While empirical data proving that surveillance prevents crime is lacking, there is evidence to support the fact that surveillance changes the behaviour of people who feel they are being observed. Chadderton argues that surveillance practices 'recognizing' Muslim, Arab or Middle Eastern pupils as non-citizens reinforce the ethnic dynamics in schools. This process can be interpreted as a shift from the more decentralised powers of governmentality towards the more overt power of sovereignty, which can suspend existing laws.

In the eighth chapter, Aina Tarabini analyses the power of teachers and other school staff to define reasons for the phenomenon of early school leavers, who constitute almost 25 percent of the population of 18–24 year olds in Spain. Her research found that the three reasons cited are not 'neutral' but packed with class and culturally-biased concepts of 'good' and 'bad' pupils and students. 'Lack of commitment' is premised on an individual's free choice rather than social, economic or individual school circumstances; 'family deficit' faults working-class families without considering the resources required for proper participation in schools; and finally a pathologisation of early school leavers is based on ideas of 'normality'.

The fourth part of this volume is dedicated to the area of empowerment, but in contrast to Arendt's universal concept of education enabling human power, the authors demonstrate clearly that this effect depends largely on social conditions. Sara C. Motta argues that pedagogical practices are central to emancipation; by unlearning the dominant social relationships, we may build a counter-hegemonic knowledge. She cites two examples – a landless rural workers' movement in Brazil that became one of the country's largest social movements and a feminist theatre collective in Colombia – to demonstrate how political and pedagogical practices can question and replace traditional suppressive forms of colonial and patriarchal power, and remove their universally accepted superiority.

Mike Cole's tenth and final chapter ties into and expands Motta's findings by pointing to the Bolivarian Revolution in Venezuela. He claims it as an example of societal change in which a specific form of education shook off neoliberal ideas and enabled the masses to participate in political decisions and thus power, creating a much more democratic society.

As a whole, this collection equips us with theoretical perspectives and empirical analytical practices that will enable social scientists and educationists to question policies, to reveal the structures and social conditions that maintain hierarchies throughout and within education, and to name the conditions under which educational processes may lead to emancipation.

References

Apple, M. (1995) [1982] *Education and Power*. Boston, London: Ark Paperbacks.

Ball, S. J.(2013) *Foucault, Power, and Education*. New York, London: Routledge.

Bishop, R.; Glynn, T. (2003) [1999] *Culture Counts. Changing Power Relations in Education*. Palmerston North: Dumore Press.

Bowles, S.; Gintis, H. (1976) *Schooling in Capitalist America*. London: Routledge and Kegan Paul.

Cossa, J. A. (2008) *Power, Politics, and Higher Education in Southern Africa*. International Regimes, Local Governments, and Educational Autonomy, Amherst, New York: Cambria Press.

Darder, A. (1991) *Culture and Power in the Classroom. A Critical Foundation for Bicultural Education* Westport: Greenwood Publisher.

De Lissovoy, N. (2008) *Power, Crisis, and Education for Liberation. Rethinking Critical Pedagogy*. Basingstoke, Palgrave Macmillan.

Freire, P. (1973) *Pedagogy of the Oppressed*. New York: Seabury.

Karabel, J. Halsey, A. H. (eds) (1977) *Power and Ideology in Education*. New York: Oxford University Press.

Laginder, A.-M. et al. (eds) (2013) *Popular Education, Power and Democracy. Swedish Experiences and Contributions*. Leicester: National Institute of Adult Continuing Education.

Moore, R. et al. (2012) *Knowledge, Power and Educational Reform: Applying the Sociology of Basil Bernstein*. Oxon: Routledge.

Parsons, M. D. (1997) *Power and Politics. Federal Higher Education Policy Making in the 1990s*. Albany: State University of New York Press.

Popkewitz, T. S. (ed.) (1993) *Changing Patterns of Power: Social Regulation and Teacher Education Reform*. New York, State University of New York.

Robertson, S. et al. (2002) 'GATS and the Education Service Industry: The Politics of Scale and Global Reterritorilization', *Comparative Education Review*, 46(4), 472–496.

Rosen, L.; Farrokhzad, S. (eds) (2008) *Macht – Kultur – Bildung*. Festschrift für Georg Auernheimer, Münster: Waxmann.

Stensaker, B.; Harvey, L. (eds) (2011) *Accountability in Higher Education. Global Perspectives on Trust and Power*. New York and London: Routledge.

Venger, A. (2007) 'The constitution of a new global regime: higher education in the GATS/WTO framework', in: D. Epstein et al. (eds) *World Yearbook of Education 2008, Geographies of Knowledge, Geometries of Power: Framing the Future of Higher Education*, New York and London: Routledge, pp. 111–127.

Youdell, D. (2009) *School Trouble: Identity, Power and Politics in Education*. Oxon: Routledge.

Young, M. F .D. (ed.) (1971) *Knowledge and Control. New Directions for the Sociology of Education*. London: Collier-Macmillan.

Young, M. F. D. (2008) *Bringing Knowledge Back In: From Social Constructivism to Social Realism in the Sociology of Education*. London: Routledge.

Young, M. F. D. (2014) 'Powerful knowledge as a curriculum principle', in Young, M. and Lambert, D. (eds) *Knowledge and the Future School. Curriculum and Social Justice*, London: Bloomsbury, pp. 65–88.

Part I
Theories

1
Arendt, Power and Education
Wayne Veck

Introduction

In an interview with the novelist, Gunter Grass, in 1964, Hannah Arendt responded to a question prompting her recollections of being a child in a Jewish family in Germany at the beginning of the twentieth century with the following words:

> You see, all Jewish children encountered anti-Semitism. And the souls of many children were poisoned by it. The difference with me lay in the fact that my mother always insisted that I not humble myself. One must defend oneself! When my teachers made anti-Semitic remarks – usually they were not directed at me but at my other classmates, particularly at the Eastern Jewessess – I was instructed to stand up immediately, to leave the class, go home, and leave the rest to school protocol. My mother would have written one of her many letters, and, with that, my involvement in the matter ended completely. I had a day off from school, and that was, of course, very nice. But if the remarks came at me from other children, I was not allowed to go home and tell. That did not count. One had to defend *oneself* against remarks from other children. (Original emphasis, Arendt cited in Young-Bruehl, 2004, pp. 11–12)

How might we begin to think about a school where hostility and cruelty are not only exchanged between the young but are given a voice by adults as they address children? What sort of questions might we venture to ask about these anti-Semitic teachers, the school they taught in and the society they lived in? We could immediately ask questions about how power operated in and upon this school.

It is possible to think of schools as sites where we cannot avoid observing power at work (see, for example, Giroux, 1992; and Apple, 1993), as *fields* where force or violence (symbolic or otherwise) are present and where social and actual capital are reproduced (see Bourdieu & Wacquant, 1992; Thomson & Holdsworth, 2003; Gibbs & Garnett, 2007; Mills, 2008; Azaola, 2012), and as organisations where identities are governed, created and conducted in and through disciplinary practices (see Foucault, 1977; 1982; 2003). But this chapter attempts to advance an account of the relation between power and education that is quite distinct from those accounts offered by critical theorists, Bourdieu, Foucault and the multitude of educationalists they have influenced. Indeed, this account rejects entirely the idea that what Arendt experienced as a young student might in any way be illuminated by thinking of the school as either an object or a site of power. Divided into three sections, the chapter considers Arendt's insights into education, power and political life to distinguish the many ways educational practices descend into forms of violence from the kind of education that might prepare young people for what Arendt (1998, p. 241) names 'the potentialities of human power'. The first section engages with this distinction between power and violence in relation to Arendt's (1993a) concept of natality, the fact that each child by virtue of being born has the potential to sustain and renew a world that is already established. In the second section, Arendt's view of authority in education is examined in relation to violence and power. The final section considers the connections Arendt illuminates between power, plurality and consent, to advance a view of education as a site where young people are *prepared* to act with others and thus to actualise power in a plural world.

Power, violence and natality

The English political theorist, Thomas Hobbes, famously contended that 'during the time men live without a common Power to keep them all in awe, they are in that condition which is called Warre; and such a warre as is of every man against every man'(1985, p. 185). In this condition, Hobbes (1985, p. 189) insisted, each individual will 'use his own power, as he will himself for the preservation of his own Nature'. Two aspects of power are assumed here. First, there is the idea that power can be amassed, owned and used by rulers to subdue their subjects. Second, power is presented as a resource that individuals can call upon whenever they are in peril. The concept of power advanced by Arendt suggests that Hobbes was wrong on both accounts. In the first, he has failed to distinguish power from violence and in the second, power from individual strength. So while Hobbes's account of sovereign rule and its degradation into a war of all against all might have much to tell us about how violence acts on and through individuals, it can, from Arendt's perspective, tell us nothing whatsoever about power.

Let us consider Arendt's distinctions in detail. First and foremost, power, unlike violence, which always relies on tools and implements to undo what has been established, and unlike 'strength, which is the gift and the possession of every man in his isolation against all other men' (Arendt, 2006a, p. 166), depends only upon the existence of plurality of men and women. Indeed, Arendt (1998, p. 200) insists that power 'exists only in its actualization' and that it is actualised only where men and women act and speak to each other and witness words and deeds, only, that is, in the *public realm* (Arendt, 1969; 1970). In fact, it is Arendt's view that power not only arises in the public realm but serves also to generate and sustain it (Allen, 2002; Gordon, 2001; Parekh, 1981; Penta, 1996). This is significant, for where violence effectively destroys, power is essentially creative (Arendt, 1946; 1969; 1970; 2006a). Arendt evokes the image of a table to illustrate the plurality that characterises the public realm or the polis, which 'is not the city-state in its physical location' but is rather 'the organisation of people as it arises out of acting and speaking, and its true space lies between people living together for this purpose, no matter where they happen to be' (Arendt, 1998, p. 198). The table is an equally apt image for Arendt's concept of power. As people gathered around a table share a space with others but retain a distinct place within it, so in the *polis* persons are united by a power that 'relates and separates men at the same time' (Arendt, 1998, p. 52). Wherever 'people are with others and neither for nor against them – that is, in sheer human togetherness' (Arendt, 1998, p. 180), it is power that sustains the distance between them and it is power, at the same time, that ensures they act together in and for a 'common world' (Arendt, 1993a; 1998). When we are for ourselves and for those people we identify as being of our kind and against those we designate Other, our relationship to our fellows is characterised by force or violence. When we are *with* others, in the absence of all fear of falling behind and all zeal for getting ahead of them, power, in Arendt's (1970, p. 52) phrase 'springs up'.

It is precisely because she conceived the public realm as the space where persons are 'oriented to reaching agreement and not primary to their respective individual successes', that Habermas (1977, p. 6) is able to write:

Hannah Arendt disconnects the concept of power from the teleological model; power is built up in communicative action; it is a collective effect of speech in which reaching agreement is an end in itself
for all those involved.

But if power is its own end, education, for Arendt (1993a), *is* teleological. Education aims at preparing the young for their contribution to the
renewal of the world that is common to all. Immediately, this significant
distinction requires us to think carefully about how schools, far from
being sites where power relations play out, might prepare the young for
participating with others in power. One way of making sense of this idea
of the school as a place of preparation *for* power is offered by Arendt in
the form of her concept of natality.

Arendt locates education between two births. Beyond our initial,
natural birth there is our first contribution to the world we share with
others, a contribution that is, in Arendt's (1998, p. 176) words, 'like a
second birth'. Poised between these two births, the young turn restlessly
to the adults before them, since, like 'everything that is alive', they have
'an *urge to appear*' (original emphasis, Arendt, 1971a, p. 29). However,
it is the educator's role, in Arendt's (1993a) view, to form a bridge that
simultaneously guides young persons to and distances them from that
realm of appearances itself, that is, for Arendt, the common world.
An education that guides young people from their first birth to their
appearance in the public realm is one that prepares them, at the same
time, for action and for spectatorship, for the announcement of their
newness and for witnessing the newness of others. Thus Arendt (original
emphasis, 1993a, p. 174) insists that 'the essence of education is natality,
the fact that human beings are *born* into the world'.

In his discussion of Arendt's concept, Brunkhorst (2000, p. 188) notes
that 'natality implies both activity and passivity: we can never choose
the time, the place, or the circumstances of our birth and life; nevertheless, we must make our own decisions and lead our own lives'. Levinson
(2001) speaks of a 'paradox of natality' that arises from both the active
and the passive dimensions of natality. If we respond to the newness
that each young person represents by guiding them with force towards
a predetermined place in the world, we thereby 'strike from their hands
their chance of undertaking something new, something unforeseen by
us' (Arendt, 1993a, p. 196). If we respond to this same newness with
passivity and simply 'expel them from our world and leave them to their
own devices' (Arendt, 1993a, p. 196), the danger is that young people,
unprepared for action, will merely attempt to force their way into

the world. Too active a response to the passive dimension of natality threatens to overwhelm young people with what already exists in the world, too passive a response to its active dimension risks allowing the young to overwhelm what has been established. The answer Arendt gives to this paradox and to the dilemma that it creates comes in the form of authority.

Authority and education

Arendt (1993a), in an essay that was first published in 1958, insists that education has fallen into a 'crisis'. Arendt located, at the roots of this crisis, which, she maintained, had reached its most critical stage in America, the emergence of a mass society and the accompanying collapse of the public and the private realms into one another. This state of affairs, she contends, has seen the majority of adults simply give up their role in sustaining and protecting the world that is common to them all. Disconnected from the public and from their responsibility for its existence and survival, absorbed in pursing individual interests and pursuits, it is Arendt's contention that adults no longer meet young people as persons of authority. 'Authority has been discarded by the adults,' Arendt (1993, p. 190) reflects, 'and this can mean only one thing: that the adults refuse to assume responsibility for the world into which they have brought the children'.

Whenever what 'has always been accepted as a natural necessity' (Arendt, 1993b, p. 92), the authority of adults in education, is relinquished, two possibilities emerge. First, the responses of adults to the active dimension of natality, to the young person's urge to appear, can become passive and thus ineffectual. Second, responses to the passive dimension of natality, to the young person's need to be protected from and guided to the world, can take the form of violence as adults simply *demand* that young people listen to and respect them. Let's now address each of these possibilities in turn.

Arendt, who declares that it is 'the essence of...educational activity...to cherish and protect...the child against the world' (Arendt, 1993a, p. 192), is equally adamant that 'the world, too, needs protection to keep it from being *overrun and destroyed* by the onslaught of the new that burst upon it with each new generation' (emphasis added, Arendt, 1993a, p. 186). If we give up on the idea of education as a preparation for power and, instead, conceive of the school as site of power, where young and old alike are all equally political actors, we risk ushering into the world not a powerful but rather a forceful generation. To understand

Arendt's insistence on this point is to grasp the significance she places on spectatorship in the life of the polis. Arendt maintains: 'Nothing and nobody exists in this world whose very being does not presuppose a *spectator*' (emphasis in the original, 1971a, p. 19). This means that action and the political freedom it announces is always reliant upon and always conditioned by spectators and their capacity to receive others in and through their actions. Where there are no spectators, where actions are neither witnessed nor recorded and words neither heard nor acted upon, no actor and no speaker can *appear* as a distinct person with a unique contribution to make to the world. Hence, a generation that believes its place in the public is assured merely by what it does and not at all by how it receives, registers and responds to the actions of others is a generation that contradicts its own urge to appear.

However, it is hardly likely that educators will be able to meet the child's potentially disruptive insistence on appearing in the world too early until they have tempered their own urge to act and to be, at all times, political actors. Arendt notes that 'where force is used, authority itself has failed' (Arendt, 2006b, p. 93), and we might further observe that where authority fails to emerge, force is a persistent possibility. In relation to education, the crucial point is that force and violence can enter into schools to fill the void created when responsibility and authority absent them. So, while the indifference of adults to the world does not inflict a direct violence upon young people, it nevertheless opens a door through which violence might creep into education, a door that responsibility and authority would have locked closed. Consider, for example, the 'personal authority' that exists 'between teacher and pupil', which is secured and maintained by 'neither coercion nor persuasion', since:

> To remain in authority requires respect for the person or the office. The greatest enemy of authority, therefore, is contempt and the surest way to undermine it is laughter. (Arendt, 1970, p. 45)

There is no surer way for a teacher to induce dismissive laughter in the young than by attempting to persuade them of their authority, and no quicker way of diminishing respect to mere obedience than by attempting to coerce young people to learn. 'Our hope always hangs on the new which every generation brings', Arendt (1993a, p. 192, emphasis added) writes, before adding crucially: 'but precisely because we can base our hope only on this, we *destroy* everything if we so try to control the new that we, the old, can dictate how it will look'.

Plurality, trust and power

Any education that prepares young people for either the violent assertion of their will over others or compliance, ill serves them for a life of participating in power. A life, that is, in which separate persons attend to, and make their appearances among, the plurality and excellence of action and speech. Arendt (1993a, p. 189) writes that 'in relation to the child, school in a sense represents the world, although it is not yet actually the world'. In relation to power and its possibilities, a crucial question is: Does a school represent a world of plurality or a narrow world? Herein dwells a further depth to the educator's already deep responsibility to the young people they encounter. The educator is responsible for representing a world where plurality and not sameness is the law.

In Arendt's (1998) characterisation of it, the public realm in an organised space where persons meet each other in the midst of their becoming stories. In this space, any final word, any formal or informal category or label applied as if an immutable truth, is an insult to the capability of each person to act, and thereby to reveal to themselves and to others *who* they are uniquely becoming as opposed to merely *what* they have been deemed to be (Arendt, 1998), and an assault upon the existence of this human sphere, in which persons are both actors and the spectators of acts, the results of which it is not possible for them to predict. Indeed, if it were suddenly possible to know in advance what sort of influence our words and deeds were to have upon others, our actions would instantly lose their quality of newness, we, our uniqueness, and the world, its plurality. And yet, precisely this possibility has arisen with the emergence of what Arendt names 'the conditions of mass society' (Arendt 1993a, p. 191), a society that is characterised by a paradox that has seen shared spaces and activities become progressively more standardised and predictable to the same degree that they are valued for what individuals or groups of individuals might separately gain from them. Living within a mass society, we are thus in danger of finding ourselves akin to members of an orchestra who, desperate to secure private glory in the performance of their particular instruments, lose sight of the production that unites them until sound surges onto sound and music is replaced by noise. With no distances between us, we seem 'fated to enter an era in which the space where our public voice should be heard will be a raucous babble that leaves the civic souls of nations forever mute' (Barber, 2001, p. 65).

The triumph of society has, according to Arendt, seen bureaucracy elevated to the supreme organising principle of human interaction. This state of affairs 'excludes the possibility of action', since 'society expects from each of its members a certain kind of behaviour, imposing innumerable and various rules, all of which tend to 'normalize' its members' (Arendt, 1998, p. 40).Given these conditions, is education condemned to be merely a preparing ground for life in mass society, a life of behaviour and not action, of self-concern and not plurality? What would the imposition of the social into education, an occurrence that would merely reflect the boarder mass insertion of bureaucracy into the polis, mean for young people and their preparation for a life of participation in power?

Barring the too heavy weight of what Levinson (2001, p. 15) calls 'belatedness', some young people can feel themselves to be defined by what others tell them are the facts of their abilities or 'their social positioning', and thus 'see no point in attempting to transform the meanings and implications that attach to their position'. In and of themselves, such processes of labelling might signal the encroachment of mass society into education, since society, Arendt (1998, p. 42) insists, always attempts to secure 'certain patterns of behaviour' that can be drawn upon to identify people who fail to 'keep the rules' and thus to classify them as 'asocial or abnormal'. Social and quasi-medical categories can inform a host of assumptions about what young people can and (more typically) cannot do or achieve. Greene (1995: 39) speaks, for example, of young people 'who are labelled as deficient, fixed in that category as firmly as flies in amber,' before concluding: 'Marginalized, they are left to the experience of powerlessness unless (usually with support) they are enabled to…reach beyond'. To speak of young persons with a vocabulary that extends merely to *what* they are is to determine for them what their difference is, and this is a negation of the promise of their birth, that they were born to *perpetually* appear and *become* their difference within and to the world. Young people can certainly come to feel themselves entirely disconnected from a world where people make decisions and implement changes, a world, that is, of creative actors and attentive spectators, but does it, even in these circumstances, make sense to speak of young people experiencing 'powerlessness'? It is not surprising then, that young people, for whom education is no longer a bridge that might lead them to the world but a wall that blocks them from it, experience powerlessness. Having never experienced power, young people cannot be expected to know how it feels to be divested of it. Rather, they experience a disconnection from possibilities, a closing down, not merely of what they are capable of doing now, but of what they might be able to do in the future. And so the stereotypes, the labels and the stigmas, all the talk of 'boys with Attention Deficient Hyperactivity Disorder', of 'girls with Emotional and Behaviour Difficulties' and 'kids from *that* neighbourhood', write over narratives before narratives have emerged. This is the brutal fact of exclusion in education: the arresting of newness before it has begun to breathe in the world. In an education where young people are met with hostility or find themselves defined by how adults assess the young people and consequently what they will predict for them, what is experienced is not powerlessness but *power alienation*. The alienation of young people from power means estrangement from the reality of their potential, the fate of which is indistinguishable from the potential of power in a world of plurality. With none of the visibility of the active imposition of the adult's will onto the young, the long, slow reduction of education to a series of bureaucratic procedures that all aim at measurable, behavioural targets, might also be deemed as a violence against the newness of the young.

Resisting this infringement of mass society into education means remembering that the distinctiveness of a young person is inseparable from the difference their actions and words will make to the world. It means remembering that this distinctiveness cannot be contained within the parameters of mere factual, measurable difference, located at the level of 'what' they are deemed to be capable of now and in the future. Such resistance entails a positive responsibility in education, the ability, that is, of educators to represent the world to the young in all its plurality and to respond to the distinct and unique potential of each of the young people they educate. Let us consider this responsibility in rela-tion to Montaigne's complaint that too many people fall into the error of thinking that the entirety of the earth must be afflicted by stormy conditions as soon as hail begins to fall down upon them. To answer this error, Montaigne (2003, p. 177) contends, is the work of education:

> Only a man who can picture in his mind the mighty idea of Mother Nature in her total majesty; who can read in her countenance a variety so general and so unchanging and then pick out therein not merely himself but an entire kingdom as a tiny, feint point: only he can reckon things at their real size. This great world of ours...is the looking-glass in which we must gaze to know ourselves from the right slant...I want it to be the book our pupil studies. (Montaigne, 2003, p. 177)

Encountering an authoritative educator who represents the world in its entirety, young people are presented with a representation of this book in a living, human form. The young are, in this way, invited to learn about the world from one who is perpetually learning, but more than this, they are gifted a living proclamation of trust. From the perspective of the young person, Arendt (1993a, p. 189) writes, the authoritative educator appears as 'a representative of all adult inhabitants, pointing out the details and saying to the child: This is our world'. And this world is no possible or partial world, the kind of world a teacher proclaiming themselves either a generalist or a specialist might represent, but the actual, plural world. Indeed any educator attempting to represent the world to the young must first shun the temptation to delimit their comprehension of it in accordance with what it happens to mean at any given time to be a specialist teacher, specialising only in one area of human understanding and achievement. Worse still, would be a teacher who specialises in delivering specialist learning and teaching to young people designated special. To address young people with the words, 'This is *our* world', is to say that this is the world we, the adults, have created, and it is this world whose renewal we will entrust to you. Thereby, the educator invites the young to learn from the book of the world, and in so doing, places trust in the young that this book, perpetually unfinished, is one to which they can contribute.

What is needed for this expression of trust is not simply teachers, who Arendt (1993a) tells us have qualifications that testify to their knowledge of the world, but educators, who have taken responsibility for and represent the contents of the world for the sake of the world itself and the young who will appear within it. All kinds of people can know all sorts of information about the world but this hardly endows them with the authority to educate. An educator with authority reassures the young person that the world is as it is because of women and men who have both taken and failed to assume responsibility for it. It is in this way, moreover, that young people might be reassured that the world itself is not indifferent to them, that it is open to be changed and that they might be the ones to change it. It is possible to witness the living out of this authority in the example of all those educators who daily inspire in young people the trust that their questions will met, not with condescension or ridicule, but with thoughtful attention.

To grasp the significance of trust as a necessary condition of power, it is useful to reflect, once again, on Arendt's distinction between power and violence. It is Arendt's (1969; 1970; 2006a) contention that in the absence of popular and active support, a revolt, no matter how violent, is doomed to fail, while any rebellion conducted with the consent of a multitude of people can be devastatingly effective without relying upon a single violent act. Writing about Arendt's concept, Young (2002, p. 271) notes: 'Power only exists as long as it is actively sustained by the plural participants in the endeavour who self-consciously coordinate with one another'. While in his discussion of Arendt's concept, Parekh (original emphasis, 1981, p. 160) observes: 'Power consists in others' *support* or active co-operation, and not mere *compliance* or passive conformity'. However, when the young participate in an education that is so estranged from the world that it aims merely at achieving what Dewey (1966, p. 49) describes as 'external efficiency of habit, motor skill without accompanying thought', they might thereby learn to give their consent without active commitment. To prepare young people to become experts at meeting standardised targets is to risk that they develop entirely socialised minds, minds that falter before each new set of deeds, words or events, and minds that can be restored only by fitting and fixing every unusual occurrence into pre-established categories. It is to risk, in short, preparing the young to *comply* with bureaucratic procedures in a world divested of power. In sum, there is no power without consent, and there is no consent without trust, and trust cannot develop in young people so long as adults refuse to meet them as representatives of the world.

Conclusion

In the account of her experiences of anti-Semitism at school, Arendt emphasises the distinction her mother drew between how she was to respond to the remarks of teachers, and how she was to react to the comments of other children. Having considered Arendt's concept of power in relation to her views about education, we might now be in a position to understand why the distinction contained within in her mother's instructions was to persist in Arendt's memory.

Arendt, who insists that power and violence are opposites, nevertheless claims that they can and often do operate at the same time and in the same place. Young offers a way of addressing this apparent contradiction. 'By interpreting Arendt's distinction between violence and power not only as conceptual, but also as *normative*,' Young (original emphasis, 2002, p. 269) claims, 'we can make sense of this'. So, though there is 'nothing...more common than the combination of violence and power' (Arendt, 1970, pp. 46–47), we can follow Young's (original emphasis, 2002, p. 269) insight, and grasp that, for Arendt, 'they need not, and they *ought not*' occur at the same time. In the same way, we can hardly deny that it is common for violence either to arise in or to impose itself upon schools. But this *should* not mean that we can answer this violence only by conflating it with power or by identifying power as a solution to the presence of violence in schools. As Arendt's mother understood, the anti-Semitic teachers in her daughter's school not only enacted violence upon the Jewish students, but also destroyed the school as an institution that protects and guides all young people to the world. It is for precisely this reason that we might commend her for instructing her daughter to leave her school whenever its teachers made anti-Semitic remarks and return to the sanctuary of the home.

What Arendt's *normative* distinction between power and violence tells us about violence in education is that it *must* be answered not by power, but by *authority*. An educator with authority represents something more for young people than amassed knowledge of the world, since this person educates, not simply by imparting what they know, but also from their very commitment to the world and to the young. This authority is announced whenever educators admit to their continued role in representing the world as it is. The authority is reaffirmed daily by the commitment of these same educators as they invite the young to know the world in all its intricate diversity and, in this way, prepare them for their opportunity to renew it. With this authority, educators can address the terrible spectre of violence in education and prepare young people for power.

References

Allen, A. (2002) 'Power, Subjectivity, and Agency: Between Arendt and Foucault'. *International Journal of Philosophical Studies*, 10(2), 131–149.

Apple, M. A. (1993) 'The Politics of Official Knowledge: Does a National Curriculum Make Sense?' *Teachers College Record*, 95(2), 221–241.

Arendt, H. (1993) 'The crisis in education' in *Between Past and Future. Eight Exercises in Political Thought*, New York: The Viking Press, 173–196.

Arendt, H. (1946) 'Expansion and the Philosophy of Power', *The Sewanee Review*, 54(4), 601–616.

Arendt, H. (1969) 'Reflections on violence', *New York Review of Books*, February 27.

Arendt, H. (1970) *On violence*, London: Harvest.

Arendt, H. (1971a) *The life of the mind: Thinking*, London: Harcourt.

Arendt, H. (1971b) *The life of the mind: Willing*, London: Harcourt.

Arendt, H. (1992) 'Lectures on Kant's political philosophy', in Beiner, R, (ed.) *Lectures on Kant's political philosophy*, Chicago: The University of Chicago Press, 7–77.

Arendt, H. (1993a) 'The crisis in education', in *Between past and future: Eight exercises in political thought*, New York: The Viking Press, 173–196.

Arendt, H. (1993b) 'What is authority?' in *Between past and future: Eight exercises in political thought*, New York: The Viking Press, 91–141.

Arendt, H. (1998) *The human condition*, Chicago: The University of Chicago Press.

Arendt, H. (2006a) *On revolution*, London: Penguin.

Arendt, H. (2006b) 'What is authority?' in *Between Past and Future*, Penguin Books, 91–141.

Azaola, C. M. (2012) 'Revisiting Bourdieu: alternative educational systems in the light of the theory of social and cultural reproduction', *International Studies in Sociology of Education*, 22(2), 81–95.

Barber, B. R. (2001) 'Blood Brothers, Consumers, or Citizens? Three Models of Identity – Ethnic, Commercial, and Civic', in Gould, C. and Pasquino, P. (eds) *Cultural Identity and the Nation State*, Lanham: Rowman and Littlefield, 57–65.

Bourdieu, P. and Wacquant, L. J. D. (1992) *An Invitation to Reflexive Sociology*, Chicago: University of Chicago Press.

Brunkhorst, H. (2000) 'Equality and elitism in Arendt' in Villa, D. (ed.) *The Cambridge companion to Hannah Arendt*, Cambridge: Cambridge University Press, 178–198.

Dewey, J. (1966) *Democracy and education: An introduction to the philosophy of education*, New York: The Free Press.

Foucault, M. (1977) *Discipline and Punish*, Harmondsworth: Penguin.

Foucault, M. (1982) 'The Subject and Power' in Dreyfus, H. and. Rabinow, P (eds) *Michel Foucault: Beyond Structuralism and Hermeneutics*, Chicago: University of Chicago Press, 208–226.

Foucault, M. (2003) *Abnormal: Lectures at the College de France 1974–1975*, Ewald, F. and Fontana, A. (eds), (trans.) G. Burchell. London: Verso.

Gibbs, P. and Garnett, J. (2007) 'Work-based learning as a field of study', *Research in Post-Compulsory Education*, 12(3), 409–421.

Giroux, H. (1992) *Border Crossings. Cultural Workers and the Politics of Education*, New York: Routledge.

Gordon, N. (2001) 'Arendt and social change in democracies, *Critical Review of International Social and Political Philosophy*, 4(2), 85–111.

Greene, M. (1995) *Releasing the Imagination: Essays on Education, the Arts, and Social Change*, San Francisco: Jossey-Bass Publishers.

Habermas, J. (1977) 'Hannah Arendt's Communications Concept of Power', (trans.) T. McCarthy. *Social Research*, 44(1), 3–24.

Hobbes, T. (1985) *Leviathan*, London: Penguin.

Levinson, S.C.(2001) 'Language and Mind: Let's Get the Issues Straight!,' in Gentnerand D. , Goldin-Meadow S. (eds), Language in Mind. Advances in the Study of Language and Thought, Cambridge, MA, MIT Press, 25–46.

Mills, C. (2008) 'Reproduction and transformation of inequalities in schooling: the transformative potential of the theoretical constructs of Bourdieu', *British Journal of Sociology of Education*, 29(1), 79–89.

Montaigne, M. de. (2003) 'On educating children', in *The complete essays*, Screech, M. A. (ed. and trans.) London: Penguin, 163–199.

Parekh, B. (1981) *Hannah Arendt and the search for a new political philosophy*, London: Macmillan Press.

Penta, L. J. (1996) 'Hannah Arendt: On Power', *The Journal of Speculative Philosophy*, 10(3), 210–229.

Thomson, P. and Holdsworth, R. (2003) 'Theorizing change in the educational "field": re-readings of "student participation" projects', *International Journal of Leadership in Education: Theory and Practice*, 6(4), 371–391.

Young, I. M. (2002) 'Power, violence, and legitimacy: A reading of Hannah Arendt in an age of police brutality and humanitarian intervention' in Rosenblum, N. L. (ed.) *Breaking the cycles of hatred: Memory, law and repair*, Princeton: Princeton University Press, 260–287.

Young-Bruehl, E. (2004) *Hannah Arendt: For love of the world* (2nd edn), New Haven: Yale University Press.

2

Symbolic Violence: Education as Concealed Power

Antonia Kupfer

Introduction

In 1970, Pierre Bourdieu and Jean-Claude Passeron published *La repro-duction. Élements pour une théorie du système d'enseignement*. The English translation *Foundations of a theory of symbolic violence* was published in 1977 as the first part of the widely referenced book *Reproduction in education, society and culture*, commonly called *Reproduction*. It is a diffi-cult text, written paragraph by paragraph, similar to a juridical text. I could find little secondary literature dealing with it; most analysis and discussion of the book refers to the second part. This neglect deprives English-speaking readers of an important contribution to social theory. The present chapter aims to rectify this omission.

Bourdieu and Passeron's concept of symbolic violence is critical in understanding why social hierarchy is accepted by those who suffer from it. The publication *Foundations of a theory of symbolic violence* was the starting point. It focuses on the key role of education and schools in maintaining domination and social inequality, problems that have hardly deceased since the 1970s. On the contrary, I will present argu-ments to explain an actual increase. Bourdieu and Passeron's expla-nation of how pedagogic work produces the objective conditions for domination turns their concept of symbolic violence into a societal theory. Their account of power and education is the polar opposite of Arendt's understanding of power as the ability to act, and education as enabling children to renew the world. These two perspectives delimit the spectrum of approaches to the relation of power and education set out at the beginning of this volume.

In what follows, I restrict my discourse to this early text, not its development in Bourdieu's *The State Nobility* (1996 [1989]), *Pascalian*

Meditations (2000 [1997]), or *Masculine Domination* (2001 [1998]), in order to focus on the role of education and schools in the act of domination. I will first place Bourdieu and Passeron's concept of symbolic violence in the sociological discussion on power, showing how it ties in with, and further develops previous concepts. I will then explain what symbolic violence means and the role education and schools play in sustaining it. In the fourth section, I will raise points of critique, and finally draw conclusions.

The concept of symbolic violence as part of a sociological debate on power

In his excellent introduction to Bourdieu's concept of symbolic violence, Mauger (2005) reminds us that Bourdieu was neither the first nor the only person who tried to determine why those who suffer oppression nevertheless agree to, and/or participate in, oppressive power. In fact, Durkheim and Mauss, Marx and Engels, and Weber offer three different explanations for dominance being maintained when no direct physical violence is threatened, and Bourdieu and Passeron integrate all three into their concept of symbolic violence.

Durkheim and Mauss (2009) base their answer on human structures of thinking. According to them, in order to make sense of the world, people create classifications, but because they do so as a society rather than individually, these classifications inherently express relations of dominance:

> The pressure exerted by the group on each of its members does not permit individuals to judge freely the notions which society itself has elaborated and in which it has placed something of its personality. Such constructs are sacred for individuals. Thus the history of scientific classification is, in the last analysis, the history of the stages by which this element of social affectivity has progressively weakened, leaving more and more room for the reflective thought of individuals. But it is not the case that these remote influences which we have just studied have ceased to be felt today. They have left behind them an effect which survives and which is always present; it is the very cadre of all classification, it is the ensemble of mental habits by virtue of which we conceive things and facts in the form of co-ordinated or hierarchised groups. (p. 51)

As a consequence, dominance is experienced unconsciously, and people develop an affirmative attitude, seeing oppressive social conditions as natural and not questioning them. Bourdieu holds that one of the most important tasks of sociology is to reveal these fundamental structures of thinking, and thus, his and Passeron's account of education and schools as locations of idea transmission is crucial for the revelation of power relations and dominance in societies.

A second strand of their concept of symbolic violence adopts Marx and Engels' perspective on the creation of consciousness. In their critique of German ideology, Marx and Engels argue against Hegel and Feuerbach, who developed *ideas* about human beings and their lives instead of analysing how people actually live. Abstract ideas about human nature do not form consciousness; an analysis of people's consciousness requires an analysis of their empirical living conditions as Marx and Engels stipulate: 'Consciousness [*das Bewusstsein*] can never be anything else than conscious being [*das bewusste Sein*], and the being of men is their actual life-process' (Marx and Engels, 1976, p. 36).

A second and related point which Marx and Engels make in their critique of German ideology is that dominant ideas and ways of thinking are the ideas and perspectives of the dominant class. Not only are ideas and thinking patterns neither neutral nor independent of socio-economic living conditions, but the power of the dominant class extends beyond material, economic areas to the realm of ideas, perspectives, worldviews, even ways of thinking. 'The class which has the means of material production at its disposal, consequently also controls the means of mental production, so that the ideas of those who lack the means of mental production are on the whole subject to it' (Marx and Engels, 1976, p. 59).

Education is one of the primary arenas where ideas are produced, taught, and acquired in societies. Consequently, if ideas, thoughts, models, theories, and worldviews are not independent of the thinkers' socio-economic position and develop strictly according to intrinsic aspects and the logic of the dominant class, educational institutions are restricted, conveying only special knowledge, views, ideas, and approaches. Bourdieu and Passeron note in Marx and Engels' analysis that special knowledge is declared general knowledge, masking its origin as knowledge of the dominant people. The confusion of special with general knowledge contributes to the acceptance and maintenance of domination. I will discuss this point in detail later.

According to Weber, domination cannot exist without a creed that legitimises it. He differentiates three forms of dominance based on the different claims to legitimacy. Legitimation can be primarily rational, which means people believe that regulations are lawful; or it can be traditional, which means people believe in the worth of past practices. Finally it can be charismatic, which means people believe in the leader's sanctity or the leader as a role model. We might think that rational domination above all requires a conscious agreement to the domination, and Weber mentions that an interest in obeying is necessary to each relation of dominance although he does not further define these interests. However, he also states:

> In general, it should be kept clearly in mind that the basis of every authority, and correspondingly of every kind of willingness to obey, is a *belief*, a belief by virtue of which persons exercising authority are lent prestige. The composition of this belief is seldom altogether simple. In the case of 'legal authority', it is never purely legal. The belief in legality comes to be established and habitual, and this means it is partly traditional. (1978, p. 263)

He means that all domination is at least partly a product of practiced traditions, without conscious agreement. Bourdieu's concept of habitus emphasises the dimension of unconsciousness because practising something without reflecting on it makes it much more powerful. Weber (1978, p. 215) points explicitly to schools as an area of domination that is influenced by social relations and culture. Similarly, Bourdieu and Passeron demonstrate how the distinction between pedagogical authority and pedagogical action legitimates domination in schools.

Finally I want to mention Foucault, who created a concept of power at about the same time as Bourdieu and Passeron created their concept of symbolic violence. All three authors emphasise the involvement and participation of all people affected by domination, but Foucault resists drawing a clear distinction between dominant and oppressed people, as Naomi Hodgson explains in her chapter on Foucault in this volume.

The concept of symbolic violence and the role of education and schools in domination

The concept of symbolic violence defines power as domination. It is not restricted to the area of education but explains how education contributes to maintaining dominance. Bourdieu closely aligned his theories with empirical practices and developed them over time. Thus he created the concept of symbolic violence with a focus on schools and education. Later in *The State Nobility* (1996), he focused more on the agreement of the dominated and in *Pascalian Meditations* (2000) and 'Masculine domination' (2001) emphasised the embodiment of perceptions as critical aspects of symbolic violence (Mauger, 2005). The concept of symbolic violence, then, did not arise as some pure abstraction that was then applied to the concrete example of education. Instead, education and schools are central to the creation and manifestation of power that goes beyond these realms to contribute to the maintenance of social inequality.

Bourdieu and Passeron (1977) start with axiom zero:

> *0. Every power to exert symbolic violence, i.e., every power which manages to impose meanings and to impose them as legitimate by concealing the power relations which are the basis of its force, adds its own specifically symbolic force to those power relations.* (p. 4, italics original)

This axiom defines symbolic violence – power that imposes meanings as legitimate by concealing the power relations that support its strength – and implies much more. First, a power that is not symbolic violence supports symbolic violence. It consists in social hierarchies. The upper classes use symbolic violence to maintain their domination, wielding it as an instrument. To find out how domination works, we must identify class backgrounds and the characteristics of actors and institutions, such as schools.

Second, symbolic violence always has a specific meaning and specific content. Therefore, it is variable and must be analysed within its specific social context, which must also be analysed. The content taught at school is both relatively autonomous and dependent on power relations. It is *duplicitous*: it seems to be meaningful on its own, independent from the way it is created and presented, but it conceals the influence and extends the prestige of those in power because certain content is regarded as *true*, without admitting questions about whether it always applies or how it came to be taught.

At this stage in the development of the concept of symbolic violence, *symbolic power* refers to different educational institutions that Bourdieu and Passeron see as systems of logical relations. When they mention, for example, the institution of school authority (SAu), they are not referring to individuals, such as headmasters, or institutions, such as school boards or local authorities, but to complex systems of relations; they mean a whole set of practices to which people ascribe authority, based on images, concepts and relations that are embedded in traditions and political and cultural contexts as well as unwritten and written rules. The concept of symbolic violence describes the relations between the various institutions that together form school authority. Clearly, the concept is extremely complex, and in what follows, I will explain its main dimensions and their relationships.

Broadly speaking, Bourdieu and Passeron's educational institutions can be divided into two categories, one related to their agency and the other to legitimation of their agency. In developing their concept of symbolic violence, Bourdieu and Passeron name the relevant institutions and explain their characteristics, products/outputs and the degree of their influence. Pedagogic action (PA), pedagogic work (PW) and work of schooling (WSg) are categories of agency, while pedagogic authority (PAu) and school authority (SAu) are categories that legitimate the former. Educational system (ES) is an overarching category that maintains the institutional conditions to secure the agency.

I will start with the category of pedagogic action, followed by an explanation of the pedagogic authority that legitimates it. I will then return to the level of agency to explain the category called pedagogic work and its legitimation by outlining the authors' understanding of the educational system, touching briefly on the category work of schooling, understood as pedagogic work in secondary schools. I will end with the legitimation category of school authority and then explain the authors' argument that there can be no alternatives to pedagogical action as violence.

Pedagogic action

Bourdieu and Passeron start from the generally acknowledged essence of school: pedagogic action. First, I will outline their definition; second, I will explain what pedagogic action creates, evokes and does; third, I will focus on its influence.

Components of pedagogical action

Pedagogical action has two elements: the teaching content and the teaching context, which are based on the dominant culture and the class-specific culture of the students. Thus, to analyse teaching in schools, we must grasp the interrelations among the curriculum, the dominant culture in which schools are located and the pupils' class-specific habitus. If we follow Bourdieu and Passeron in rejecting the simple view of education as a straight line in one direction from a powerful teacher to a dependent pupil in favour of a much more complex process, we can see that domination cannot work apart from the conditions of the dominated. Here, their view is similar to Foucault's. The authors' conception of pedagogical action demonstrates that education is a wider social process, not exempt from society in protected, cloistered institutions, or ivory towers.

Since pedagogical action is so tightly linked to society, its dependence relations differ with historical and geographical context. It does not have the same shape over time and space but is shaped by specific power relations of specific social contexts.

What pedagogical action creates and evokes

According to Bourdieu and Passeron, pedagogical action is the 'chief instrument of the transubstantiation of power relations into legitimate authority' (p. 15) or symbolic violence. It creates the illusion that teaching content is purely subject-related and does not convey a certain perspective, a specific meaning. This illusion is created by masking the fact that teaching takes always place in social contexts that are shaped by, and composed of, the dominant culture and the class-specific culture. Context influences content. Bourdieu and Passeron see societies as hierarchically organised with upper and lower strata that support social inequalities. Teaching takes place in a hierarchical society and is used by the powerful to secure their privileges. To manifest their power, they impose the content of what is being taught (see Marx and Engels). Teaching content and curricula are not neutral. They do not follow an intrinsic logic or express an independent truth because such things do not exist, according to Bourdieu and Passeron. All knowledge is socially created and thus related to social hierarchy. The content taught in schools is imposed by the powerful but in a way that conceals their overall power and their influence on content.

Later Bourdieu and Passeron specify that the main 'thing' pedagogical action transmits is not content but the legitimacy of the dominant culture as a fait accompli. As their concept of symbolic violence primarily addresses power, not knowledge, they focus on the ways that social hierarchies are created and maintained. Part of this modus operandi is to differentiate 'superior' or 'valuable' knowledge or teaching content from the 'inferior' or 'non-valuable'. Pedagogical action makes the dominated 'internalize the legitimacy of their exclusion; by making those it relegates to second-order teaching recognize the inferiority of this teaching and its audience' (p. 41) and 'by inculcation…a transposable, generalized disposition with regard to social disciplines and hierarchies' (p. 41). They do not discuss whether there are indeed different levels of quality in knowledge and teaching content because they exclude the existence of an independent perspective from which anyone can evaluate the qualities of knowledge and teaching content.

Degrees of influence/power in pedagogical action

Not only the shape, but also the degree of influence of pedagogical action depends on the specific social context and the power relations in which it takes place. The degree of influence rises when the state 'hinders the dominant classes from invoking the brute fact of domination' (p. 14); that is, when the dominant classes are not allowed to physically assault or exclude others. The degree of influence also rises with 'the degree of unification of the market on which the symbolic and economic value of the products of the different PAs is constituted' (p. 14). For example, the more economic value in terms of access to employment positions attached to cultural products, such as school-leaving degrees or diplomas, the more powerful and influential pedagogical action is.

The degree of influence of pedagogical action also differs according to the students' social class. The strongest influence is exerted on members of social classes whose dispositions and cultural capital are similar to the teachers' and the teaching content and weakest where students' dispositions and cultural capital diverge most from their teachers' and the content taught. As a consequence, actors for change are farthest from the powerful and the least ideologised, or fooled.

Pedagogical authority

The social condition for the existence of pedagogical action is pedagogical authority, which is essential for the legitimating domination. What is pedagogical authority? We cannot understand it in such material terms as a person with power – for example, the education minister or a headteacher – but as the abstract beliefs that teachers are necessary and what they teach is right. Here we are reminded of Weber to whom legitimation and the belief in authority are the preconditions for domination. These beliefs are unconscious; no one explains or debates and agrees to them. Bourdieu and Passeron mainly explain pedagogical authority by its *effect,* which is its substance: '*PAu ... reinforces the arbitrary power which establishes it and which it conceals*' (p. 13, italics original). Again, pedagogical authority reinforces arbitrary power by misrecognising it as legitimate; it both constitutes and conceals arbitrary power. We might say that it is the social recognition of the accomplishment of teaching and learning, or pedagogical activity, so it ensures that teaching and learning take place and that communication between teachers and students takes place so that students attend and behave in the classroom. Pedagogical authority is 'in reality, automatically conferred on every pedagogic transmitter by the traditionally and institutionally guaranteed position he occupies in a relation of pedagogic communication'

(p. 21). Bourdieu and Passeron make clear that pedagogical authority is *socially* established by a whole system that creates and supports teachers. The authority attained in the position of *teacher* eliminates the possibility that individual teachers will not be seen as capable authorities. In other words, the *position* enables teachers to exercise authority and at the same time creates the impression that their authority derives from the content they teach or a charisma that results from veiling the true sources of pedagogical authority. Pedagogical authority has no normative content because the teachers' authority is accepted regardless of whether students actually learn anything. In fact, pedagogical authority aims to exclude any questioning of the content or information of the teaching and succeeds because '*the pedagogic receivers are disposed from the outset to recognize the legitimacy of the information transmitted...hence to receive and internalize the message*' (p. 21, italics original). Pedagogical action is always tied to pedagogical authority, but they are not the same. Pedagogical authority largely functions to conceal the agency and to legitimate the violent act. To clarify how the agency operates, Bourdieu and Passeron created a third category, *pedagogic work*.

Pedagogic work

By pedagogic work (PW), Bourdieu and Passeron refer to the process of inculcation, which first takes place in the family (primary pedagogic work), and later in school (secondary pedagogic work). The category strongly refers to society, indicating that the authors' concept of symbolic violence must be understood as a societal theory (*Gesellschaftstheorie*) and not restricted to educational institutions.

What does pedagogic work create or produce?

Pedagogic work produces 'a lasting habitus' (p. 31), which is needed to maintain hierarchical societal structures. Since structures cannot exist without agency, and agency is always situated within structures, the habitus links them: '*PW tends to reproduce the social conditions of the production of that cultural arbitrary (...) through the mediation of the habitus, defined as the principle generating practices which reproduces the objective structures*' (pp. 32–33, italics original). Bourdieu and Passeron also refer to the social conditions as 'the objective conditions for misrecognition of cultural arbitrariness' (p. 37). Primary pedagogic work differs in families of different social classes, and when added to secondary pedagogic work at school, which enables middle- and upper-class children to meet demands but fails working-class children, pedagogic work establishes societal hierarchy.

The objective conditions for maintaining societal hierarchy rely on the double outcomes of pedagogic work: a 'legitimate product' (p. 39); and 'the legitimate need for this produce' (p. 38, not italic A.K.) producing the legitimate consumer, a person equipped with the disposition to consume the product in a legitimate manner. Since pedagogic work is a dynamic process, its effect – concealment of the habit of internalising symbolic violence – is amplified with more inculcation.

Conditions for productivity of pedagogic work

Bourdieu and Passeron posit three tightly linked measures of the specific productivity of pedagogic work: the durability, transposability, and exhaustivity of the habitus produced. They do not go into the details of these rather technical measures but compare the productivity of the pedagogic work in schools between pupils of different classes, who developed different habits as products of different primary pedagogic work in their families. They conclude that secondary pedagogic work is stronger (more productive) when it takes place in a setting in which explicit inculcation is organised in alignment with formal transferability of the habitus, which is true for middle- and upper-class children.

Bourdieu and Passeron also differentiate between a more traditional mode of teaching, which tends to be practical and carried out unconsciously, and a more modern way that includes theory and space for reflection on the practice. Traditional and modern ways of teaching have different effects on pupils of different social classes and habitus. Pedagogic work carried out in a traditional way fails pupils who are not familiar with the practice the teacher demands. For example, a teacher asking them to interpret a poem assumes they know how to interpret a poem, and those who do not know cannot meet the demand. Traditional school teaching that does not explicitly teach the prerequisites to carry out the demands, legitimates certain ways of obtaining and mastering the prerequisites.

Educational systems and the work of schooling

While pedagogic work establishes one dimension of the societal conditions that shape pedagogical action based on the family habitus, the educational system establishes another: the institutional conditions that shape the exercise and reproduction of secondary pedagogic work, or the work of schooling. Educational systems equip their agents with standardised instruments, such as uniform teacher education or national curricula that also work as instruments of control and tend to exclude practices that do not contribute to the reproduction of existing hierarchical teaching methods. As part of symbolic violence, educational systems must (re)produce the institutional conditions that cloak the source of power and the influence it exerts.

School authority

Finally, Bourdieu and Passeron define the category of school authority as 'the institutionalized form of pedagogical authority' (p. 63 without italic A.K.), which means it provides authority to teachers as agents, giving them 'a legitimacy by position...guaranteed by the institution and which is socially objectified and symbolized in the institutional procedures and rules defining...training, the diplomas which sanction it and the legitimate conduct of the profession' (p. 30). School authority impedes the recognition of power relations and thus is a very powerful element of symbolic violence.

Bourdieu and Passeron's argument against alternatives to education as symbolic violence

Bourdieu and Passeron assert that pedagogical action must transmit societal power relations to legitimate authority. They state: '*All* **pedagogic action** *(PA) is...the imposition of a cultural arbitrary*' (p. 5, italics and boldface original). By 'cultural arbitrary' they mean that teaching content 'cannot be deduced from any principle' (p. xi). In the Foreword to the French edition, they explain what motivates this assumption:

> ...we simply give ourselves the means of constituting pedagogic action in its objective reality, by recourse to a logical construct devoid of any sociological or, a fortiori, psychological referent. We thereby pose the question of the social conditions capable of excluding the logical question of the possibility of an action which cannot achieve its specific effect unless its objective truth as the imposition of a cultural arbitrary is objectively misrecognized. (p. xi)

Since all societies have hierarchies, we cannot separate the analysis of education, teaching and pedagogy from an analysis of the power relations of their social context.

Bourdieu and Passeron claim to argue on a logical level and offer an illustration:

> The paradox of Epimenides the liar would appear in a new form: either you believe I'm not lying when I tell you education is violence and my teaching isn't legitimate, so you can't believe me; or you believe

I'm lying and my teaching is legitimate, so you still can't believe what I say when I tell you it is violence. (p. 12)

Either way, teaching must be violence and further, pedagogical action is never conscious, so it remains beyond our control.

The authors also exclude the possibility that any alternative educational praxis can solve the problem of violence. Various attempts, such as non-repressive education, are still acts of repression because they conceal their own arbitrariness. Again, since pedagogical action is not conscious, students cannot agree or refuse to be taught arbitrary content in an arbitrary fashion.

Finally, Bourdieu and Passeron deny the possibility that dominated people can be liberated through education. First, dominated people who acquire the dominant culture cannot gain emancipation because this culture devalues theirs and requires their alienation from it. Second, to glorify the dominated culture by declaring it 'popular culture' cannot lead to liberation since this culture is as arbitrary as the dominant culture, and people cannot hope to gain liberation from any arbitrary culture. The text does not clarify the reason; do Bourdieu and Passeron simply presuppose that liberation cannot be gained from an arbitrary culture, or do they hold that liberation in a hierarchical society is impossible? Since Bourdieu focuses on power relations rather than epistemological questions, the latter interpretation is more plausible. Furthermore, when he and Passeron discuss whether a democratic education would be *theoretically* in the interest of all dominated people, they conclude it would not *as long as education is a positional good* since some members of the dominated groups might aspire to and actually move upward socially.

In sum, Bourdieu and Passeron's estimation of the possibilities for emancipation through education contrasts both with Arendt's, as outlined in Wayne Veck's chapter, and a Marxist view, as explained by Mike Cole.

Critique of the concept of symbolic violence

I would like to raise two critiques of Bourdieu and Passeron's concept of education as symbolic violence. The first relates to the nature of pedagogical action, the second to the teaching content.

Bourdieu and Passeron assert that pedagogical action never works consciously. I would agree in regard to families that most parts of socialisation are probably not carried out or received consciously. However, in schools, pupils and students are older and may develop a consciousness of what and how they are taught. Teachers may also reflect on their own education, their roles and their teaching. In my view, human beings are able to tolerate contradictions to a larger extent than presumably Bourdieu and Passeron would acknowledge and therefore my critique rests on a different estimation of human nature. I think people can do both: that is, to teach and learn unconsciously and have moments in which they realise how the school and the teaching content are shaping them. These moments of realisation may spark personal crises but not necessarily immediate change. Social structures are enduring, and the next day, teachers and students might go on with an exam.

My second critique is related to the first. According to Bourdieu and Passeron, we cannot gain liberation from an arbitrary culture, and since all culture, and therefore all teaching content is arbitrary, education cannot lead to emancipation. In an absolute way, I would agree, but again in my view, certain facets or degrees of liberation are meaningful. I hold that people can gain a certain degree of liberation by obtaining the best knowledge that exists at that moment, knowing consciously that it has been created and may be developed further and change or become outdated. This knowledge could enlarge the scope for action and thinking and therefore affect life chances towards a higher degree of liberation or even power as Young (2014) would say. In the 'Report of the Collège de France on the Future of Education', originally published in 1985, Bourdieu contributes suggestions for changes to the French educational system. His view differs from the one outlined with Passeron in *Reproduction*, acknowledging instead that education develops a critical spirit which can be used against the abuses of symbolic violence. It holds teachers responsible for enabling students to criticise, and advises schools to teach the social history of cultural performances in an intercultural way. To increase social equality, it calls for a greater variety of socially recognised forms of cultural performances. I do not read this report as negating the formal theoretical argument expressed in *Reproduction* but rather as a political statement to propose policy changes.

Conclusions

Foundations of a theory of symbolic violence has two key messages. First, schools are not primarily a place of learning but of (re)producing hierarchical power relations. Second, learning does not happen independently of (re)producing hierarchical power relations.

Are these messages up-to-date? We still live in a hierarchical society, and compared to the 1970s when the text was first published, social inequality and inequalities in power relations have increased. Today, income disparities have increased, and wealth accumulates in the hands of increasingly fewer people. With the rise of financial capitalism, democracy diminishes and power-sharing becomes more and more unequal. Today, more people are in formal education and participate longer than ever before. The amount of years for compulsory schooling has increased, and large parts of lifelong learning are conducted in formal settings, which means that formal education praxis impacts our lives longer and to a larger extent. Education has crucial significance in terms of individuals and societies. An analysis of education is largely an analysis of social and individual life trajectories.

A third reason why I consider Bourdieu and Passeron's text still relevant is the fact that despite various reforms and the creation of alternative schools, the vast majority of students continue to receive a conservative formal education. By conservative, I mean that very little social history of cultural performances is taught; lessons still focus on cultural performances themselves and not on their creation. In recent decades, new technologies have been introduced to assist teaching and learning, but they are mainly implemented and used in a rather uncritical way. Ben Williamson's chapter illustrates clearly that 'learning to code' lessons enable children to use new technologies rather than to understand their inherent and implicit powers and the content they convey.

To conclude, Bourdieu and Passeron open our eyes to a trap: we cannot escape from power relations in a hierarchical society, not even in schools or universities. We should not forget this observation, taking power relations into account in all our teaching and learning and working towards a more egalitarian society outside the realm of education.

References

Bourdieu, P. (1992) [1985] 'Vorschläge des Collège de France für das Bildungswesen der Zukunft' (Report of the Collège de France on the Future of Education), in: ibid. *Die verborgenen Mechanismen der Macht*, Hamburg: Schriften zu Politik and Kultur 1, 111–122.

Bourdieu, P. (1996) [1989] *The State Nobility. Elite Schools in the Field of Power*, Stanford: Stanford University Press.

Bourdieu, P. (2000) [1997] *Pascalian Meditations*, Stanford: Stanford University Press.

Bourdieu, P. (2001) [1998] *Masculine Domination*, Cambridge, Polity Press.

Bourdieu, P. and Passeron, J.-C. (1977) [1970] 'Foundations of a Theory of Symbolic Violence', in: ibid. *Reproduction in Education, Society and Culture*, London and Beverly Hills: Sage, 1–68.

Durkheim, E. and Mauss, M. (2009) [1903] *Primitive Classification*, London, Cohen and West.

Marx, K. and Engels, F. (1976) [1845–1846] 'The German Ideology. Critique of Modern German Philosophy According to Its Representatives Feuerbach, B. Bauer and Stirner, and of German Socialism According to Its Various Prophets', in ibid. *Collected Works*, 5, London, Lawrence and Wishart.

Mauger, G. (2005) 'Über symbolische Gewalt', in Colliot-Thelene, C. et al. (eds) *Deutsch-französische Perspektiven*, Frankfurt: M., Suhrkamp, 208–230.

Weber, M. (1978) *Economy and Society. An Outline of Interpretive Sociology*, Berkely, Los Angeles, London: University of California Press.

Young, M. (2014)' Powerful knowledge as a curriculum principle', in Young, M. et al., *Knowledge and the Future School, Curriculum and Social Justice*, London: Bloomsbury, 65–88.

3
Gramsci, Education and Power

Peter Mayo

Introduction

Antonio Gramsci (born in Ales, Sardinia, 1891; died in Rome, 1937) is widely regarded as one of the foremost social and political theorists of the twentieth century. Raised in Sardinia, he subsequently moved to Turin to take up a scholarship at the University of Turin. The city was a hotbed of political mobilisation and was part of the industrial heartland of the Italian North. Despite his great promise as a philologist, having been heralded by one of his teachers, Matteo Bartoli, as 'the archangel' set to 'defeat the grammarians',(Gramsci, 1973, 80),[1] Gramsci never completed his studies. He dropped out of university to engage in revolutionary socialist politics being prominent in workers' education circles and in socialist journalism, among other things. He eventually emerged as one of the most prominent figures in the radical left of the Italian Socialist Party and later the first Secretary General of the Italian Communist Party, following the split which occurred in Leghorn (Livorno) in 1921. Arrested in 1926 following the Fascist rise to power, he would spend the rest of his life in prison. According to the chief prosecutor, his brain was meant to be 'stopped from functioning' for 20 years (Hoare and Nowell Smith, in Gramsci, 1971, p. lxxxix) in a ruthless, clinical process publically described by Enrico Berlinguer, fellow Sardinian and successor as PCI Secretary General, as intended to 'assassinate' the Communist leader 'scientifically'[2]. This comment by the Prosecutor proved to be wide off the mark. In actual fact, Gramsci's ten years of imprisonment enabled him to bequeath to posterity one of the most prominent compilations of notes in twentieth century political thought. Some taking the form of essays, these notes would have a great influence on a variety of fields including Political Science, Anthropology,

Philosophy, Sociology, Literary Theory, Education Studies, History and Cultural Studies. Education, in its broadest sense, featured prominently in Gramsci's thinking. He himself was an indefatigable organiser of education courses even when awaiting trial on the island of Ustica, an open 'island prison' at the time. Gramsci and other political detainees would mingle with the locals and even invite them to attend the school they set up there – a landmark in the development of education on the island. Gramsci wrote not only about the Unitarian school but also about different routes to education, such as non-formal education routes *–altre vie* (other routes) – including the short-lived Institute of Proletarian Culture and a 'correspondence school' for the newly set up Italian Communist Party.

This essay

This essay focuses on Gramsci's ideas concerning the relationship between education and power. It starts off with an exposition of Gramsci's conceptualisation of power, focusing primarily on the concept of Hegemony. This leads to a discussion around the role which education plays in configurations of power as conceived by Gramsci. Due consideration is attached to the notion of the state, a construct viewed, from a Gramscian perspective, in its various forms. The importance which Gramsci attaches to language and culture, in addition to political economy, in the context of consolidating or challenging hegemonic relations, is underlined in this section. The significance Gramsci attached to the strong political agency of different types of intellectuals in this struggle is also reflected here.

The discussion moves from a focus on social relations, with their educational dimension, as highlighted by Gramsci, to highlighting educational content, again from a gramscian perspective, one which developed in his writings and partly emerged from his experiences as activist and organiser of different political and educational projects. The paper concludes with a discussion on some of the ramifications of Gramsci's ideas for a social justice-oriented educational practice.

Gramsci's conceptualisation of power

Gramsci draws on Macchiavelli's *Il Principe* (The Prince) for his conceptualisation of power. His notion of power centres on the fifteenth- to sixteenth- century Florentine thinker's 'Twin Heads of the Centaur,' namely force and consent. The relationship between the two varied

from state to state. For purely heuristic purposes, Gramsci conceptually separates political and civil society. This separation applies to the
different types of societies of his time (irrespective of the geographical
location, which could be Germany or Russia, for example), the difference between them lying in the degree of development of civil society
(Thomas, 2009). Gramsci's conception of 'Civil Society', which has a
long history, is no longer current today, however (Boothman, 2014). In
the Gramscian sense, civil society is understood as the entire complex
of knowledge and culture, and of religious and social institutions (Pala,
2014), This broad spectrum includes agencies ranging from schools,
churches, the press and cultural centres to others like the Red Cross,
Oxfam, Caritas and social clubs[3] that all exist alongside (some even
interacting with) the repressive forces (army, police etc.) of the 'political
society' that sustains the state. Again, the usage of this term differs from
the contemporary one, the latter referring to the third space between
the state and industry. As Gramsci argued, with respect to the state and
civil society in Western countries in his time:

> there was a proper relation between State and civil society, and when
> the State trembled a sturdy structure of civil society was at once
> revealed. The State was only an outer ditch, behind which there
> stood a powerful system of fortresses and earthworks: more or less
> numerous from one State to the next, it goes without saying – but
> this precisely necessitated an accurate reconnaissance of each indi-
> vidual country. (Gramsci, 1971, p. 238)

When and where a strong 'civil society' of this type exists, it is futile
to attempt to change the state simply by a direct offensive as this
is bound to fail (see the cases of the *Spartakusbund* – the Spartacus
League – uprising in Weimar Germany and more recently the late
1970s urban guerrilla warfare in Germany and Italy). In these kind of
societies, a movement or alliance of movements for change needs to
operate in and across the whole spectrum of civil society, engaging in
a lengthy process of 'intellectual and moral reform' involving, among
other things, widespread cultural and educational work, to help lay
the foundations and create the conditions for a transformation of the
state (the final transformation can however occur only after the state
is conquered).

> ...every revolution has been preceded by an intense labour of criti-
> cism and by the diffusion of culture and the spread of ideas among

masses of men (*sic*) who are at first resistant and think only of solving their own immediate economic and political problems for themselves[, and] who have no ties of solidarity with others in the same condition. (Gramsci, 1977, p. 12)

The situation in Czarist Russia, site of the Bolshevik revolution, was quite different from that obtaining in Germany, France or Italy, for example. *Burgherlich gesellschaft* (bourgeois civil society) was not strong in this specific historical and geographical context. A frontal attack (war of manoeuvre) on the repressive repositories of the state and its institutions was therefore much more straightforward: 'In the East (*meaning Russia* – my italics) the state was everything, civil society was primordial and gelatinous' (Gramsci, 1971, p. 238).

The revolution in Russia had to be characterised by the building of civil society, and therefore the apparatuses that could consolidate hegemony. Hegemony is the main concept, running through Gramsci's prison notes, without, one must say, any systematic exposition being provided (Borg, Buttigieg and Mayo, 2002a, p. 1). Hegemony refers to a situation in which most arrangements, marking a particular social reality, are conditioned[4] by and tend to support the interests of a particular class or social grouping.

Prima facie, there appear to be ambiguities in Gramsci's writings as to whether hegemony refers solely to this aspect of power or also combines this aspect with the coercive elements. One should keep in mind that Gramsci was simply jotting down notes in prison for a future work. This might well explain the inconsistencies in the use of terminology. These inconsistencies have, however, given rise to different uses of the term 'hegemony' by different writers and commentators. In short, hegemony is often said to refer to either one of the heads (consent) or both twin heads (coercion and consent) of Macchiavelli's Centaur: force (coercion) + consent or else force + hegemony (consent). I personally favour the more comprehensive conception of hegemony, that is, consent + coercion, since it is very much in keeping with Gramsci's notion of the 'Integral State' (Gramsci, 1971, p. 239). Gramsci delineated the two aspects of consent and repression in this all-encompassing state for simply heuristic purposes. In reality, one cannot separate the two since there is no entirely repressive apparatus and, likewise, no completely ideological apparatus. Schools, for instance, may appear prima facie to be ideological but also be repressive at the same time; the degree of repression varying from state to state: for example, with flunking, state-slapped fines for absenteeism, heavy-handed approaches by security guards in US schools (Giroux, 2009), and reprisals against striking teachers.

Hegemony, a frequently-used word in critical education, is not one of Gramsci's original concepts. In fact, few of his concepts are actually original. The word dates back to the ancient Greeks and was later used by revolutionary political figures such as Lenin and Plekhanov, as well as in linguistics debates to which Gramsci must have been exposed during his philology studies (see Ives, 2004). Gramsci's concept of hegemony is rooted in Marx's theory of consciousness (Allman, 1999, 2010). The latter is best captured in the following assertions by Marx (and Engels) in *The German Ideology.* 'The ruling ideas are nothing more than the ideal expression of the dominant material relationships, the dominant material relationships grasped as ideas; hence of the relationships which make one class the ruling one, therefore the ideas of its dominance' (Marx and Engels, 1970, p. 64). Not only does the ruling class produce the ruling ideas, in view of its control over the means of intellectual production (ibid.), but the dominated classes produce ideas that do not necessarily serve their interests; these classes, that 'lack the means of mental production and are immersed in production relations which they do not control', tend to 'reproduce ideas' that express the dominant material relationships (Larrain, 1983, p. 24). After all, as Marx and Engels had underlined, '...each new class which puts itself in place of one ruling before it, is compelled, merely in order to carry through its aim, to represent its interest as the common interest of all the members of society, that is expressed in ideal form: it has to give its ideas the form of universality, and represent them as the only rational, universally valid ones'(Marx and Engels, 1970, pp. 65, 66). Hegemony, concerned with the exercise of influence and winning of consent, involves the very same process as described by Marx and Engels.

Education and power

For Gramsci, education is conceived of in its broadest context and is not limited to schooling but is central to the workings of hegemony; every relationship of hegemony being a pedagogical relationship:

> Every relationship of 'hegemony' is necessarily an educational relationship and occurs not only within a nation, between the various forces of which the nation is composed, but in the international and world-wide field, between complexes of national and continental civilisations. (Gramsci, 1971, p. 350)

At its most basic level, this notion of hegemony as a pedagogical social relationship deals with the social relations of capitalist production. In changing these relations, one can go some way towards changing the mode of production itself. Gramsci's early and later writings on the factory councils are instructive here. These factory councils, conceived of as educational agencies in the technical and administrative fields among others, were intended to supersede the trade unions in terms of enabling workers to transcend the capitalist wage relation, to usher in a new conception of workers' control at the workplace. This view was consonant with the Turin workers' act in occupying the Turin factories. In so doing, they brought that part of the Italian peninsula close to a revolution. The factory councils were conceived of as educative agencies intended towards industrial democracy *tout court*. In Gramsci's view, they were to constitute the basis of the new workers' socialist state:

> The Socialist State already exists potentially in the institutions of social life characteristic of the exploited working class. To link these institutions, coordinating and ordering them into a highly centralized hierarchy of competences and powers, while respecting the necessary autonomy and articulation of each, is to create a genuine workers' democracy here and now. (Gramsci, 1977, p. 66)[5]

In arguing thus, Gramsci emphasises the 'relational' aspect of that construct called 'the State'. The capitalist state is therefore characterised by legitimised hierarchal relations, and the struggle to create a democratic socialist state involves the struggle to confront the legitimacy of such relations and to contribute to generating democratic and socialist relations at different sites of practice, including the workplace. Transforming the social relations of production, eliminating, for instance, the hierarchical separation between the conception and execution of work, through which workers can gain a broader rather than partial knowledge of the production process and can collectively be involved in such things as overall strategy, constitutes an important step towards transforming the state through its constitutive social relations. By this I mean, in keeping with a particular reading of Marx, the state conceived of as an ensemble of legitimised social relations.

To transform relations of hegemony, one must operate within the interstices of the hegemonic apparatuses themselves and across the whole spectrum of civil society, once more used in the gramscian sense (Pala, 2014). Again, one ought to remember, even in this context (working across the spectrum of civil society), that the separations between ideology/consent, and repression/coercion, are heuristically conceived and that the two exist within most of these very same institutions of civil society, albeit to differing degrees.

Education constitutes an important feature of the ethical state, that is to say the state that not only enforces but also educates (Gramsci, 1971, p. 242) – the state as moral regulator[6] – through the ideological institutions that buttress it and also though the ostensibly repressive institutions that also have an ideological dimension, for example, the 'correctional' function of penal institutions, the 'moral basis' (read: justification) of police action. Once again, it is the integral state that combines the twin functions of 'consent' and 'coercion', 'ideology' and 'repression', 'civil' and 'political' society.

In so far as this wide-ranging educational work is concerned, Gramsci attaches importance to the work of intellectuals defined not by any intrinsic properties but by their function in either cementing the current hegemonic arrangements or else challenging them with a view to transforming them. The process of transformation, in this regard, is a collective process, involving intellectuals and activists with converging political goals, and the people with whom they work. The transformative effort entails wide-ranging intellectual and cultural work. For hegemony is always in a state of flux and can therefore never be complete, hence its being a conditioning, rather than a determining, force.

These intellectuals carry out this work through a variety of educational means, involving forms of what Henry A. Giroux calls 'public pedagogy'. These include popular culture, adult education and the media. Antonio Gramsci's conception of the educator is, however, broad enough to comprise a variety of practitioners, some of whom might not immediately identify themselves as such (educators).

His notion of the educator includes party activists working in the field of workers' education, something he himself engaged in, even during his early political career. It would include foremen or supervisors in the context of the factory councils, as Gramsci conceived in his writings on industrial democracy. It would also include people of different technical and cultural backgrounds who were invited as speakers to the *Ordine Nuovo* group (the group surrounding the similarly named periodical of socialist culture), or who collaborated at the *Club di Vita Morale*, an adult education agency intended for members of the working class. It can also include any intellectual, whether publically visible or not. The former group includes those we call today 'public intellectuals'; the latter, 'subaltern intellectuals'. The 'public intellectuals' are national or international household names, like Benedetto Croce and Giustino

Fortunato in Gramsci's time, or well-known national and global TV pundits, spokespersons for industry (for example, Sergio Marchionne of FIAT in contemporary Italy[7]) or activists who hog the spaces of the various international and national media. The more progressive activists would include people such as Noam Chomsky, the late Howard Zinn, the late Tony Benn, the late Bob Crow, Naomi Klein, the late Edward Said, Carol Becker, the late Pierre Bourdieu, Henry Giroux and Slavoj Žižek. More generally, the group of 'public intellectuals' involves those of different political persuasion and social location, including high-profile politicians, journalists, op-ed writers, trade unionists, industrialists, spokespersons for social movements and lobby groups.

The subalterns are those engaged in intellectual work, conceptualising and generating consent for particular definitions and constructions of 'reality' in restricted sites. One can include here schoolteachers, journalists in local or provincial media, parish and other priests, managers in particular firms, marketing experts etc. In short, 'subaltern' is used, in this context, to define intellectuals operating at a restricted territorial level, rather than a national or global reach.

All these intellectuals, whether high-profile or subaltern ones are not defined as 'intellectuals' due to the inherent characteristics more usually associated with them, as with the case of traditional intellectuals such as academics and 'men/women of letters', but because of their function in shaping opinions and promoting particular conceptions of the world through their affirmations, strictures and actions. They are influential in many ways, often in support of or opposed to the current state of affairs. They would fall within the range of Gramsci's broad strata of 'organic intellectuals'.

Gramsci's conception of the educator can also include 'traditional intellectuals' whose organic purpose seems to be over, since they are residual specimens of an earlier and possibly outdated hegemonic set of arrangements, and therefore assume the appearance of a 'neutral' category, identified by their immanent features, when in effect they serve to maintain and legitimise the status quo. These traditional types might also lure potentially progressive intellectuals from their immediate cultural context with a status and language that would, consequentially, render the latter alien to that very same terrain. Peter Ives (2004) has discussed this with respect to intellectuals and language development. There is always the danger that these intellectuals absolutise their activity.

Organic intellectuals had an important role to play in elaborating and creating connections between the 'spontaneous grammars' (regional languages and dialects) of the popular classes. This was not happening in Gramsci's time. In Gramsci's view, people who would have otherwise provided intellectual leadership among the subaltern classes were being co-opted, by the dominant class, partly through their being equipped with a normative grammar (various forms of standard language, including esoteric language) that was alien to the subordinated classes. This process of allurement therefore served to alienate potential organic intellectuals from these classes, rendering them traditional intellectuals instead – intellectuals whose activity appeared, deceptively, to be devoid of any social moorings, when in fact this activity served to consolidate the hegemony of the dominant groups. A classic example would be scientific and other experts, including social scientists, claiming to be either 'objective' or 'detached,' trading in purportedly politically 'neutral' knowledge, when in actual fact this knowledge helps, in many ways, to retain the status quo. Paulo Freire's well known observation that there is no such thing as neutral knowledge comes to mind.

This broad notion of intellectual workers, including both traditional and organic, and, to use a term very much in vogue at present, 'cultural workers', including educators, has had an impact on the manner in which educational and cultural activity are being viewed today in progressive sections of the literature on education and culture in the Anglo-American influenced world (see Mayo, 2014a).[8]

Content of learning and curricula

In Gramsci, one finds interest in both established and popular forms of knowledge and cultural production. Contrary to those who adhered to the *proletkult*, with its complete break from the past, Gramsci, like Lenin, placed the emphasis on learning the dominant culture and the forms of 'powerful knowledge' (Young, 2013) but in a manner that highlights their ideological basis:

> Proletarian culture is not something that has sprung from nowhere, it is not an invention of those who call themselves experts in proletarian culture. That is all nonsense. Proletarian culture must be the result of the natural development of the stores of knowledge which mankind has accumulated under the yoke of capitalist society, landlord society and bureaucratic society. (Lenin, in Entwistle, 1979, p. 44)

For example, while Gramsci suggests that this 'national' language needs to be learnt so that people are not kept at the margins of political life, the case with all standard 'national' languages, he feels that it needs to be learnt so that people are not kept at the margins of political life. He also expressed belief in the validity of manifestations of the 'popular creative spirit'. He saw, in this manifestation, the creative energy for cultural transformations, which at the time appeared to exist outside the realm of capitalist commodification. Many of these forms of the creative spirit were later not immune to commodification by Capitalism, however. Then there are his controversial writings on the Unitarian school that have been described by Mario Alighero Manacorda (1972) as an epitaph on what this school was but can no longer be, since society has changed (p. xxix). But Gramsci was critical of the Gentile reforms, introduced by Fascist Minister of Education, Giovanni Gentile, which Gramsci saw as a retrograde step. Subjects such as Latin had to be replaced. But the problem with that was that it would take quite a substantive area, capable of imparting similar rigour, to become a worthwhile substitute in a society undergoing change (Borg and Mayo, 2002b) A key concept here is the critical appropriation of dominant forms of knowledge.[9] As I argue elsewhere (Mayo, 2014a and b), the notion of cultural appropriation, as part of a 'war of position' (a process of advancement and retreat), as opposed to a 'war of manouvre' (frontal attack), applies both to the presently dominant forces and those attempting to change this particular situation of domination. For instance, capitalism can appropriate processes, figures and ideas, which originally appeared to be revolutionary, to suit its own ends. Yesterday's revolutionary anti-capitalist figure became today's commercial icon to appeal to the revolutionary cravings of youth. The image of Che Guevara is a case in point, recently appropriated to market an energy drink branded 'revolutionary energy'. Potentially revolutionary concepts such as 'workers' participation', very much at the heart of the Soviets in Russia and in the factory council movement in Gramsci's early politically active years in Turin, besides 'self-management' processes in socialist countries such as the former Yugoslavia, have more recently been repackaged. They have been repackaged in a management-driven initiative to suit the Capitalist concern for, among other things, greater productivity and employees' loyalty to the firm, to smother any possible tension arising from the basic dialectical capital-labour relation. While Gramsci spoke of the need for a critical appropriation of the dominant culture, the capitalist hegemonic class, through its political and cultural think tanks and intellectuals, including marketing experts, is always ready to prey on popular sensibilities and tastes in its quest for new markets and products, and therefore in its fetishisation of new commodities. These commodities include the many items, images and concepts, including potentially revolutionary ones as indicated above, that appeal to the imagination of various sectors of society, especially youths. The potentially revolutionary fervour of youths can easily be channelled in the direction of such commercially-appropriated products, in an 'individualising consumer culture ideology', for which they become a captive niche market. The revolutionary and hegemonically disruptive (in terms of the heterosexual regulation discussed in Notebook XXII on 'Americanism and Fordism') potential of a gay section of the population electing to live in 'alternative living' quarters can be snuffed by a capitalist system that is always dynamic and sees such quarters as the repository of a niche market for particular kinds of products. Examples of this situation abound in places such as San Francisco and Seville.

These cultural forms, especially those constituting mass popular culture, have been the focus of attention in cultural studies, showing how hegemony works. The focus is on the contradictory nature of these types of culture, especially popular activities and leisure commodities. The concern in such messages is with converting 'common sense' to 'good sense', the former characterised by a mixed contradictory consciousness which connects with people's quotidian experience but which is incoherent. 'Good sense' is the term used by Gramsci to refer to a more coherent type of consciousness which is diluted of its 'false consciousness' elements while retaining and solidifying its potentially revolutionary and socially transformative ones. Gramsci observed how hegemony occurs through different forms of culture including popular culture, which, though often manifesting the finer aspects of the 'popular creative spirit', is, like any other culture, not to be romanticised; it contains potentially disempowering elements. For instance, cultural manifestations of regional identity can exhibit an obliviousness to the deep class divisions that exist in each territory. This can lead to false alliances between people on both sides of the social class divide. A case in point is Gramsci's reference, in his essay on the 'Southern Question', to the abortive attempt at creating a 'Giovane Sardegna' alliance, on the Italian mainland, between exploited Sardinian peasants and their offspring both on the island and mainland and the offspring of the exploiting Sardinian gentry (Gramsci, 1995), as the local (Sardinian) overseers of capitalist exploitation (Mayo, 2007, p. 7).

This focus on the contradictory and potentially empowering aspects of popular culture is given prominence in the contemporary critical pedagogical literature (Mayo, 2014a), where Gramsci's influence, via the impact of cultural studies, continues to be felt.

Meaning for educational practice

Gramsci discussed, in his notes on schooling, the then emerging trendy 'progressivist' form of pedagogy, perceived as a dilution of the Rousseau legacy. He saw signs of this underlying some of the reforms introduced by Fascist Minister, Giovanni Gentile. Gramsci stated that the romantic school, associated with Rousseau, must enter the classical phase, that is to say a phase characterised by a balance between what is new and apparently emancipatory and what is regarded as traditional but still powerful in terms of its ability to enable one to handle life effectively and negotiate the intricacies of power.

While one should teach what Michael Young (2013), almost echoing Gramsci, would call 'powerful knowledge', one should expose this knowledge's ideological basis. The language question is a case in point. In denying learners this powerful knowledge, Gramsci would argue, one would be selling them short. Knowledge of this language would prevent learners from remaining at the margins of political life. One should however demonstrate, at the same time, the manner in which 'ideology resides in language' to echo Paulo Freire. Taking the example of my home country, the former British colony of Malta, one should emphasise the colonial basis of the predominance of the English language without denying people from all classes of Maltese society access to this language of international currency. In former colonies, language issues are complex, as Freire discovered in his work in Portugal's African colonies where the many tribal languages had to play a subservient role to the standard colonising Portuguese language, which served as a lingua franca, although not spoken by all but. This standard language became a noticeable means of social differentiation (see Freire, 1978; Freire and Macedo, 1987).

As for teaching, one can read, in his notes on the 'Unitarian School – Notebooks 1V and XII (Gramsci, 1975), that Gramsci would rather prefer a 'mediocre' teacher who dwells on facts to someone who engages in a kind of laissez-faire pedagogical approach which will always benefit those who have the cultural capital to learn what is powerful from other sources, not least their own cultural milieu.

Some basic implications

The above considerations deriving from Gramsci's writings lead me to argue that:

- Education is about learning basic skills and knowledge that are historically contingent and have strong underlying ideological elements but which have stood the test of time. Such an educational engagement, however, entails doing so in a critical manner, and involves the critical reflection that constitutes the basis of praxis.

- In seeking to teach within an emancipatory context, educators should be careful not to throw out the knowledge baby with the knowledge bathwater.

- Critical pedagogy has much to learn from the above consideration and insights from Gramsci. Critical pedagogues need to deal extensively with Young's (2013) discussion around 'powerful knowledge'. In short, critical pedagogy must deal with the need for educators to teach thoroughly and correctly that knowledge which can provide access to power and therefore help foster among learners the consciousness, skills, knowledge and attitudes to operate effectively in the system with a view to collectively transforming it. I see this as applying also to emerging 'powerful knowledge' such as 'coding', discussed by Ben Williamson elsewhere in this volume. I see the importance of 'coding, as explained by Williamson, as part of the dominant hegemonic, rather than 'post-hegemonic', condition. In my view, software shapes what is presented, disseminated and therefore constructed digitally as 'reality', a modern manifestation of digitally-mediated hegemony. It constitutes another manifestation of Capitalism's ability to construct and circulate ideas, and shape notions of 'reality' through its information structures. As always, and in keeping with Gramsci's notion of hegemony, these structures can be subverted through critical appropriation of the very same means involved. Critical knowledge of coding can play an important role in this process.

- For this reason, 'powerful knowledge' should not be transmitted simply in a 'technical-rational' manner but should be taught in a way that also makes the learners aware of its ideological basis and biases, intimated by Williamson in his chapter. For example, taking the issue of language, so dear to Gramsci's heart, learners should learn speak a dominant language thoroughly. They should, however, do so in a manner that enables them to recognise the role it played and often still plays in engendering colonial and neo-colonial relations and creating social differentiation, owing to the fact that knowledge of the language is a form of materially rewarding cultural capital.

- The last mentioned approach is an example of how one can acquire knowledge in an emancipatory manner. What renders such an approach emancipatory is the way this knowledge is transmitted, taking into account the best traditions of Freirean pedagogy, which space does not permit me to describe here, though much has been written on this (Mayo, 2004). This pedagogical approach entails the avoidance of an authoritarian mode of communication. It is the sort of pedagogy that instils in the learners the commitment to sharing this knowledge with others across the social spectrum, rather than jealously guarding it as some prized individual possession, a positional good, in a culture of 'having' rather than 'being'.

Conclusion

Uncritically imparting and reproducing the dominant forms of knowledge would remain problematic for a democratic education. Gramsci was opposed to this. In the 'Unitarian School' notes, Gramsci refers to teachers who limit themselves to delivering facts as 'mediocre' (Gramsci, 1971, p. 36). He prefers this to simply a laissez-faire approach, which he feared the reform of his time would encourage, especially among working-class kids. This however does not mean this type of teaching constitutes the desired form of alternative teaching. He is well aware that, no matter how useful subjects such as Latin are in inculcating rigour, they have to be replaced because times have changed.

> It will be necessary to replace Latin and Greek as the fulcrum of the formative school, and they will be replaced. But it will not be easy to deploy the new subject or subjects in a didactic form which gives equivalent results in terms of education and general formation, from early childhood to the threshold of adult choices of career. (Gramsci, 1971, pp. 39, 40)

This conviction connects with his views regarding established forms of culture and emerging or popular ones. The existence of one type does not preclude the other, with 'synthesis' being the desideratum for cultural renewal and development. The point to register for critical pedagogy, and which was well captured by Gramsci's sense of a classical phase (conceived of as 'balance') needing to replace the romantic phase in education, is that any change, with a democratic purpose in mind, should be carried out warily, that is, not denying the sort of 'powerful knowledge' that would allow learners to make inroads into the political power structure with a view to changing it, albeit collectively. In other words, a critical pedagogy should ensure that one develops the skills, attitudes and right knowledge base to act as an important agent capable of negotiating, with others, change in the hegemonic ensemble of social relations with a view to rendering them more democratic and socially just.

Notes

In this essay I have used some material from Mayo (2015).

1. Letter to Tania, dated March 19, 1927. Original in Italian in Gramsci (1996, p. 56). See also the discussion in Peter Ives, (2004: 47–53). In this letter, Gramsci discloses to his sister-in-law his intention to embark on a work 'für ewig' (forever), and tentatively outlines the areas he seeks to develop. The entries in what have become known as 'The Prison Notebooks' (*Selections from the Prison Notebooks*, Gramsci, 1971) and *Quaderni del Carcere* (Gramsci, 1975) were meant to provide the foundation for this work.
2. Enrico Berlinguer expressed this view in a televised debate, on Italy's state station Rai TV, focusing on Fascism and its legacies. The remark was made as a rider to the assertion that, had Nazi-Fascism (a frequently-used Italian term) been successful, it would have rendered Europe one large concentration camp. See: www.youtube.com/watch?v=vHFkQu8VBBM [accessed 7 March 2015].
3. I am indebted to my good friend Joseph A. Buttigieg for the provision of these examples.
4. In the words of D. W. Livingstone, hegemony is 'a social condition in which all aspects of social reality are dominated by or supportive of a single class' (Livingstone, 1976: 235). Taking my cue from this volume's Editor, Antonia Kupfer, my preferred language, in this context, would be more prudent, to avoid giving hegemony the overly deterministic weight suggested by Livingstone's choice of verb ('dominated'). Otherwise, this definition would contradict the notion that hegemony is fluid and constantly open to negotiation and renegotiation.
5. Adapted from Mayo (2004b)
6. In the words of Corrigan and Sayer (1985: 3), it is a state which 'states', with the rider that it 'never stops talking' (ibid.).
7. Sergio Marchionne: CEO of Fiat S.p.A., Chairperson and CEO of Chrysler Group LLC, and Chairman of CNH(California, Nevada, Hawaii) Industrial N.V, and 2012 Chairman of the European Automobile Manufacturers Association.
8. This section on intellectuals draws on Mayo, P (2014).
9. It has often been argued that, whenever there is an appropriation of any cultural form by one social group from another, a transformation of that cultural product occurs. In *Culture & Society*, Raymond Williams (1958, 1982) refers to poet, playwright and critic T. S. Eliot who argued that the transformation from something traditionally elite to something more widely diffuse entails a dilution, 'cheapening' or 'adulteration'. Williams argued otherwise (p. 239). Like Gramsci, he must have had faith in the working class' potential for cultural renewal as the appropriated product is made to relate to its 'way of life'.

References

Allman, P. D. (1999) *Revolutionary Social Transformation: Democratic Hopes, Political Possibilities and Critical Education*, Westport, CT and London: Bergin and Garvey.

Allman, P. D. (2010) *Critical Education against Global Capitalism, Karl Marx and Revolutionary Critical Education*. Rotterdam and Taipei: Sense Publishers.

Boothman, D. (2014) 'Una Lunga Preistoria: Adam Ferguson, L'illuminismo Scozzese e le Radici della Società Civile' [A long prehistory. Adam Ferguson, the Scottish Enlightenment and the roots of Civil Society] in Pala, M. (ed.) *Narrazioni Egemoniche. Gramsci, Letteratura e società civile* (Hegemonic Narratives. Gramsci, Literature and Civil Society), Bologna: Il Mulino.

Borg, C., Buttigieg, J. and Mayo, P. (2002a) 'Introduction: Gramsci and education, a holistic approach', in Borg, C., Buttigieg, J. and Mayo, P. (eds) *Gramsci and Education*, Lanham, MD: Rowman and Littlefield, pp. 1–23.

Borg, C., and Mayo, P. (2002b) 'Gramsci and the Unitarian School. Paradoxes and Possibiities', in: Borg, C., Buttigieg, J. and Mayo, P. (eds) *Gramsci and Education*, Lanham, MD: Rowman and Littlefield, pp. 1–23.

Corrigan, P. and Sayer, D. (1985) *The Great Arch: English State Formation as Cultural Revolution*, Oxford: Blackwell.

Entwistle, H. (1979) *Antonio. Gramsci. Conservative Schooling for Radical Politics*, London, Boston and Henley: Routledge and Kegan Paul.

Freire P. (1970) *Pedagogy of the Oppressed*, New York, NY: Continuum.

Freire P. (1978) *Pedagogy in Process: The Letters to Guinea Bissau*, New York, NY: Continuum.

Freire, P. and Macedo, D. (1987) *Literacy: Reading the word and the world*, Massachussets: Bergin and Garvey.

Giroux H. A. (2001) *Public Spaces/Private Lives: Beyond the Culture of Cynicism*, Lanham, MD: Rowman and Littlefield.

Giroux, H. (2009) 'Brutalising kids: Painful lessons in the pedagogy of school violence,' *Truthout* 8 October. Available from: http://truthout.org [Accessed 13 January 2013].

Gramsci A. (1971) *Selections from the Prison Notebooks*, (eds) Hoare, Q. and Nowell Smith, G., New York, NY: International Publishers.

Gramsci, A. (1972) *L' Alternativa Pedagogica* (The Pedagogical Alternative), (ed.) Manacorda, M. A., Florence: La Nuova Italia.

Gramsci, A. (1973) *Letters from prison. Antonio Gramsci*, (ed.) Lawner, L., New York: Noonday Press.

Gramsci A. (1975) *Quaderni del Carcere, Edizione Critica* [Prison Notebooks: Critical Edition], (ed.) Gerratana, V., Torino: Einaudi. (In Italian)

Gramsci, A. (1977) *Antonio Gramsci, Selections from Political writings (1910–1920)*, (eds) Hoare, Q. and Matthews, J., New York, NY: International Publishers.

Gramsci, A. (1995) *The Southern Question*, (ed. and trans.) Verdicchio, P., Lafayette, W., Bordighera Inc.

Gramsci, A. (1996) *Lettere dal Carcere 1926–1937, Vol. 1*, Palermo: Sellerio.

Ives P. (2004) *Language and Hegemony in Gramsci*, London: Pluto Press.

Larrain, J. (1983) *Marxism and Ideology*, New Jersey: Humanities Press.

Livingstone D. W. (1976) 'On hegemony in corporate capitalist states', *Sociological Inquiry* 46(3–4), 235–250.

Manacorda, M. A. (1972)'Introduzione' [Introduction], in Gramsci, A, *L'Alternativa Pedagogica*, Manacorda, M. A. (ed.), Florence: La Nuova Italia.

Marx, K. and Engels, F. (1970) *The German Ideology*, (ed,) Arthur, C. J., London: Lawrence and Wishart.

Mayo, P. (2004) *Liberating Praxis: Paulo Freire's Legacy for Radical Education and Politics*, Santa Barbara, CA: PraegerPublishers.

Mayo, P. (2007) 'Gramsci, the Southern Question and the Mediterranean', *Mediterranean Journal of Educational Studies*, 12(2), 1–17.

Mayo, P. (2014a) 'Gramsci and the politics of education', *Capital and Class*, 38(2), 385–398.

Mayo, P. (2014b) 'Antonio Gramsci's Impact on Critical Pedagogy', *Critical Sociology* (forthcoming in hardcopy), Published online before print February 7, 2014, doi: 10.1177/0896920513512694 *Crit Sociol February 7, 2014 0896920513512694*

Mayo, P. (2015) *Hegemony and Education under Neoliberalism. Insights from Gramsci*, New York and London: Routledge.

Pala, M. (ed.) (2014) *Narrazioni egemoniche. Gramsci, Letteratura e societa` civile*, Bologna: Il Mulino.

Thomas P. D. (2009) *The Gramscian Moment: Philosophy, Hegemony and Marxism*, Amsterdam: Brill.

Williams, R. (1958, 1982) *Culture & Society*, London: The Hogarth Press..

Young M. (2013) 'Overcoming the crisis in curriculum theory: a knowledge-based approach', *Journal of Curriculum Studies* 45(2), 101–118.

Part II
Knowledge

4
Programming Power: Policy Networks and the Pedagogies of 'Learning to Code'

Ben Williamson

Interest in the educational value of learning to write and programme computer code has grown from a minority concern among computing educators, grassroots computing organisations, and computer scientists into a major policy discourse. Originating with activist and grassroots campaigning groups such as Computing at School, 'learning to code' is now being actively promoted in England by cross-sector organisations including Nesta (National Endowment for Science, Technology and the Arts) and the Nominet Trust that are increasingly seeking to participate in educational governance. As a result, learning to code has been recognised as desirable amongst politicians and educational policymakers, as evidenced by the scheduled 2014 replacement in the English National Curriculum of the subject ICT (Information and Communication Technology), which critics claim over-emphasises basic functional skills for using computers, with a new computing programme of study that focuses instead on computer science, programming skills and computational thinking (Department for Education 2012). Learning to code has been transformed from a grassroots campaign into a major policy agenda in a remarkably concentrated period, yet the powerful actors mobilising it into curriculum policy are largely unrecognised in educational policy research, and the material practices of coding promoted through the pedagogies of learning to code have not been subject to detailed research.

Learning to code is additionally embedded in a contemporary societal context in which software codes and algorithms are understood as increasingly powerful influences on the world. The rapid expansion of 'Big Data', 'machine learning' and 'data analytics' reflect a contemporary situation in which software code and algorithms are being put to work as powerful technologies right across social, political, cultural and economic contexts and governmental, civil society and industrial sectors, as well as in science, social science, and humanities disciplines (Kitchin, 2014). A form of technical 'solutionism' is emerging across sectors, fields and disciplines that tends to assume that all social, scientific, governmental and human problems can be addressed through the application of the right code and algorithms (Morozov, 2013). As a consequence, a critical social scientific debate (largely among sociologists, geographers and 'software studies' researchers, for example, Fuller, 2008) has developed around code, algorithms, and software. Researchers increasingly recognise software code and algorithms as an 'invisible structural force' that can 'pattern and coordinate everyday life' (Mackenzie, 2006, p. 45). Terms such as 'algorithmic power', 'code as law', and 'algorithmic ideology' have proliferated (for example, Mager, 2012). As the title of the new book *Software Takes Command* by media theorist Lev Manovich (2013) asserts, the contemporary world has undergone a transformational 'softwarization' into a 'software society' in which all social, economic, and cultural systems of modern society now run on software and its constitution through code (Manovich, 2013). Like electricity and combustion in the industrial society, he claims, software enables a global information society.

To date, little critical attention has been given to software code or digital data in educational research, though, as Selwyn (2015, p. 72) notes, there is now increased emphasis on 'the "modelling" of education through digital data' and 'algorithmically-driven "systems thinking" – where complex (and unsolvable) social problems associated with education can be seen as complex (but solvable) statistical problems.' Moreover, Williamson (2015, p. 84) has identified how the 'algorithmic power' of 'network-based and database-driven software' is 'increasingly augmenting, mediating and governing educational practices.' Thus the rise of a major global market in online courses and e-learning products is seen as a solution to widespread pedagogic problems, while politicians and policymakers increasingly mobilise sophisticated data analysis tools and techniques to enable statistical identification of problems at national, regional and institutional scales. These examples suggest that software code has been increasingly positioned as the solution to educational problems, whether specific pedagogical problems for the teacher in the classroom or a policymaker's problem with tracing and modelling national educational progress and outcomes, and indicate the extent to which new forms of computational thinking, the understanding of how to construct problems so they can eventually be expressed in binary mathematics, are infusing educational thought. It is in this context that a variety of organisations and actors have coalesced around learning to code and the related skills of computational thinking, although this is not a coherent or stable network, but a messy hybrid of intentions, ambitions, and interests.

In this chapter, I trace the policy developments, discourses, and cross-sectoral and interorganisational connections that have translated learning to code into curriculum policy. The chapter is organised around two clusters of questions. The first is about power and policy networks. What organisations are involved in seeking to influence and negotiate policy around learning to code? Is this an example of how power in the educational policy-making process is being displaced to new networks of actors? The second cluster of questions is about the power of software itself as an actor in education. With computer code and programming activities increasingly prominent, are we seeing the emergence of new nonhuman sources and configurations of power? How might we understand the power of computer-coded devices themselves? Can these influence what learners do? And how do the pedagogies of learning to code configure and activate the capacities of the learner? These are questions central to the aim of this book: to explore new actors and agents of power in education, and to explore new forms of power operating in different contexts. The chapter combines aspects of policy studies with software studies approaches in the social sciences to consider the power of learning to code in education.

Policy network analysis

The chapter draws on a study of the participation in education of cross-sector organisations, think tanks, and other 'policy intermediaries' and 'policy labs'. The focus is specifically on the organisations Nesta and the Nominet Trust, and on the ways they have established networks of governmental, civil society and commercial actors to promote and campaign for learning to code. Nesta was established as the National Endowment for Science, Technology and the Arts with an £80 million endowment by the UK New Labour government in 1998 but became independent in 2011 with a remit to innovate in public services. Nesta works with various philanthropic organisations as well as with commercial businesses, civil society organisations, and in collaboration with government departments including the Cabinet Office, with whom it is in a joint venture to run the Behavioural Insights Unit. 'Digital education' is one of Nesta's key themes and the platform on which it advocates a range of learning to code initiatives. Nesta's activities around learning to code are all managed within its 'Public Innovation Lab' which seeks to solve social challenges through the application of new technologies. For example, in its work on health, Nesta's innovation lab focuses on wearable and mobile monitoring devices, while its work on 'digital education' involves projects on remote tutoring and online video resources as well as learning to code, computing and related forms of *digital making* discussed later. The Nominet Trust was established in 2008 as the philanthropic outgrowth of Nominet, the internet registry which maintains the UK register of domain names. The Nominet Trust invests in projects and programmes 'using the internet to address big social challenges' and describes itself through the discourse of social investment, social innovation and social technology entrepreneurship. The Nominet Trust hosts the 'Social Tech Guide' website which showcases technology projects that 'address complex social challenges, from health and education to poverty and climate change'. It positions technology as a 'social good' and its steering committee consists of both the chief executive of the Nominet Trust and the chief executive of Nesta. In collaboration, Nesta and the Nominet Trust initiated the 'Make Things Do Stuff' campaign which promotes a wide range of activities and organisations associated with learning to code and other forms of digital making.

Organisationally, these bodies are neither solely governmental nor commercial actors, but straddle sectors and broker projects with connections between them. Nesta and the Nominet Trust both act as 'hubs' for a variety of partnerships and networks. They are prototypical of 'public and social innovation labs' (*psilabs*) or innovation teams (*i-teams*) as Nesta documents describe them (Mulgan, 2014; Nesta, 2014). Public and social policy innovation labs seek to put 'smart software' and digital data to work deep within the activities of government, alongside new forms of 'sociable governance' through relationships and collaborations, particularly in the redesign of public services, education, health, and social services (Williamson *forthcoming*). Nesta's own public innovation lab and the Nominet Trust's emphasis on social innovation and 'social tech' are evidence of how such organisational reconfigurations are enabling them to position themselves as solution-providers for public and social policy problems. Policy labs, or psilabs and i-teams, are a new organisational format combining a variety of 'sociable' methods of co-design, rapid prototyping, and citizen entrepreneurship with 'smart' coded methods, such as data mining, data analytics, and predictive 'machine learning' techniques in the redesign of services such as education. In this emerging sector, code and algorithms are seen as computational solutions to the problems of re-engineering government services, as 'hack events' sponsored by Nesta, such as *hackathons* for public sector redesign, clearly demonstrate (Merrett, 2014).

These organisations criss-cross the borderlines between the public and private sectors and are contributing to new forms of 'network governance' and 'policy networks' in public education in England (Williamson, 2014). 'Networked governance' is characterised by decentralisation, mobility, fluidity, looseness, complexity and instability, by the criss-crossing of sectoral borderlines and the hybridisation of ideas, discourses and materials from bureaucratic, academic and media fields. While conventional policy instruments have not been completely overturned, the shift to networked governance in education, as Ball and Junemann (2012) have documented, is evident from the entry of new participants into policy processes, changes in prevailing policy discourses, and changes in the relationships between the state and non-state, non-public sector organisations. Educational 'policy networks' are an interorganisational materialisation of network governance. Made up primarily of 'experts' from think tanks, policy institutes, multilateral agencies, media consultancies, political lobbying and public relations, policy networks 'perform the role of conveying ideas between different areas of the production, distribution, or circulation of ideas' in order to 'influence the decision-making process' (Lawn and Grek, 2012, p. 75). While the concepts of network governance and policy networks are not uncontentious, Ball and Junemann (2012) claim that in England, education policy certainly is now being dispersed and enacted by increasingly heterogeneous and sometimes unstable networks of governmental, civil society and commercial actors.

In seeking to demonstrate how education is increasingly being governed through network governance, and through associated interorganisational configurations of 'policy labs' and 'social innovators', this chapter is focused on how intermediary policy actors are promoting the practices of learning to code in schools. Learning to code is both a set of pedagogic practices and a contemporary policy discourse being enacted by a mixture of actors from policy labs, governmental agencies, and commercial companies, through a variety of projects, partnerships and campaigns. Through such networks, learning to code is being constructed as a hybrid product of different discourses, interests and agendas. Adopting methods of 'policy network analysis', I focus on the reports, pamphlets, websites and other documents that articulate these intermediaries' ideas and aspirations. As Ball and Junemann (2012, p. 14) articulate it, the method of policy network analysis seeks to identify actors, their associations and relationships, and their power and capacities to contribute to policy decision-making. The specific focus below is on identifying key organisations from government, business and civil society involved in promoting various activities around 'learning to code' (primarily in England), and on analysing the ways in which they discursively construct and mobilise learning to code.

The central argument is that intermediary organisations such as Nesta and the Nominet Trust are promoting computer programming activities in ways which might embed young people firmly in the coded infrastructures and material practices of today's digitally-mediated landscape. This demands a consideration of how power is being displaced both to intermediary actors and to the coded infrastructures and programming practices they promote. These intermediary actors and the technologies and practices they promote all combine to organise the pedagogic experiences of school children and configure their capacities and abilities. In the next section, I seek to understand 'code' as an increasingly pervasive source of power in the world, before proceeding to examine the formation of the 'learning to code' agenda.

Programming power

Computer code is commonly understood as the machine-readable language programmed to instruct computer software. It is the substrate to software, and is constructed through programming – the art and science of putting together algorithms and instructions that can be automatically read and translated by a machine in order to do something. A growing recognition of the power of code is reflected in popular science publications like *9 Algorithms that Changed the Future* (MacCormick, 2012) which demonstrate the vast reach of code and its algorithmic ordering structures into contemporary everyday practices. The algorithms of the title refer to search engine indexing and ranking; the cryptographic algorithms required by secure websites; pattern recognition algorithms for recognising handwriting, speech and faces; data compression of files like MP3s and JPEGs; and the transactional changes made to databases, such as those required for online banking and social networking sites like Facebook. All of these algorithms and their rules and sequences are written in code, making code itself into a significant contemporary technical device, the coders that script it into significant expert actors, and the coding they do into a significant material practice.

Beyond its technical and material existence, code also exerts important social effects. Computer code is thoroughly entangled in contemporary practices of surveillance, enterprise, consumption, leisure, economics, politics and much else, as developments such as government snooping, 'smart cities', personalised targeted advertising, and the transformation of online popular culture attest (Mackenzie, 2006; Beer, 2013). As code is wired out into the world in software products, it is now understood among many social scientists as more than just the written script that instructs and controls computing devices. As Manovich (2013, p. 15) phrases it, software is *'a layer that permeates all areas of contemporary socie-ties'* (original italics). Through the software it instructs, code organises, disrupts and participates in contemporary social, economic, political and cultural activities and practices. It may even be 'reassembling social science' itself (Ruppert, Law and Savage 2013) as new digital methods and search algorithms make possible new analyses, configurations and visu-alisations of the world. Sociotechnically understood as both a product of the world and a relational *producer* of the world, code *acts*: it interpo-lates, mixes with and ultimately *produces* collective political, economic and cultural life (Kitchin and Dodge, 2011). It is inseparable from its social, cultural, political and economic processes of *production*, and its socially, culturally, politically and economically *productive* effects.

Moreover, people view and understand code through the deployment of powerful and consistent discourses that promote, justify and natu-ralise software across a whole array of domains (Kitchin and Dodge, 2011). Indeed, for Mackenzie and Vurdubakis (2011, p. 16), software is the 'hybrid progeny of computer code and social codes of conduct': not just the technical fact of lines of code that instruct software, but sets of social codes with the power to 'direct how citizens act' (Thrift, 2005, p. 173). All of these things add up to a pervasive system of thought within which the procedures and processes written in code and sequenced in algorithms may be taken as a new set of rules and mundane routines to live by. The power of code is not just in its technical operations but in how it sinks into everyday cultural, economic and political discourse, thought and action.

We need to consider here the idea that code acts as a 'vital source of social power' that augments society (Kitchin and Dodge, 2011, p. 246). As the substrate to software, code is significant as a source of power because it is invested through the command structure of its program-ming with some degree of autonomy to perform its work. It can 'make things happen' by virtue of its 'execute-ability', its ability to perform tasks according to patterns of encoded instructions constructed through programming (Mackenzie and Vurdubakis, 2011, p. 6). Everything from typing in a word processing software package to running a complex scientific simulation ultimately depends on code performing the work it has been instructed to do. Software code is not inert but fundamentally performative. The performativity of code to make things happen and to produce outcomes autonomously lies at the heart of many recent accounts of the power of software in modern life, to the extent that some researchers consider software code and algorithms as a challenge to human agency itself. As Beer (2009, p. 987) claims, 'algorithmic power' may be 'becoming a part of how we live, a part of our being, a part of how we do things, the way we are treated, the things we encounter, our way of life'.

Scott Lash (2007) has described the power of software code in a technologically mediated world as 'power after hegemony'. His article is an ambitious reconsideration of cultural theory. Lash (2007, pp. 55–56) argues that in cultural studies 'hegemony means domination through consent as much as coercion', through ideology and discourse, and 'that cultural power is largely addressed to the reproduction of economy, society and polity.' The hegemonic era that Lash characterises is one defined by technologies of reproduction such as film, television, records, radio and print media, which cultural studies has long subjected to ideological critique. For Lash, our new era, however, is even more thoroughly technologically mediated. In an era of networked technologies, software ubiquity, and social media, more and more of everyday life is experienced through technologies that have been constructed by programmers according to the logic of computer science. Where hegemony is based on a logic of reproduction, contemporary new technologies involve users in acts of content creation and in the generation of traces of data. Users live with software code and algorithms that can trace every interaction and transaction they make online, trace their physical movement through location-aware mobile devices, and even predict their tastes, relationships, and activities. Consequently, computer science, computer code and its algorithms are introducing new computational 'rules' into human societies. These rules are 'generative' and 'inventive' rather than reproductive. Thus, as algorithms increasingly pervade the social fabric as new kinds of social rules, they have the generative and inventive capacity to shape and configure social formations and individual lives. In contrast to the reproductive logic of hegemony, in a new epoch 'posthegemonic power operates through a logic of invention, hence not of reproduction but of chronic production of economic, social and political relations' (Lash, 2007, p. 56). As such, how code and algorithms are programmed can extend into the ordering, structuring and sequencing of the social world itself. In this sense, we are moving into a 'society in which power is increasingly in the algorithm' (Lash, 2007, p, 71); where power is in the software we use, and where, as Beer (2009, p. 995) adds, 'information is harvested about us' in order to generate new experiences. Thus, we move in a world where software 'learns' about us:

> Rather than power at a distance, this is power up close.... This is undoubtedly an expression of power, not of someone having power over someone else, but of the software making choices and connections in complex and unpredictable ways in order to shape the everyday experiences of the user. (Beer, 2009, p. 997)

Whereas hegemonic power sought to secure consent from the 'outside' through ideology and discourse to the reproduction of economy, society and polity, a post-hegemonic form of algorithmic power works from 'inside' as part of our 'being', living with us and reacting to everything we do. This is the case, for example, when Amazon's algorithms generate recommendations for consumer purchases; when Google's PageRank algorithm orders search query results; or when Facebook's NewsFeed algorithm configures or manipulates users' social network feeds; but even more significantly when algorithmic data analytics systems automate such things as the provision of government services, organise transport and utilities infrastructures, coordinate social control mechanisms, and enable real-time governmental and commercial surveillance. In all these cases, the generative rules of algorithms work from inside everyday life rather than from outside, in the form of a dominant ideology or discourse. They constitute 'grammars of action' for new forms of social ordering and governance, and are endowed with the power to 'actively reshape behaviour' (Kitchin and Dodge, 2011, p. 109). As Beer (2013, p. 70) explains, 'algorithms create realities, they constitute the world in different ways and they present us with limitations and boundaries that we then live by.' Hegemonic power from outside is being elided by post-hegemonic power that, through the ubiquity of devices programmed in code and algorithms, acts as a 'technological unconscious' deep within everyday activity (Thrift, 2005).

It is important to note that these accounts from the literature on code and algorithmic forms of power emphasise how these technologies are themselves socially produced, by programmers and coders working according to the computational rules and styles of thought associated with computer science. As such, Mager (2012) has argued that the kind of code and algorithms that facilitate everyday social practices, such as using search engines or accessing a social media news feed, are based on particular social models of the world and reflect certain kinds of assumptions and politics that she terms 'algorithmic ideology'. In order for an algorithmic system to function, Neyland (2014) claims, the world outside of the system has to be mathematically modelled by its programmers in such a way that it can be built-in to the social world of the algorithmic system. Google's driverless car, for example, relies on ultra-precise digitised maps to navigate the physical world – a compelling case of the ways in algorithms and their code are involved in building 'a world out there into a world in here, in the algorithmic machine' (Neyland, 2014, p. 11). Software code and algorithms are, then, through and through social *products* as well as *producers* of the world. The rules of computer science, code and algorithmic forms of power are being projected into the social world in ways which subsequently do work in that world. They model the world in particular ways, and provide grammars of action that make it possible then to act on it. In this sense, power runs through the code and algorithms that increasingly structure and organise everyday life and all kinds of social institutions.

In the next sections, I explore how this understanding of code might enable us to better understand emerging developments around programming and learning to code in schools. Learning to code inculcates young people in the material practices of code production, whilst also embedding them firmly in a heavily software-mediated environment structured and ordered by code and algorithmic power.

Programming pedagogies

Today there is a growing interest in promoting computer programming to young people. In this section I explore the ways in which 'learning to code' has been discursively constructed and promoted by cross-sector intermediary organisations, including Nesta and the Nominet Trust, which act as conduits for a network of interests from the governmental, commercial and civil society sectors. As we shall see, the result is that 'learning to code' has become a contingent, hybrid and elastic concept. As the *Observer* newspaper columnist Naughton (2012) has stated, the growth of interest in programming comes with a variety of different assumptions from advocates across different sectors. The dominant policy interest, he argues, is in promoting and growing computer entrepreneurship for the economic competitiveness of 'UK plc'. The alternative perspective, which Naughton advocates, is learning to code for *informed citizenship* in a world where computation has become ubiquitous. Naughton draws specifically on a catchy slogan from Douglas Rushkoff (2011), who states that 'if you are not a programmer, you are one of the programmed', and argues that learning to code is essential if we wish to understand how our technologies work and how they work on us. These arguments certainly appear to acknowledge that the world is increasingly governed by coded products, and suggest that 'learning to code' is a way of giving learners some agency to counteract its pervasive power.

The evidence that such arguments for learning to programme computer code has been taken up in educational discourse is in the fast growth of 'Code Club', a volunteer-based grassroots initiative that places computer programmers in after-school clubs in primary schools to teach young children basic programming and coding. According to the organisers of Code Club:

> Learning to code is an important skill now we're living in a digital age. It's not just enough for children to know how to use technology. They should know how it works too. ... They should understand that they're in charge of the computer, and can (and should) make it do what they want, not the other way around. (Code Club 2013)

Code Club was established in April 2012 and has quickly grown into a nationwide network of clubs (at the time of writing in summer 2014) in over 2000 UK primary schools, as well as a Code Club World network. Code Club is sponsored and promoted by Nesta and the Nominet Trust with funding from the Department for Education, as well as support from computing corporations like Microsoft and Google. It is marketed simultaneously in terms of its educational benefits and the economic benefits of upskilling children as computer programmers. The organisers of Code Club are extremely active on social media such as Google Groups and Twitter, where they coordinate many activities such as 'Code Pub' meet-ups for volunteers, have been profiled frequently by the press, and appear at many events including practical workshops and conferences. Code Club is not just a set of educational activities but a whole culture of programming, including participants from infancy up to the professional programming domain, materialised in practices ranging from basic coding tutorials and games to high-level advanced programming.

Code Club is one among many grassroots initiatives that, during 2013, were increasingly clustered and networked together as part of a concerted campaign to promote young people learning to code. In May 2013, the Public Innovation Lab at Nesta, in partnership with the not-for-profit 'social innovator' the Nominet Trust and the internet company Mozilla, launched an initiative called Make Things Do Stuff that promotes various forms of learning to code, programming and 'digital making':

> Make Things Do Stuff aims to mobilise the next generation of digital makers. We want to help people to make the shift from consuming digital technologies, to making and building their own. Because when all kinds of different people start hacking, re-mixing and making things with technology, the possibilities get really interesting. Make Things Do Stuff will enable people to … navigate a path that will take them from being a digital consumer, to being a digital maker. (Make Things Do Stuff, 2013a)

These activities are justified through a combination of discourses about the powerful role of computer code in the contemporary world, and the need of commercial computer companies. The Make Things Do Stuff website states that: 'In a world where everything from fridges to cars, bank accounts to medical diagnoses are becoming powered by computing, understanding how digital technologies are made (and how to make your own) is vital to full participation in society' (Make Things Do Stuff 2013b). Furthermore, it juxtaposes a constructionist understanding of 'making something, sharing it and getting feedback' as ' a powerful way to learn', with a commercial discourse of how 'digital technologies are developed in the real world [and how to] get something made, get it out there, get feedback, learn, and make it better' (Make Things Do Stuff 2013b). The Make Things Do Stuff campaign is the hybrid progeny of educational, governmental, commercial, and grassroots discourses and the actors and organisations that actively promote them.

Make Things Do Stuff is primarily organised and governed by its three major partners, Nesta, the Nominet Trust and Mozilla, though its activities are distributed among a wide cross-sectoral network of government, civil society and commercial actors. As a source of funding, support, and campaigning, Make Things Do Stuff has distributed funding and support to Code Club as well as a number of related coding and digital making activities such as CoderDojo clubs in Scotland and Technocamps in Wales. The initiative is described as an 'open movement' and is partnered with a range of technology companies, education businesses, third sector organisations, and government. These include Facebook, Microsoft, O2, Mozilla, and Virgin Media; Codecademy, Coding for

Kids, Decoded; and HM Government, the Scottish Government and the Teacher Development Trust. The government Chancellor of the Exchequer, George Osborne MP, launched the initiative in May 2013 claiming that 'this campaign is backing the entrepreneurs of the future and helping ensure that Britain is equipped to succeed in the global race' (HM Treasury, 2013).

There is a clear cross-sectoral policy narrative around programming as an economically valuable skill in evidence here. To give some more detail to this narrative, these entanglements of computer companies with government via intermediaries such as Nesta and the Nominet Trust have influenced the scheduled 2014 replacement of 'ICT' with 'computing' in the National Curriculum in England. In contrast to the basic functional skills of using computers, which critics claim were characteristic of the ICT curriculum, such as how to use a word-processor or a database, the computing programmes of study explicitly focus on programming and coding along with 'computational thinking' and core knowledge from computer science (Department for Education, 2013). The impetus to replace ICT with computing in the curriculum was led by a Royal Society (2012) report *Shut Down or Restart* which was directly commissioned by Microsoft, Google, and university computer science departments, the new computing curriculum having been developed by the British Computer Society and the Royal Academy of Engineering with leadership from a Microsoft senior executive.

The Cambridge academic and Observer newspaper columnist John Naughton (2012) has contributed to the debate with a high-profile series of articles including a 'Manifesto' for reintroducing computer science in schools. Naughton uses the expression 'program or be programmed', the title of a book by Douglas Rushkoff (2011), who also works as an adviser for Codecademy, itself a Make Things Do Stuff partner organisation. Rushkoff's book itself has spawned a number of online 'study guides' that aim to make its key ideas accessible to a much wider and younger audience. There has also been considerable grassroots support for programming in the curriculum from Computing at School, a member-led subject association for computing teachers, which is chaired by a senior Microsoft researcher and is funded by Microsoft, Google and the Chartered Institute of IT. The Computing at School 'white paper' of 2010 was among the first documents to argue for the replacement of ICT in the National Curriculum with computing. The paper from Computing at School (2010) argued that 'computing is the study of how computers and computer systems work, and how they are constructed and programmed', and it suggested that a new computing curriculum would include the study of 'how computers work', how algorithms, data structures, systems and networks are used to solve computational problems, as well as teaching the knowledge and skills of programming. This is largely the message of the new computing curriculum itself, and the Department for Education (DfE) has subsequently awarded funding (alongside Microsoft, Google and others) for Computing at School to support a 'Network of Teaching Excellence in Computer Science' to grow teaching capacity in advance of its implementation (Computing at School, 2014).

However, it was only in 2011 when Nesta published a report entitled *Next Gen* (Livingstone and Hope, 2011) that the key messages about computing and learning to code took on policy significance. *Next Gen* demanded more 'rigorous teaching of computing in schools' and recommended putting computer science into the national curriculum. The report did not originate, however, from a concern with the teaching of computing in schools. Rather, it was commissioned as a review of the skills needs of the video games and visual effects industries, which have long been seen as economically valuable and innovative sectors of the UK economy. The authors are industry leaders in the videogames and visual effects sector, and the report was commissioned by Ed Vaizey, the Conservative Party Minister for Culture, Communications and the Creative Industries. The importance of *Next Gen* was signalled after Eric Schmidt from Google used the platform of the MacTaggart Lecture at the Edinburgh television festival in 2011 to express his dismay that computer science was not taught as standard in UK schools, a message repeated by Google around the world urging governments to support young people to learn to code in order to produce a skilled workforce for a digital economy (Cave and Rowell, 2014).

As a partner in Make Things Do Stuff, the Nominet Trust, too, has produced a series of reports, events, projects and blogs dedicated to the topic of learning to code. Echoing political discourse on the subject, the Nominet Trust chief executive argued there is a 'serious and economic imperative' besides the 'fun and learning that digital making offers young people,' namely that the 'UK and global jobs market are crying out for digital skills and we need to make sure that the next generation can meet this need' (Nominet Trust, 2013). Nominet Trust has distributed funding through a 'Digital Makers Fund' in partnership with Nesta. The beneficiaries include a number of start-up organisations and grassroots organisations involved in various digital making and learning to code activities. Nominet Trust also commissions reports and 'state of the art' reviews on key areas such as digital making, big data, and the politics of computers (for example, Sefton-Green, 2013; Krotoski, 2014). It represents a messy mix of advocacy for the digital economy, support for grassroots organisations, the social economy and civil society, as well as journalistic and academic commentary on aspects of digital culture, within which its campaigning for learning to code is entangled.

Make Things Do Stuff, Code Club and related activities in the UK have been mirrored at an international scale. In the US, during 2013, a campaign called 'Hour of Code' was launched that called for all school children to learn some programming skills, based on a clear argument about the economic benefit of equipping young people for jobs in computer science related jobs. Promotional material produced in early 2014 claims the campaign reached 20 million young people in December 2013 alone, and aims to involve over 100 million in 2014 through a mix of online courses, tutorials and video lectures made available to schools (code.org, 2014). In terms of governance, Hour of Code was set up and run by code.org, 'a non-profit dedicated to expanding participation in computer science by making it available in more schools.' Its 'vision is that every student in every school should have the opportunity to learn computer programming' (code.org 2014). A non-profit organisation, code.org was founded by the entrepreneurs Ali and Hadi Partovi, twins with a long history of 'angel investment' and venture capitalism in Silicon Valley, and has been partnered with or sponsored by donations from Microsoft, Google, Amazon, Dropbox, Facebook and many others, as well as by philanthropic individuals from across commercial computing and venture capitalism (see https://code.org/about for a full and extensive list of organisational and individual partners and donors).

Back in the UK, a similar campaign was launched in January 2014. The 'Year of Code' was established to coincide with the introduction of the new computing curriculum in England, which puts coding in the curriculum for every schoolchild, and is an active campaign to promote a variety of programming and coding initiatives both in and out of school, to help people 'learn code & create exciting things on computers' (Year of Code 2014). The Year of Code website (http://yearofcode.org/) provides links to a range of start-up organisations and grassroots campaigns related to learning to code, as well as an extensive network of partners from across government, commercial media, and civil society. Year of Code is chaired by Rohan Silva, a former senior policy advisor to prime Minister David Cameron, and an 'entrepreneur-in-residence' at Index

Ventures, an international venture capital firm whose mission statement is that 'every aspect of human life and economic activity can be transformed by technology and entrepreneurial passion' (http://indexventures.com/firm). Its executive director and advisors are almost all drawn from the fields of entrepreneurship, venture capital, and computing. Its only explicitly educational advisor is from the Education Foundation, an 'independent think tank for education' that advocates and champions digital innovation in education and acts as a partner with other technology companies, notably Facebook, to introduce their products in schools. As the *Guardian* columnist John Naughton (2014) argued, 'Year of Code is a takeover bid by a corporate world that has woken up to the realization that the changes in the computing curriculum...will open up massive commercial opportunities.' The BBC journalist Rory Cellan-Jones (2014) revealed that one of its founders, Saul Klein, also of Index Ventures, when pushed to discuss whether Year of Code was a government or Index Ventures initiative, claimed that: 'We live in a world where the intersection of public policy and commerce is often needed to drive an important social agenda.' The development of Hour of Code in the US and Year of Code in the UK is evidence of how initial grassroots movements and activities, such as Computing at School and Code Club, have been mediated by increasingly powerful cross-sectoral policy innovation labs and absorbed into the entrepreneurial mission of venture capital companies.

For the commercial sector, there may be clear economic benefits to be gained from supporting learning to code. As Morozov (2014) has written, the 'learning to code', educational 'hacking' and the 'maker movement' are all highly desirable to some of the most powerful agencies and organisations in the world. Google, Facebook and Microsoft have all supported high-profile campaigns like the Hour of Code, while DARPA (the defence research wing of the American military complex) has spent over $13 million promoting the maker movement and 'makerspaces' to high schoolers, and in China, the Communist Youth League has been actively recruiting participants to 'Maker Carnivals'. The desirability of such activities is most obviously in the upskilling of a future workforce, as many advocates for learning to code demonstrate. In their book on political lobbying in the UK, Cave and Rowell, (2014, pp. 260–261) describe the various activities surrounding the learning to code movement and the reform of the computing curriculum as a 'lobbying tool for technology firms with a clear, vested interest in digitizing learning, as well as enthusing a new generation of coders.' They claim that this campaign of 'business-backed think tanks' and 'education technology lobbyists' 'intent on reshaping education' (p. 249) has now 'got what it wanted' in the shape of computer science in the curriculum, twinned with much great political acceptance by the Department for Education of technology being 'integrated and embedded across the whole curriculum' and its desire to build a strong UK educational technology market (p. 261). Beyond general arguments about upskilling for the digital economy or growing the educational technology market, learning to code is also embedded in concerns about the capacity of businesses and government agencies to make use of Big Data sources and more intelligent, connected devices, as outlined in a report by the government Design Commission (2014), which recommends further governmental support for the teaching of code in the curriculum as well as digital making and shared 'makerspaces/hackspaces' in schools, colleges and universities.

Learning to code is no longer simply an after-school activity run by volunteer programmers, as originally envisioned by Code Club and other like-minded grassroots organisations such as Computing at School. As these sets of entanglements between government, businesses, intermediaries, lobbyists, and educational organisations demonstrate, learning to code has become the focus for the development of complex new cross-sectoral alignments and networks. Year of Code and Make Things Do Stuff exemplify the kind of cross-sectoral 'policy networks' that are increasingly participating in educational governance in England, especially around new technologies, Big Data and new media agendas. The learning to code policy domain and its discourse is not merely a government product, but the hybrid and ultimately messy result of pronouncements produced by computing specialists, entrepreneurs and investors, journalists, policymakers, lobbyists, and corporate computing companies, brokered by intermediary partnering organisations and policy innovation labs such as Nesta and the Nominet Trust. It demonstrates clearly how educational governance is increasingly being displaced to powerful new actors from outside of the educational sector itself, influenced by powerful interests and ambitions, with complex links between governmental, business and civil society organisations and practices.

Programmers and prosumers

The underlying assumptions about learning to code have gone largely unquestioned, despite its rapid growth. Clearly coding carries into the classroom a specific set of assumptions about knowledge and forms of knowing and doing. As noted earlier, programming is not just a technical procedure but is related to systems of thought about the way the world works, and about how it might be modelled in order to further shape people's interactions with it. Mirroring the notion discussed earlier that code and algorithms project the 'rules' of computer science into the world, Kitchin & Dodge (2011, p. 26) argue that the material practice of programming is 'an expression of how the world can be captured, represented, processed and modelled computationally with the outcome subsequently doing work in the world'. For example, the ways in which banking can be captured in online banking systems, or how biometric systems are constructed to facilitate automated border control, subsequently shape how these activities take place. In other words, programming code captures ideas about how the world works, in order to then augment, mediate and regulate people's lives. Though, as Kirschenbaum (2009) has pointed out, any act of programming may contain biased, distorted, caricatured, or merely partial selections from the world it claims to model; in that sense, programming is a persuasive or perhaps rhetorical act. The material practice of programming, therefore, possesses the power to shape how people know and act in the social world.

Moreover, material practices of learning to code assume a certain image of the desirable individual learner to be produced. As the researcher of code cultures Mackenzie (2006) argues, the work of computer programmers is premised on notions of flexibility, speed, virtuality, just-in-time-production, teamwork, and other aspects of 'immaterial labour'. Make Things Do Stuff, Code Club, Year of Code and the like anticipate learners' entry into a network-based digital economy for which the work of programmers stands as a prototypical practice. Thus an emphasis on learning to code is part of what Barry (2001) describes as the contemporary political preoccupation with sculpting a mind and body with the technical skills, knowledge and capacity to meet the demands of new flexible work routines. Consistent with much recent education policy discourse, learning to code activities 'govern by activating the capacities of the individual' to contribute to the digital economy (Ozga, Segerholm and Simola, 2011, p. 88). In this sense, learning to code may be interpreted as a material practice of 'algorithmic ideology' (Mager, 2012), a kind of inculcation into the codes of conduct, practices, assumptions, and knowledges that underpin production in the digital economy. Thus, learning to code embodies a host of assumptions and working practices based on ideas such as computational thinking, statistical modelling, systems thinking, scientific rationality, and algorithmic logic that have their origins in the working practices of the computer science professions. These are very particular kinds of social practices imbued with 'particular values and contextualized within a particular scientific approach', and often reductionist, functionalist and technicist modes of thinking that see the world in computational terms rather than in relation to cultural, economic or political context (Kitchin, 2014, p. 5). To adapt Lash's (2007, p. 75) terms, what are being rehearsed through learning to code are the 'hands-on' practices and epistemologies of 'coders, writing algorithms,' working in 'ephemeral project-networks' in 'laboratories and studios'. In a culture where power is in the algorithm, Lash argues, status goes to those actors with the material skills, social values, and expert epistemologies to construct those algorithms. At its most basic, such practices amount to the fantasy of technical 'solutionism' where the right code and algorithms may be seen as the solution to complex problems. Learning to code thus seeks to inculcate learners into the systems of thought associated with the professional regime of programmers and the computer science disciplines, and with the knowledge and philosophies of the world, with all their biases, prejudices, ideological assumptions and modes of perception, that are materialised in software products.

It is clear that for its advocates at Nominet Trust and Nesta, as well as both the governmental and business actors with which they are networked, that coding is positioned as a rewarding, desirable and skilled occupation, not least in terms of providing technical engineering solutions to public and social policy problems. As already noted, both Nesta and Nominet Trust support 'hack' events, which put teams of computer programmers together, using code-sharing tools, to engineer solutions to government and public sector problems (Merrett, 2014). The Nominet Trust's 'Social Tech Guide' provides ample evidence of how technology entrepreneurship, twinned with practices of coding and hacking, has been positioned for 'social good' (Nominet Trust, 2014). According to Morozov (2013) this kind of solutionist thinking originates in the Silicon Valley hacker culture of technological innovation, which has recast complex social phenomena like politics, public health, and education, as neatly-defined problems with definite, computable solutions that can be optimised if the right algorithms are in place. The overall digital making, coding and hacking discourse is embedded in this social, cultural and political context of technological utopianism. Via Nesta and the Nominet Trust, and through their networks and associations with the culture of hack events, learning to code has been positioned in relation to such activities as equipping young people with the skills required to become solutions-engineers and hackers of the future.

Yet the depiction of solutionist hacking glosses over the fragility, complexity and mundanity of much coding work in the digital economy. As Mackenzie (2006, p. 14) notes, software has to be coded, and yet this job may be undertaken by 'a programmer, webmaster, corporation, software engineer, team, hacker or scripter'. The figure of the programmer often vacillates between potent creator of new worlds and antisocial, perhaps criminal or parasitic.' More prosaically, the work and material practice of coding is often dull, routinised and monotonous, as well as difficult, frustrating and dysfunctional (Kitchin and Dodge, 2011). Moreover, as Kitchin and Dodge (2011, p. 33) have argued, coding is a 'disciplinary regime' with established 'ways of knowing and doing regarding coding practices'. Yet owing to intense ongoing innovation in the field, programmers are always struggling to learn and adapt to constant change, and experience a high degree of 'ignorant expertise' and confusion about what they are doing (Ullman cited in Kitchin and Dodge, 2011, p. 35), particularly in relation to the wider possible social effects of what is incorporated into the code. Coders simply do not always know the effects of the code they are writing, and nor do they acknowledge how their own worldviews, ideologies and assumptions are embedded in the kinds of interactions and ways of doing that they make possible. The frequent failure of software projects, the *bitrot* that occurs as software packages are constantly superseded, and the regular disruptions caused by software bugs in everything from online banking to password protection are all evidence of the fragility and contingency of the code produced through the material practices of coders. Moreover, the construction of software features that breach people's right to privacy indicate how many coding projects proceed without the coder amply considering the wider social effects, as evidenced by recent European Union proposals over the 'right to be forgotten', which favour the rights of individuals rather than software companies to manage and control their personal data. The learner participating in Code Club, Year of Code, Make Things Do Stuff, or the like, is being solicited into a system of thought, ways of seeing, knowing and doing associated with a culture of coding practice that is not always as systematic, objective and expert as it is widely represented as being by learning to code advocates. The material practice of coding is more complex, contingent, confused, ignorant and distanced from concerns over its effects on the social world, and rests on the assumption that the problems with that social world can be addressed with algorithmic solutions written in code. This is about applying technical engineering to the task of human and social engineering. Learning to code is premised on a fantasy of the material practices associated with coding which simplifies and romanticises the empirical reality of disciplinary practice in the digital economy.

However, Make Things Do Stuff and Code Club justify themselves not just through the prospective economic value of children learning to code, but through a wider cultural argument about *producing* and not simply *consuming* technology. One way to analyse this preoccupation with coding clubs, programming and related digital making activities is to view it as promoting 'participatory' practices of 'co-production', 'crowdsourcing' and 'prosumption' in new social media practices. 'Prosumption' registers the alleged blurring of production and consumption as consumers of digital media increasingly also become its producers. Manovich (2013, pp. 18–19), for example, argues that 'software development is gradually getting more democratized' as a result of the recent simplification of programming environments through social media. The argument that software production, coding, and other forms of prosumption are ultimately democratising and empowering has been taken up enthusiastically by Code Club in particular, and also repeated by both the Nominet Trust and Nesta, albeit as part of a messy mix of commercial, economic and civil society discourses and arguments.

From a more critical perspective, Beer & Burrows (2013) question the apparent 'democratization' of software, claiming that this logic plays back into the hands of commercial digital media organisations. They argue that network-based social media – Facebook, Twitter, YouTube, Wikipedia, and so on – have facilitated the increasing participation of people in the formation of media content, leading to the:

> significant phenomena of the growing amount of 'labouring' people are undertaking as they 'play' with these new technologies: creating profiles, making status updates; distributing information; sharing files; uploading images; blogging, tweeting; and the rest. (Beer and Burrows, 2013, p. 49)

Ideas associated with participation in the networked cultures of social media, such as co-production, prosumption, crowdsourcing, user-centred design, and so on, have long been attractive for organisations such as Nesta, which has put such practices at the centre of its reformatory ambitions for 'digital education' as well as more widely in its proposals for 'people-powered' public services and new 'conversational' forms of 'sociable governance' (Williamson *forthcoming*). Learning to code is a logical outgrowth of this proliferation of technologies of co-construction, crowdsourcing and prosumption.

However, network-based activities of programming, prosumption and so on are also interweaving individuals more and more densely into new data-based social media infrastructures. In their analysis of social media in contemporary popular culture, Beer and Burrows (2013) argue that data accumulation does not just 'capture' culture but is recombined through feedback loops to actually shape, reconstitute and co-construct popular culture and everyday practices. They offer examples such as automated recommendations services and 'behavioural advertising' in consumption practices (techniques commonly practised by Amazon, Google, Spotify, Facebook and other social media services). These services accumulate personal and behavioural data from online transactions and run these data through predictive analytics in order to generate personalised recommendations. On the basis of users' subsequent behaviour, these systems then work recombinantly and recursively by continually harvesting users' by-product data and feeding it back into their predictive recommendations.

Through learning to code, young people are increasingly being positioned as 'prosumers' whose active production of online content – in the shape of Facebook updates, tweets, online purchases, and so on – is now the basis for the business models of most major social media companies. The job of the prosumer is to produce content from which commercial organisations can attempt to extract value. Moreover, these data can then be used to modify future services and recommendations – thus subtly and continually reshaping cultural engagement itself. In this sense, learning to code firmly embeds young people in what Kitchin and Dodge (2011, p. 6) term the 'coded infrastructures' that now orchestrate many of the patterns of everyday life, and that are subject to the commercial interests of for-profit communication corporations. Consequently, learning to code is not a neutral or depoliticised material practice, but shaped, patterned, ordered and governed by powerfully commercialised coded infrastructures. In turn, through their material participation in the coded infrastructures of prosumption, young people are being shaped and moulded with particular ways of seeing, thinking, and acting; their digital subjectivities sculpted by the systems of thought programmed into the software they use. The prosumerist individual configured by the software of social media providers is encouraged to share personal information and data; maximise sociality through horizontal networks of connected friends; extend reach, influence and collaboration through liking and sharing digital artefacts;

and to contribute through everyday participative and creative forms of digital making, software programming, and coding. Learning to code is a material practice that takes place in the coded infrastructures of contemporary algorithmic power.

Conclusion

This chapter has begun to unpack two emerging issues in terms of power in education. Through documenting and analysing the recent growth of learning to code in schools, it has shown, firstly, how education is increasingly being targeted by intermediary organisations that represent particular kinds of agendas, and concentrate a variety of powerful interests from across the commercial, civil society and governmental sectors. Education policy is being discussed and made in new places, by new actors, through new forms of network governance and through relationships among policy networks (Ball and Junemann, 2012). The introduction of the new computing curriculum in England in 2014, with its strong emphasis on computer science, computational thinking and computer programming over ICT skills, demonstrates how the networking together of commercial and governmental interests, much of it accomplished through relationships brokered by intermediary organisations such as Nesta and the Nominet Trust, and by their discursive production of reports and campaigns, is now exerting considerable influence on mainstream educational policymaking. As a policy discourse, not just a set of pedagogies, learning to code is evidence of shifting power relations in education policy and governance. Specifically it is evidence of the displacement of power to cross-sector intermediaries such as public and social policy innovation labs, and of their capacity to broker connections, conversations and new forms of 'sociable governance' among distributed 'policy networks' of governmental, civil society and commercial actors.

Secondly, the chapter has shown how, through the work of these intermediary actors, education is increasingly being embedded in coded infrastructures which demand a reshaping of young people's capacities and abilities. Through learning to code, young people are being inculcated into the material practices and codes of conduct associated with the cultures, ways of viewing the world, and values of computer programmers – particularly the assumption that technical engineering, algorithms and coding solutions can be applied for 'social good' and to 'hack' human, social and public problems. As producers and not just consumers of coded products, they are also being embedded as prosumers in the infrastructures of contemporary social media participation, making their everyday activities amenable to the extraction of value by powerful commercial social media companies and to the subtly recursive shaping of contemporary life.

The learning to code movement has been transformed from its origins among grassroots movements such as Computing at School. It has become the focus for a variety of powerful commercial, governmental and civil society actors, mediated by intermediaries and venture capital organisations that are little recognised in educational research. While some of its original enthusiasts and advocates saw learning to code as a way to give power back to users, or to stimulate informed citizenship for an increasingly digitally dense world, it has been translated into the business model of global social media and computing corporations, mobilised in political ambitions for a digital economy, and embedded as a material practice of prosumption in the coded infrastructures of a recursive digital culture. This is a culture in which, as Lash (2007) argues, power courses through the algorithm as a conduit for new computational ways of interacting with the world, as channelled through the 'rules' of computer science and the disciplinary systems of thought associated with programmers; one where, as a consequence, software and its code and algorithms are constantly generating new realities; and where young people are being configured in the conduct of coders, with the skills and capacities to write the software and algorithms that will subsequently engineer, activate and 'hack' the future.

References

Ball, S. J. and Junemann, C. (2012) *Networks, New Governance and Education*, Bristol: Policy Press.

Barry, A. (2001) Political Machines: Governing a technological society, London: Athlone Press.

Beer, D. (2009) 'Power through the algorithm? Participatory web cultures and the technological unconscious', *New Media and Society*, 11(6), 985–1002.

Beer, D. (2013) Popular Culture and New Media: The Politics of Circulation, London: Palgrave Macmillan.

Beer, D. and Burrows, R. (2013) 'Popular culture, digital archives and the new social life of data', *Theory, Culture and Society*, 30(4) 47–71.

Cave, T. and Rowell, A. (2014) *A Quiet Word: Lobbying, Crony Capitalism and Broken Politics in Britain*, Munich: Bodley Head.

Cellan-Jones, R. (2014.)'Year of Code – PR fiasco or vital mission?' *BBC online*, 12 February. Available from: http://www.bbc.co.uk/news/technology-26150717 [Accessed 28 April 2014].

Code.org. (2014) 'Overview', *Code.org* website. Available from: https://code.org/files/Code.orgOverview.pdf [Accessed 28 April 2014].

Code Club. (2013) About Code Club, *Code Club* website. Available from: https://www.codeclub.org.uk/about [Accessed 13 September 2013].

Computing at School (2012) 'Network of Teaching Excellence in Computer Science', *Computing at School* website. Available from: http://www.computingatschool.org.uk/index.php?id=noe [Accessed 16 June 2014].

Computing at School (2014) 'Switched On'. *Computing at School newsletter*, Summer 2014, Available: http://computingatschool.org.uk/da [Accessed 27 August 2015].

Department for Education [DfE] (2012) '"Harmful" ICT curriculum set to be dropped to make way for rigorous computer science', *Gov.uk* website. Available from: https://www.gov.uk/government/news/harmful-ict-curriculum-set-to-be-dropped-to-make-way-for-rigorous-computer-science [Accessed 13 September 2013].

Department for Education (2013) 'The National Curriculum in England, Framework Document'. Available: http://www.education.Gov.uk/nationalcurriculum [Accesswed 20 July 2015].

Department for Education [DfE] (2014) 'National Curriculum in England: Computing programmes of study' *Gov.uk* website. Available from: http://www.gov.uk/government/publications/national-curriculum-in-england-computing-programmes-of-study [Accessed 20 June 2015].

Design Commission (2014) *Designing the Digital Economy: Embedding growth through design, innovation and technology*, London: Design Commission. Available from: http://www.socialtech.org.uk/about/ [Accessed 16 June 2014].

Fuller, M. (ed.) (2008) *Software Studies: A lexicon*, London: MIT Press.

HM Treasury (2013) '100,000 young people to become "digital makers"', Gov.co.uk. Available from: https://www.gov.uk/government/news/100000-young-people-to-become-digital-makers [Accessed 13 September 2013].

Kirschenbaum, M. (2009) 'Helloworlds!' *The Chronicle of Higher Education*, 23 January. Available from: http://chronicle.com/article/Hello-Worlds/5476 [Accessed 13 September 2013].

Kitchin, R. (2014) 'Big Data, new epistemologies and paradigm shifts', *Big Data & Society*, 1(1), 1–12.

Kitchin, R. and Dodge, M. (2011) *Code/Space: Software and Everyday Life*, London: MIT Press.

Krotoski, A. (2014) *The personal (computer) is political*, Oxford: Nominet Trust. Available from: http://www.nominettrust.org.uk/knowledge-centre/articles/personal-computer-political [Accessed 25 April 2014].

Lash, S. (2007) 'Power after Hegemony: Cultural studies in mutation?' *Theory, Culture & Society*, 24(3), 55–78.

Lawn, M. and Grek, S. (2012) Europeanizing Education: Governing a New Policy Space, Oxford: Symposium.

Livingstone, I. and Hope, A. (2011) *Next Gen*, London: Nesta.

MacCormick, J. (2012) 9 Algorithms that Transformed the Future: The Ingenious Ideas that Drive Today's Computers, Oxford: Princeton University Press.

Mackenzie, A. (2006) *Cutting Code: Software and Sociality*, Oxford: Peter Lang.

Mackenzie, A. and Vurdubakis, T. (2011) 'Codes and Codings in Crisis: Signification, Performativity and Excess', *Theory, Culture and Society*, 28(6), 3–23.

Mager, A. (2012) 'Algorithmic ideology: How capitalist society shapes search engines', *Information, Communication & Society*, 15(5), 769–787.

Make Things Do Stuff (2013a) 'About Make Things Do Stuff', *Make Things Do Stuff* website. Available from: http://makethingsdostuff.co.uk/about [Accessed 13 September 2013].

Make Things Do Stuff (2013b) 'What is Make Things Do Stuff?' *Make Things Do Stuff* blog. Available from: http://makethingsdostuff.co.uk/blog/2013/03/12/what-make-things-do-stuff [Accessed 13 September 2013].

Manovich, L. (2013) *Software Takes Command*, London: Bloomsbury.

Merrett, N. (2014) 'Public sector embraces 'hackathon' innovation potential', *Government Computing*, 30 May. Available from: http://central-government. governmentcomputing.com/news/public-sector-embraces-hackathon-innovation-potential-4281766 [Accessed 16 June 2014].

Morozov, E. (2013) 'The perils of perfection', *New York Times*, Sunday Review, 2 March. Available from: http://www.nytimes.com/2013/03/03/opinion/sunday/the-perils-of-perfection.html [Accessed 16 June 2014].

Morozov, E. (2014) 'Making it', *The New Yorker*, 13 January. Available from: http://www.newyorker.com/arts/critics/atlarge/2014/01/13/140113crat_atlarge_morozov [Accessed 16 June 2014].

Mulgan, G. (2014) 'The radical's dilemma: an overview of the practice and prospects of Social and Public Labs – version 1. Available from: http://www.nesta. org.uk/sites/default/files/social_and_public_labs_-_and_the_radicals_dilemma. pdf [Accessed 26 February 2014].

Naughton, J. (2012) 'A manifesto for teaching computer science in the 21st century', *The Observer*, 31 March. Available from: http://www.theguardian.com/education/2012/mar/31/manifesto-teaching-ict-education-minister [Accessed 13 September 2013].

Naughton, J. (2014) 'Year of Code already needs a reboot', *The Guardian*, 15 February. Available from: http://www.theguardian.com/technology/2014/feb/15/year-of-code-needs-reboot-teachers [Accessed 28 April 2014].

Nesta. (2014) 'i-teams', Nesta website. Available from: http://www.nesta.org.uk/project/i-teams [Accessed 16 June 2014].

Neyland, D. (2014) 'On organizing algorithms', *Theory, Culture & Society*, DOI. Available from: http://dx.doi.org/10.1177/0263276414530477 [Accessed 20 June 2015].

Nominet Trust (2013) 'Digital making activities to expand opportunities for UK young people', Nominet Trust website. Available from: http://www.nominet-trust.org.uk/news-events/news/digital-making-activities-to-expand-opportunities-uk-young-people [Accessed 13 September 2013].

Nominet Trust. (2014) 'About the Social Tech Guide', *Social Tech Guide* website. Available from: http://www.socialtech.org.uk/about/ [Accessed 16 June 2014].

Ozga, J., Segerholm, C. and Simola, H. (2011) 'The governance turn', in Ozga, J., Dahler-Larsen, P., Segerholm, C. and Simola, H. (eds). *Fabricating Quality in Education: Data and governance in Europe*, pp. 85–95, London: Rouledge.

Royal Society (2012) *Shut down or restart? The way forward for computing in UK schools*. Available from: https://royalsociety.org/~/media/education/computing-in-schools/2012-01-12-summary.pdf [Accessed 27 August 2015].

Ruppert, E., Law, J. and Savage, M. (2013) 'Reassembling social science methods: The challenge of digital devices', *Theory, Culture and Society*, 30(4), 22–46.

Rushkoff, D. (2011) Program or Be Programmed: Ten Commands for the Digital Age, New York: OR books,

Sefton-Green, J. (2013) 'Mapping Digital Makers', Oxford: Nominet Trust. Available from: http://www.nominettrust.org.uk/knowledge-centre/articles/mapping-digital-makers [Accessed 16 June 2014].

Selwyn, N. (2015) 'Data entry: toward the critical study of digital data in education', *Learning, Media & Technology*, 40(1), 64–82.

Thrift, N. (2005) *Knowing Capitalism*, London: Sage.

Williamson, B. (2014)' Mediating education policy: Making up the "anti-politics" of third sector participation in public education', *British Journal of Education Studies*, 62(1), 37–55.

Williamson, B. (2015) 'Governing software: networks, databases and algorithmic power in the digital governance of public education', *Learning, Media & Technology*, 40(1), 83–105.

Williamson, B. *forthcoming*. 'Governing methods: Policy labs, data and design in the digital governance of education', *Journal of Educational Administration and History*.

Year of Code (2014) 'What is Year of Code?' *Year of Code* website. Available from: http://yearofcode.org/ [Accessed 16 June 2014].

5
Researching Power and the Power in Research

Naomi Hodgson

Introduction

Over the last 25 years, Foucault has become a mainstay of Anglophone educational research, especially in analyses of power, discourse, and subjectivity (see, for example, Ball, 1990, 2013; Besley and Peters, 2007), and in particular with regards to sexuality and gender (for example, Baker and Heyning, 2004). But as theory has taken a number of 'turns' away from poststructuralism in recent years, Foucault is no longer the 'theory du jour', as Dan Butin (2006) puts it, after 'demonising' the modus operandi of educational policy. While theorists such as Bourdieu seem to have retained currency among sociologists of education, Foucault seems to have been displaced by newer mavericks such as Bruno Latour and the Actor Network theorists and socio-materialists that followed (see for example, Fenwick and Edwards, 2010; 2012).

Although educational theorists may seem to have moved away from an explicit concern with the application of Foucauldian conceptions of power or governmentality to education, this does not mean that these are no longer relevant to understanding the conditions in which we find ourselves today. Foucault's work is still explicitly and productively used throughout the social sciences and humanities in ways that update and develop his understanding of rationalities of government regarding the complexities of late, globalised neoliberalism and the modes of subjectivation this produces. Foucault's thought is also present in much of the current critical work within the fields of sociomaterialism and posthumanism. Within it, a distinctive attitude is at work, which leads to questions being posed in a particular way, to new methodologies being developed, and to original and productive modes of critique being articulated. In the field of education, such critiques manifest in a concern, informed also by Latour, with *making public*, and with what is *educational* in educational theory. A distinctive critical attitude is entailed in practices of looking, reading, and writing that are concerned, not with applying a Foucauldian theory of power to education, but with producing an educational account of power and education (see, for example, Simons et al., 2009).

While authors such as Mark Olssen have written extensively in theoretical terms about Foucault as a materialist (see for example, Olssen, 1999), new materialist scholars have criticised Foucault for not taking sufficient account of the material dimension in his analyses. Thomas Lemke (2014) refers to Karen Barad in particular as taking issue with this omission in Foucault's work, with her critique of Foucault as a traditional humanist whose account denies the production of power by, and the existence of agency in, the material. I will discuss Lemke's account of Barad here in order to illustrate the issues she raises with Foucault's work and then, in turn, to question the way in which Lemke defends it, in particular to indicate how his understanding of the material differs somewhat from Barad's and also that found in recent sociomaterialist scholarship, including that in education (for example, Decuypere et al., 2010; Noens and Ramaekers, in press). I will then draw on Barad's own work to indicate how, as well as raising issues with Foucault's analytic, she draws on and develops it. She continues a mode of critical scholarship that invites us to question our own conceptualisations of the world and thus our own research.

By drawing attention to Barad's critique, and to Lemke's defence of Foucault, we can see how a particular conception of the material and the need to attend to it relates to Foucault's conception of power and his approach to the analysis of it. To further develop a mode of analysis that permits the material aspect, I will discuss how we might proceed to study the practice of research itself and its role within current modes of governance. The concern here is not to defend a particular account of power, but to demonstrate how we might research at where and how we understand power to exist. On this basis we can update the ways in which we articulate a critique of current research practices. Thus, the concern here is not, or not only, with how we research 'power' in education but how a particular form of power is effected by the governmental concern with research itself. Before turning to contemporary concerns with the relationship between Foucault's thought and materialist analyses, I will briefly outline Foucault's understanding of power in the context of his wider thought.

Power, government, and subjectivity

It is Foucault's work on governmentality that is most often adopted in the study of education, as a model with which to explain the operation of power. This work is often read in relation to his earlier work on power in which greater emphasis is placed on domination and docility, for example, *Discipline and Punish*. The possibility of resistance is therefore overshadowed and the ascetic mode of Foucault's philosophy, more evident in his later work, is not considered.

Foucault is not concerned with creating a definitive theory of power, and how it operates, for its own sake. His concern is that the specific diagnosis of the operation of power entails a diagnosis of who we are. As Foucault has suggested:

> For some people, asking questions about the 'how' of power would limit them to describing its effects without ever relating those effects either to causes or to a basic nature. It would make this power a mysterious substance which they might hesitate to interrogate in itself, no doubt because they would prefer not to call it into question. By proceeding this way, which is never explicitly justified, they seem to suspect the presence of a kind of fatalism. But does not their very distrust indicate a presupposition that power is something which exists with three distinct qualities: its origin, its basic nature, and its manifestations? (Foucault, 1982, p. 217)

Instead he argues that 'to begin the analysis with a "how" is to suggest that power as such does not exist' (p. 217), that is, 'power assumed to exist universally in a concentrated or diffused form, does not exist' (p. 219). The question is '"How", not in the sense of "How does it manifest itself?" but "By what means is it exercised?" and "What happens when individuals exert (as they say) power over others?"' (p. 217).

A relation to others is therefore presupposed – it is necessary for the operation and production of power – but is indirect:

> In effect, what defines a relation of power is that it is a mode of action which does not act directly and immediately on others. Instead it acts upon their actions: an action upon an action, on existing actions or on those which may arise in the present or the future. A relationship of violence acts upon a body or upon things; it forces, it bends, it breaks on the wheel, it destroys or it closes the door on all possibilities. Its opposite pole can only be passivity, and if it comes up against

any resistance it has no other option but to try to minimize it. On the other hand a power relationship can only be articulated on the basis of two elements which are indispensable if it is really to be a power relationship: that 'the other' (the one over whom power is exercised) be thoroughly recognised and maintained to the very end as a person who acts; and that, faced with a relationship of power, a whole field of responses, reactions, results, and possible inventions may open up. (p. 220)

Foucault's understanding of power, then, rejects the idea of power as an entity and as dominating and repressive. For Foucault, freedom is a pre-requisite for power. As shown in the contrast between violence and power above, power exists between individuals faced with a field of possibilities for action. There is not a binary – freedom or power – but a 'complicated interplay' (p. 221). It is in this interplay that power relations are effected and wherein, also, lies the possibility of resistance. Foucault's concern with power then can only be understood in relation to his concern with the subject, or more specifically with how we as humans are made subjects. This focus, and the way in which it is pursued, not only advocate a particular form of critique but provide such a critique in the process of the work itself: 'Maybe the target nowadays is not to discover what we are, but to refuse what we are...We have to promote new forms of subjectivity through the refusal of this kind of individuality which has been imposed on us for several centuries' (p. 216). This is not a call to revolution: 'power relations are rooted deep in the social nexus, not reconstituted "above" society as a supplementary structure whose radical effacement one could perhaps dream of' (p. 222). The refusal he calls for refers to an ethical relation of the self to the self in which one's agency and one's relation to the other is acknowledged. The refusal is located in the choice to act in a particular way in our daily practices in a constant negotiation of power: 'Rather than speaking of an essential freedom, it would be better to speak of an "agonism" – of a relationship which is at the same time reciprocal in citation and struggle; less of a face-to-face confrontation which paralyzes both sides than a permanent provocation' (p. 222).

The understanding of ethics in the particular sense found in Foucault's work encapsulates how the understanding of power and its interrelationship with freedom and the subject, and the notion of critique found in the form and substance of Foucault's work, come together. Foucault's concern with ethics is explored in his later work in relation to Ancient Greek ethics in particular, a focus that marked a distinct break with earlier concerns. As Frédéric Gros puts it, with the publication of *The Use of Pleasure* and *The Care of the Self,*

> Everything had now changed, the historical-cultural framework and the reading grid of his history of sexuality; it is no longer Western modernity (from the sixteenth to the nineteenth century), but Greco-Roman antiquity; it is no longer a political reading in terms of power apparatuses, but an ethical reading in terms of practices of the self. It is no longer genealogy of systems, it is a problematisation of the subject. (Gros, 2005, p. 508)

Foucault's purpose was not to provide a history of ethics, nor is the reading of the different ethics operative in antiquity intended to provide a critique of the current operation of power in the sense of providing an alternative. Foucault was concerned to avoid the term 'alternative'. He argued: 'you can't find the solution of a problem in the solution of another problem raised at another moment by another people' (Foucault, 1986, p. 342). Foucault was attracted by the problem in Greek ethics of the aesthetics of existence: 'The idea of the *bios* as a material for an aesthetic piece of art is something which fascinates me. The idea also that ethics can be a very strong structure of existence, without any relation with the juridical *per se*, with an authoritarian system, with a disciplinary structure' (p. 348). For Foucault, then, ethics is not taken to refer to a universal set of principles. Instead he describes ethics as 'the relationship you ought to have with yourself, *rapport à soi*... which determines how the individual is supposed to constitute himself as a moral subject of his own actions' (p. 352).[1] Foucault suggests then that it is not the moral code that has shifted historically but ethics, the relationship one has to oneself.

While Foucault's work on Greek ethics relates to, and elucidates, his early concern with genealogies of government and power, it also marks a shift to a more specific focus on the problematisation of the subject (Gros, 2005, p. 508). This problematisation entailed a closer focus on the practice of philosophy and of writing itself. The interrogation of our own relationship to truth, and of our subjugation by it, is central to Foucault's understanding of critique, and more broadly of philosophy, and this entails interrogation of the production of truth, and of ourselves, in our writing. His concern with ethics and the care of the self is not, as Gros suggests, the abandonment of politics by Foucault but the complication of the study of governmentalities: 'ethics, or the subject, is not thought of as the other of politics or power', as the outline of his understanding of critique indicates (Gros, 2005, p. 512; see Foucault, 2007 [1978]).

For Foucault, then, the understanding of the relationship between power, critique, subjectivity, and truth entails a particular understanding of writing and philosophy as transformative: we might say, as educative as opposed to educational.[2]

It is an ethos, an attitude, that entails work which puts itself 'to the test of reality, of contemporary reality, both to grasp the points where change is possible and desirable, and to determine the precise form this change should take' (p. 316). Foucault describes this critical attitude as a virtue (Foucault, 2007 [1978], p. 43). He describes critique, at its core, as consisting of 'relations that are tied to one another, or one to two others, power, truth and the subject' (p. 47). The attitude of critique consists in 'the movement by which the subject himself gives himself the right to question truth on its effects of power and to question power on its discourses of truth'; it is 'the art of voluntary insubordination' (p. 47). This is not to respond to governmentalisation in the form 'we do not want to be governed like that and we do not want to be governed at all' (p. 44). Rather, seeking not to be governed like that and at that cost entails a desubjugation of the subject, seeking the limits of our knowledge. The 'question is being raised: "what, therefore, am I?", I who belong to this humanity, perhaps to this piece of it, at this point in time, at this instant of humanity which is subjected to the power of truth in general and truths in particular?' (p. 56). The historical philosophical practice central to Foucault's work therefore 'displaces the historical objects familiar to historians' and is concerned with 'the problem of the subject and the truth about which historians are not usually concerned' (p. 56).

The way in which Foucault questions the practices according to which we are made subjects forms the basis for what follows here. As the above outline has shown, Foucault's work goes beyond providing a model through which to understand society and the power relations within it, to offer a particular way of framing questions of power, in relation to truth and the subject. This questioning does not come in the form of a test against a standard of rationality, but a test of the understanding of society, and the subjectivity it produces, against the reality of that society and subjectivation. What follows from this is not the need to overlay Foucault's thought onto existing relations, but to take up the need to put our thinking to the test of reality, to draw new insights from current theory and our current conditions. This suggests, then, the need to continually consider the 'how' of power anew and to seek a different relationship of ourselves to ourselves and to matters at hand. The particular matters of concern in this chapter are those of research itself: the relationship of the university to research and the constitution of the researcher herself. I will continue the account of power in the next section by considering the relationship between education – or more specifically, learning – and power from the perspective of govern-mentality, and indicate how research is implicated and constituted in this relationship today. This will lead to a consideration of how we might further develop an analytic of power in light of current post-humanist and materialist theory, which takes issue with the limits of Foucault's work.

From learning citizen to citizen-as-researcher

Foucault's account of governmentality details the shift in the object of government from territory to population and the arts of government developed with the emergence of the modern state. Subsequent accounts drawing on the concept of governmentality have been concerned to detail the shifts in how we are governed and govern ourselves. The governance of 'men' and 'things' in the name of the nation-state, of progress, and emancipation, placed the individual, the state, and educa-tion in a particular relationship to each other. The governance of indi-viduals today in the name of the knowledge economy or learning society shifts this relationship and the make-up of its constituent parts, thus requiring a shift in the conceptual tools we use to understand it.

The policy concern with lifelong learning is illustrative and constitu-tive of a shift in the way in which the relationship between individual, education and the state are conceptualised (see Masschelein et al., 2007 for an analysis from the perspective of governmentality). The governance of men in the name of the progress of the nation-state in the nineteenth and twentieth centuries has given way to a post-national governance of resources for present needs. The orientation of the individual to the nation-state, to linear progression, and modernisation, is now an 'envi-ronmental' orientation to meeting present needs by means of adaptation and innovation (Simons and Masschelein, 2008; Simons and Hodgson, 2012). Central to this is a further responsibilisation of the individual in the age of the post-welfare nation-state, which requires a particular orientation to education, not as institutionally-situated and as a process governed by age-related achievements, but as an attitude of permanent self-improvement, within and without formal educational provision. As Maarten Simons (2009) puts it: 'Freedom and security remain the twin objectives of the government of men, however, "lifelong learning" is replacing "the social" and "innovation" and "globalisation" take the place of "progress" and "modernisation" (Simons, 2009, p. 3).

Lifelong learning then has become central to the current mode of government and self-government, in which capitalising one's life through permanent attention to skills and competencies and the efficient employment of these has become the means of sustaining what has been termed the performative (Yeatman, 1993) or competition state (Ball, 2000), in which government is effected through performance measurement and management (Simons, 2007). Government operates through the regulation of the choices of individual citizens, understood as exercisers of choice and aspirers to self-actualisation and self-fulfilment, governed through their very freedom (Barry et al., 1996, p. 41). Empowerment in this context refers to the framing of all aspects of our lives as learning opportunities. Understanding ourselves as learners relates not only to the ages of compulsory education or to formal educational institutions but also to the professional, the familial, and the social, physical, and emotional parts of our lives as well (Rose, 1999, 2007).

A further shift can be observed, however, following that from the social citizen to the learning citizen: to the citizen-as-researcher. This refers not, or not only, to the involvement of citizens in research, as volunteers in citizen science projects for example, but to a shift at the level of the relationship of the self to the self and to the state. Recent policy has increasingly focussed on the quality and qualities of research and innovation, not only in relation to those sectors more commonly associated with these, such as universities and the commercial research and development sector, but across many public and private sectors, and also at the level of the individual. It is no longer sufficient only to learn and to accrue competencies and skills; the individual, or organisation, must adapt and innovate in the practices of putting them to use.

Institutions and organisations today, both public and private, including the university, no longer retain certainty over their role, and instead must identify their own particular niche among their competitors and continually adapt to survive.[3] Their survival – or their understanding of sustainability – is dependent on their ability to adapt to current conditions in the face of finite resources. The language of environments – the learning environment and the research environment – frames discussion of the orientation of our practices today, and articulates the space in which the individual comes to understand herself environmentally. In an environmental self-understanding, a teleological narrative within a fixed temporality is displaced by the permanent confrontation with conditions to which we are asked to adapt and to take responsibility for. It demands a permanent reorientation of oneself within one's environment in response to the resources available (see Simons and Masschelein, 2008; Simons and Hodgson, 2012).

To understand power relations from this perspective, concerned with a mode of governmentality and subjectivation, it is not sufficient to provide a top-down analysis of the marketisation and privatisation of higher education and the positioning of consumers as citizens, much as these are features of the current context. The concern is with the 'how' of power: how does the university as it exists today come into being? How does the researcher come to understand herself as such? What does it mean to be a researcher? The remainder of this section seeks to begin to address these questions with reference to policies and practices constitutive of the university and the researcher today.

Current European policy seeks commonality, compatibility and comparability among member states and their constituent agents (individuals and institutions, for example). In June 2011, the European Commission Directorate-General for Research and Innovation published its 'Report of Mapping Exercise on Doctoral Training in Europe: "Towards a Common Approach"' (EC, 2011). The report is itself based on the principles of good practice in doctoral training set out by the European Universities Association (the Salzburg Principles and Recommendations).[4] The report also ties into the 'interconnected commitments' of the Europe 2020 Flagship Initiative 'Innovation Union'. This Flagship Initiative provides an overarching impetus to all policy relating to research, education, and innovation.

The report on doctoral training expresses the way in which researchers are understood in relation to the wider governance of the European Union as a competitive knowledge economy. It reads:

> Our economy needs to adequately absorb many new researchers. Cooperation between the academic sector and industry (in the widest meaning of the term), starting at the level of early research training, will strengthen the much needed research intensity of our economy. (EC, 2011, p. 1)

The notion of absorption in this excerpt evidences an environmental understanding. Like a homeostatic system, a fine balance must be maintained between the production of researchers, the needs of the economy for their knowledge and skills, and the maintenance of a competitive position in relation to other economies. 'Knowledge workers' provide the fuel for permanent innovation. But this is not a passive submission to the demands of the knowledge economy. The individual is responsible for innovating and for continuous self-improvement. This is not only a matter of academic or professional competence; this responsibility for innovation is a matter of one's citizenship.[5] The doctoral training report goes on to state:

> The issue of doctoral training has gained considerable importance in recent years. Doctoral training is a primary progenitor of new knowledge, which is crucial to the development of a prosperous and developed society. Developed economies rely on new knowledge and highly skilled knowledge workers to feed a process of continuous innovation. They rely also on adequately trained responsible citizens that can adapt to changing environments and can contribute to the common good. Grand societal challenges like climate change and healthy ageing require complex solutions based on high level frontier research carried out by new generations of researchers. (pp. 1–2)

The economy requires not only 'skilled knowledge workers' but also 'adequately trained responsible citizens that can adapt to changing environments and contribute to the common good'. The function of research is no longer the sustenance of the disciplines, or science, situated within the university, for the progress of the nation-state. Rather: 'The knowledge society requires the creativity and flexibility of the research mindset for a number of different functions and careers, also beyond those directly related to research. The doctorate has increasingly achieved recognition as a key part of this process' (EUA, 2010, p. 2). Research, then, is a productive force for the governance of the knowledge economy. To research is now a disposition required of us all in order to permanently adapt to the conditions of our environment (Hodgson, 2013a).[6]

The foregoing brief discussion of interrelated policy statements that seek comparability and compatibility between member states illustrates the ethos of the environmental-ecological self-understanding. Hierarchy, age-related stages, and linear progress have been superceded by the establishment of common measures and a streamlining of the language by which functions and qualities are referred to. Success is a matter of competition, innovation and entrepreneurialism aimed toward finding and, through adaptation, maintaining a niche, not only in research roles and institutions but in all sectors, at all levels, and in all aspects of our lives.

Foucault's thought and subsequent literature on governmentality provide a framework with which to describe the way in which a mode of subjectivation takes effect. To provide a more detailed account of this – not only of the normative discourses and practices to which we are subject but also what mode of subjectivation and what forms and practices materialise as a result – we must observe the how of power at the level of everyday practices. This challenge to text-based analyses is posed by posthumanist and materialist thought, which develops an empirical, or experimental, ontology (see Marres, 2013 for an account of this), exposing limitations of the various 'turns' in social theory and philosophy. As suggested above, the adoption of these modes of analysis in education might be seen as faddish, deposing Foucault, Deleuze, and others, in favour of Latour (and others associated with Actor Network Theory) or prominent materialist and posthumanist scholars. These bodies of work have important insights for our understanding of power, education, and subjectivity unless we understand the critiques of earlier scholarship as a thoroughgoing rejection of the value of these factors.

I will pursue such rejections below by considering a defence of Foucault by Thomas Lemke against the critique of the materialist philosopher and physicist Karen Barad. Lemke's defence draws attention to important aspects of Foucault's thought, to illustrate that the material aspects of the world are not ignored by his work. But in doing so, Lemke perhaps closes down possibilities opened up by Barad's critique. These are taken up later in the chapter.

Foucault and the new materialism

Thomas Lemke comes to the defence of Foucault in response to criticisms levelled at his account of power and governmentality by theorists of 'new materialism' who contend 'that matter itself is to be conceived as active, forceful and plural' (Lemke, 2014, p. 2). As Lemke summarises, the so-called 'material turn':

> aims at a new understanding of ontology, epistemology, ethics and politics, to be achieved by overcoming anthropocentrism and humanism, the split between nature and culture, linguistic or discursive idealism, social constructivism, positivism, and naturalism. Central to this movement is the extension of the concept of agency

and power to non-human nature, thereby also calling into question conventional understandings of life. (p. 2)

From this perspective, writes Lemke, Karen Barad identifies three particular shortcomings of Foucault's approach to the understanding of power:

1) Foucault gives 'conceptual privilege' to the social, making it 'impossible to engage with matter in a substantive way' (Barad, 2008, p. 138, cited in Lemke, 2014, p. 4), and thus he 'restages matter's passivity' and 'honors the nature-culture binary' (Barad, 2007, p. 146, cited in Lemke, 2014, pp. 4–5).
2) Foucault's analysis is one-sided as he ascribes agency 'only to the human domain'and so does not address 'the nature of technoscientific practices and their profoundly productive effects on human bodies' or their implication in 'what constitutes the human' (Barad, 2007, p. 145–146, cited in Lemke, 2014, p. 5). A post-humanist concept of performativity is needed to attend to this, according to Barad (Lemke, 2014, p. 5).
3) Foucault does not give an adequate account of how the 'precise nature of the relationship between discursive practices and material phenomena' is articulated (Barad, 2007, p. 146, cited in Lemke, 2014, p. 5) because he 'takes for granted the boundaries between nature and culture, human and non-human' (Lemke, 2014, p. 5). Matter is a 'passive resource or raw material for power relations' according to Barad (Lemke, 2014, p. 5).

But Lemke argues that within Foucault's notion of the 'government of things' lies an implicit posthumanism and an approach that answers to the concerns raised by Barad and others (Lemke, 2014, p. 6). Against the general assumption that Foucault belongs to the social constructivist, anthropocentric era, Lemke argues that 'elements of a post-humanist approach may be found in Foucault's idea of a "government of things", which he outlines in his lectures on governmentality' (p. 3). Further, Lemke suggests that the 'relational account of agency and ontology' that Foucault's idea of a 'government of things' enables, might open the way for 'a more materialist account of politics' that 'significantly differs from some problematic tendencies in the new materialism' (p. 3).

Lemke locates Foucault's idea of the 'government of things' in his 1978 lecture at the Collège de France in which he refers to Guillaume de la Perrière's definition of government as 'the right disposition of things, arranged so as to lead to a convenient end' (Foucault, 1978, cited in Burchell et al., 1991, p. 93). For Foucault this is a decisive shift in the art of government from the concern with territory and sovereignty in the texts of Machiavelli (Lemke, 2014, p. 7). Foucault writes:

> One governs things. But what does this mean? I do not think this is a matter of opposing things to men, but rather of showing that what government has to do with is not territory but rather a sort of complex composed of men and things. The things with which in this sense government is to be concerned are in fact men, but men in their relations, their links, their imbrication with those other things which are wealth, resources, means of subsistence, the territory with its specific qualities, climate, irrigation, fertility, etc.; men in their relation to that other kind of things, customs, habits, ways of acting and thinking, etc.; lastly, men in their relation to that other kind of things, accidents and misfortunes such as famine, epidemics, death, etc;.... (Foucault, 1978, in Burchell et al., 1991, p. 93)

For Lemke, the interpretation of the art of government that Foucault presents is not based on the interaction of two fixed, stable entities, 'men' and 'things', but employs a relational approach (Lemke, 2014, p. 7): 'In fact, the qualification 'human' or 'thing' and the political and moral distinction between them is itself an instrument and effect of the art of government, and does not constitute its origin or point of departure... [T]he art of government determines what is defined as subject and object, as human and non-human' (Lemke, 2014, p. 7). Lemke suggests that Foucault implies a symmetry of sorts in the understanding of humans and things in the art of government;[7] as there is 'no pre-given and fixed-off borderline between humans and things, it is possible to state that "humans" are governed as "things"' (p. 8). This might risk exacerbating the problem that Barad identifies – denying agency not only of things but also of humans – but Lemke argues that this is not the case.

> Foucault does not mean a global and all-pervasive process of reification 'reducing' men to passive and inert things; quite the contrary, the interests, sensations, and affects of men are essential facts that political reason – a rational knowledge that no longer relies on a divine order of things or the principles of prudence and wisdom – has to take into account. (p. 8)

Foucault further distinguishes the government of things from sovereignty using the notion of 'milieu', to refer to the 'intersection between a multiplicity of living individuals working and coexisting with each other in a set of material elements that act on them and on which they act in turn' (Foucault, 2007, p. 22, cited in Lemke, 2014, p. 8). This concept, for Lemke, 'eschews any simple and uni-directional concept of causality or focus on human agency' (p. 10). The milieu 'provides the "point of articulation" between the "natural", the "artificial", the physical and the moral' (p. 10). Non-human nature is not taken for granted; Foucault is interested in how it is 'articulated within practices' that he refers to as 'more-than-human' practices (Lemke, p. 10). This approach illustrates Foucault's concern with the 'how' of power (Foucault, 2002, p. 336), that is, with how power is produced in the relations between 'partners' (p. 337). The concern is with looking at how, that is, in what relationships, power is produced.

Lemke provides a strong defence of Foucault's posthumanism and materialism in response to Barad's critique. While doing so in support of the need to take the material into account, Lemke also raises issues with Barad's account of matter. In the examples Lemke provides of Barad's work, there is a risk, it seems, of matter being privileged in the account and for it to be imbued with inherent qualities. For example, when Barad refers to 'matter's dynamism' and calls for 'a return to matter', arguing that restricting our understanding of power to the domain of the social denies matter of 'the fullness of its capacity' (Barad, 2008, p. 128). This raises questions, Lemke suggests, about what this 'fullness' and 'capacity' might consist in, if not 'the idea of a singular and stable substance and an originary force' (Lemke, 2014, p. 13). It could also be argued that in seeking to provide a new way of studying power, the focus and force of what Foucault was doing are ignored: the work of Foucault to which Barad refers in her critique was historical and text-based, and not attending to the same political issues with which Barad is concerned. But the concern here is not to defend Foucault at any cost. Rather it is to illustrate what is made possible in the account of agency and materiality that Foucault does provide for the understanding of power, while acknowledging that his accounts relate to the politics of a particular point in history and that we must adapt the understanding of power to take account of who we are today. We must 'put our thinking to the test of reality' (Foucault, 2000, p. 316), not the other way around.

For Lemke, Foucault's reference to the government of things provides evidence that his account of power does permit the material dimension. It is not clear, however, where the emphasis lies for Lemke. He refers to Foucault's description of governing things as a 'complex composed of men and things', things such as 'wealth, resources, means of subsistence', 'climate, irrigation, fertility', 'customs, habits, ways of acting', 'famine, epidemics, death, etc.' (Foucault, 1978, cited in Burchell et al., 1991, p. 93). Here, then, it might be argued that what are being referred to are sociological and demographic categories and events. They are constitutive of and constituted in a mode of governing but are perhaps not 'things'. Here, the emphasis is on *the* government *of* things: government as the designation of objects to be rendered measurable and manageable and thereby governable and in relation to which men are governed. The notion of *a* government of *things*, however, changes the emphasis, to consider things in themselves as operative in governing us in particular ways, intentional or not. A government of things implies things governing – conducting our conduct – and constituting a mode of government, and thus the emphasis is similar to that of 'the internet of things'. Broadening the notion of things in this way enables us to consider philosophically and empirically the production and operation of power relations in education following Foucault, drawing on the insight of posthumanists that build on his work, such as Barad, and also in line with a sociomaterial approach, such as that of Decuypere et al. (2010), for example. We will now consider Barad's work in relation to that of Foucault, to indicate how hers is not a thoroughgoing refutation of it but rather draws on some of its insights, and develops them to take account of the how of power by addressing its materiality.

How Foucault matters to materialism

Barad seeks to address the treatment of matter as if 'passive and immutable' that has led, in the numerous theoretical 'turns', to language being 'granted too much power' (Barad, 2003, p. 801). As a corrective to 'the representationalist belief in the power of words to represent pre-existing things' (p. 802), Barad offers 'a materialist, naturalist, and posthumanist elaboration' of performativity 'that allows matter its due as an active participant in the world's becoming' (p. 803). As a physicist, matter is fundamental to Barad's understanding of what she terms the 'intra-activity' of the world. As Lemke suggested, there is a risk that the role of matter is overstated, but our concern here is with what is made possible by the shift in thinking that Barad introduces. In line with Foucault and others critical of representationalism, Barad displaces the idea that 'beings exist as individuals with inherent attributes, anterior to their representation' (p. 804) and, more generally, an anthropocentric view of the world.

Barad does not merely point out the shortcomings of Foucault's account of power, but rather develops it by means of her critique. She acknowledges that 'Foucault's analytic of power links discursive practices to the materiality of the body' (p. 808) but suggests that its limitations prevent 'an understanding of precisely *how* discursive practices produce material bodies' (p. 808). She shares Foucault's concern with the how of power, but elaborates an analytic that might more fully account for it. Barad refers to Foucault's positioning the body as 'the locus of productive forces, the site where the large-scale organization of power links up with local practices' (Barad, p. 809).She refers to his stating that 'the deployments of power are directly connected to the body', that the biological and historical are 'bound together', and his seeking a history of 'the manner in which what is most material and most vital in [bodies] has been invested' (Foucault, 1980a, pp. 151–152, cited in Barad, 2003, p. 809). But Barad seeks a more detailed 'how', an account of how the body's very 'materiality plays a role in the workings of power' (p. 809).

For Barad:

> Crucial to understanding the workings of power is an understanding of the nature of power in the fullness of its materiality. To restrict power's productivity to the limited domain of the 'social', for example, or to figure matter as merely an end product rather than an active factor in further materializations, is to cheat matter out of the fullness of its capacity … If we follow disciplinary habits of tracing disciplinary-defined causes through to the corresponding disciplinary-defined effects, we will miss all the crucial intra-actions among these forces that fly in the face of any specific set of disciplinary concerns. (Barad, 2003, p. 810)

Barad's work exemplifies this 'materiality' or 'matter', bringing physics to bear on philosophy and social theory, and vice versa. These concerns are also addressed by Science and Technology Studies, for example. For all the concern with interdisciplinarity in educational research, however, the fields of sociology of education and philosophy of education remain quite distinct (though of course this is changing and there are exceptions). To read the world through the lens of disciplinary-defined categories, questions, and causes is to put the world to the test of our theories. Barad, as Foucault did, puts thinking about human existence to the test of reality and thus seeks an 'agential realism' to provide 'a robust account of the materialization of *all* bodies – "human" and "non-human" – and the material-discursive practices by which their differential constitutions are marked' (Barad, 2003, p. 810).

Conclusion: how does research materialise?

Foucault's analytic of power is presented here as having enduring relevance to the understanding of the conditions we find ourselves in today. His work, and scholarship that has developed his account in the last forty years, provides a nuanced narrative of the how of power, the ways in which discourses and practices constitute a mode of governmentality and thus a particular mode of subjectivation. Foucault's work instantiates a critical attitude that asks who we are and what we do, and what we do, does. Agency is fundamental to this understanding of power relations and the understanding of philosophy, of writing – and so potentially of research – as transformative points to the particular educational – or educative – force of this approach. This critical attitude to the present requires us, however, to permanently attend to the 'how' of power, and thus to refine the conceptual tools with which we conduct studies of governmentality.

The discussion here of the university and the researcher illustrates both the insights into the how of power this approach produces and the need to permanently revise how we conceptualise this. The discussion outlines the shift that has taken place in the role of the university as part of a wider shift in the relationship between the individual, the state, and education. The lifelong learning citizen, addressed in policy and constituted in formal educational practices, and the framing of all areas of our lives as learning problems, is subject to an environmental self-understanding, in which she must continually adapt, seek and respond to feedback, and invest herself in learning opportunities in all aspects of her life. Further shifts in recent years, however, have seen a movement away from needing the workforce to upskill themselves to enable employment, to needing the workforce to create that employment themselves. That is, it is not sufficient to gain qualifications; today one needs to innovate in how and where to employ the knowledge and skills gained. This approach furthers the responsibilisation of the individual that has been a feature of modern government – the individual is governed in terms of her freedom – to require an orientation not only to learning but also to research. This feature also has implications for how we understand research. Its traditional association with the university, or the commercial research and development sector, and its orientation to particular scientific or commercial ends has shifted. In the knowledge economy, the 'outputs' of research, and a workforce equipped with research skills are vital resources. Research must be responsive, its focus adaptable to present needs, its outputs short-term and measurable, and it must provide a further resource, of knowledge, skills, or economic and social benefit. The knowledge and skills required for research are defined in policy and curricula, providing a framework for comparability and competition.

The analysis of the university and the researcher in this chapter is based on policy documents and the discourses of research operative in our current practices. The perspective of posthumanist and materialist scholarship, that draws on and updates Foucault's analytic of power, provides a further level of detail to the analysis of the how of power, challenging us at once to again rethink what it is we are researching – the physical matter of it – and our very relationship to it: how are we implicated in the how of power? The interrelationship of power, subjectivity and ethics in Foucauldian work entails that the analysis is both a critique of existing conditions and of ourselves.

Notes

1. Foucault elaborates this understanding according to four aspects. The first is the aspect of the self concerned with moral conduct, termed the ethical substance (*substance éthique*), that which is worked on by ethics (Foucault, 1986, p. 353). The second is the mode of subjection (*mode d'assujettissement*), 'the way in which people are invited or incited to recognize their moral obligations', for example, in relation to divine law, natural law, or a rational rule (p. 354). The third aspect he describes as 'the means by which we can change ourselves in order to become ethical subjects', or how we work on the ethical substance (p. 354). He terms this the 'self-forming activity' (*pratique de soi*) or '*asceticism* in a very broad sense' (p. 355). Finally:

   > The fourth aspect is: Which is the kind of being to which we aspire when we behave in a moral way? For instance, shall we become pure, or immortal, or free, or masters of ourselves, and so on? So that's what I call the telos (*téléologie*). In what we call morals, there is the effective behaviour of people, there are the codes, and there is the kind of relationship to oneself with the above four aspects. (p. 355)

2. This distinction marks a difference in attitude, between education as *educere*, as leading out, and education as teaching and expertise; the former critical and transformative, the latter fixative. Foucault makes this distinction with reference to his own writing, describing his books as experience books, not truth books designed to teach (Foucault, 2002, p. 246; see also Masschelein, 2006).

3. It is conceptually difficult to refer to the university today as an institution, as this implies its modern sense, but this is the subject of further work. See Decuypere et al. (2010) for one re-conception of the university as 'Virtual-Entrepreneurial-Networked' using a sociotechnical analysis.

4. http://www.eua.be/Libraries/Publications_homepage_list/Salzburg_II_Recommendations.sflb.ashx

5. For a more detailed analysis of the relationship between citizenship and learning in European policy from the perspective of governmentality, see Hodgson (2011).
6. For a more in-depth analysis of these policies see also Hodgson, N. (2013b).
7. The notion of symmetry is prominent in Actor Network Theory. See, for example, Latour (2007).

References

Ball, S. J. (1990) [2013] *Foucault and Education: Disciplines and Knowledge*, London: Routledge.

Ball, S. J. (2000) 'Performativities and fabrications in the education economy: towards the performative society', *Australian Educational Researcher*, 272, 1–23.

Barad, K. (2003) 'Posthumanist performativity: Toward an Understanding of How Matter Comes to Matter', *Signs: Journal of Women in Culture and Society*, 28(3), 801–831.

Barad, K. (2007) *Meeting the Universe Halfway: Quantum Physics and the Entanglement of Matter and Meaning*, Durham, London: Duke UniversityPress.

Barad, K. (2008) 'Posthumanist performativity: Toward an understanding of how matter comes to matter', in Alaimo, S. and Hekman, S. (eds) *MaterialFeminisms*, Bloomington, Indianapolis: Indiana University Press, pp. 120–154.

Barry, A., Osborne, T. and Rose, N. (eds) (1996) *Foucault and Political Reason: Liberalism, Neo-Liberalism and Rationalities of Government*, Chiacgo: University of Chicago Press.

Baker, B. M. and Heyning, K. E. (eds) (2004) *Dangerous Coagulations? The Uses of Foucault in the Study of Education*, New York: Peter Lang.

Besley, T. (A. C.) and Peters, M. A. (2007) *Subjectivity and Truth: Foucault, Education, and the Culture of the Self*, New York: Peter Lang.

Burchell, G., Gordon, C. and Miller, P. (eds) (1991) *The Foucault Effect: Studies in Governmentality*, Chicago: University of Chicago Press.

Butin, D. (2006) 'Review Article: Putting Foucault to Work on Educational Research', *Journal of Philosophy of Education*, 40(3), 371–380.

Decuypere, M., Simons, M. and Masschelein, J. (2010) 'The virtual in the university and the university in the virtual? A socio-technological perspective on academic practice', paper presented to EASST Conference, Trento, 2–4 September 2010.

EC (European Commission) (2011) *Report of Mapping Exercise on Doctoral Training in Europe 'Towards a common approach'*, EC: Brussels.

European Universities Association (2010) *Salzburg II Recommendations*, Brussels: European Universities Association. Available from: http://www.eua.be/Libraries/Publications_homepage_list/Salzburg_II_Recommendations.sflb.ashx [Accessed 3 July 2014].

Fenwick, T. and Edwards, R. (2010) *Actor-network Theory and Education*, London: Routledge.

Fenwick, T. and Edwards, R. (2012) *Researching Education through Actor-network Theory*, Oxford: Wiley Blackwell.

Foucault, M. (1978) 'Governmentality' in Burchell, G., Gordon, C. and Miller, P. (eds) (1991) *The Foucault Effect: Studies in Governmentality*, Chicago: University of Chicago Press.

Foucault, M. (1980a.) *The History of Sexuality. Vol. 1, An Introduction,* (trans.) Robert Hurley, New York: Vintage Books.

Foucault, M. (1982) 'Afterword: The Subject and Power' in Dreyfus, H. and Rabinow, P. (eds) *Michel Foucault: Beyond Structuralism and Hermeneutics,* Brighton: Harvester.

Foucault, M. (1986) 'On the Genealogy of Ethics: An Overview of a Work in Progress' in Rabinow, P. (ed.) *The Foucault Reader,* London: Penguin.

Foucault, M. (2000) 'What is Enlightenment?' in Rabinow, P. (ed.) *Essential Works of Foucault, 1954–1984, Vol. 1, Ethics,* London: Penguin.

Foucault, M. (2002) 'Interview with Michel Foucault' in Faubion, J. (ed.) *Michel Foucault, Essential Works of Foucault 1954–1984, Volume 3, Power,* London: Penguin.

Foucault, M. (2007) [1978] 'What is Critique?' in *The Politics of Truth,* Los Angeles: Semiotext(e).

Gros, F. (2005) 'Course Context' in Foucault, M., *The Hermeneutics of the Subject: Lectures at the Collège de France 1981–1982,* New York: Picador.

Histoire de la sexualite, II: l'usage des plaisirs (1984; trans. 1985) and *Histoire de la sexualité, III: le souci de soi* (1984; trans. 1986).

Hodgson, N. (2011) *Educational Research, Subjectivity and the Construction of European Citizenship,* unpublished Ph.D. Thesis, Institute of Education, University of London.

Hodgson, N. (2013a) 'From Entrepreneurialism to Innovation: Research, Critique, and the Innovation Union' in Smeyers, P. and Depaepe, M. (Eds) *Educational Research: The Importance and Effects of Institutional Spaces,* Dordrecht: Springer.

Hodgson, N. (2013b) 'Materials that shape researchers' in Smeyers, P. and Depaepe, M. (eds) *Educational Research: Material Culture and the Representation of Educational Research,* Dordrecht: Springer.

Latour, B. (2007) *Reassembling the Social: An Introduction to Actor-Network Theory,* Oxford: Oxford University Press.

Lemke, T. (2014) 'New materialisms: Foucault and the "government of things"', *Theory, Culture and Society,* 32(4), 1–23, DOI: 10.1177/0263276413519340.

Marres, N. (2013) 'Why political ontology must be experimentalized: on eco-show homes as devices of participation', *Social Studies of Science,* 43(3), 417–443, DOI: 10.1177/0306312712475255.

Masschelein, J. (2006) 'Experience and the Limits of Governmentality', *Educational Philosophy and Theory,* 38(4), 561–576.

Masschelein, J., Simons, M., Brockling, U., and Pongratz, L. (eds) (2007) *The Learning Society from the Perspective of Governmentality,* Oxford: Blackwell.

Noens, P. and Ramaekers, S. (2014) (in press) 'The family as a "gathering": how the life of an object "makes" a family'. *International Journal of Child, Youth, and Family Studies,* 5 (4.2), 722–740.

Olssen, M. (1999) *Michel Foucault: Materialism and Education,* Westport, CT: Bergin and Garvey.

Rose, N. (1999) *Powers of Freedom,* Cambridge: Cambridge University Press.

Rose, N. (2007) *The Politics of Life Itself: Biomedicine, Power, and Subjectivity in the Twenty-First Century,* Princeton: Princeton University Press.

Simons, M. (2007) '"To be informed": understanding the role of feedback information for Flemish/European policy', *Journal of Education Policy,* 22(5), 531–548.

Simons, M. (2009) 'The Public/Private Lives of European Citizens: Lifelong Learning, Global Positioning, and Performance Spectacles', paper presented to Europe Conference on Educational Research, Vienna, Austria, 27–29 September 2009.

Simons, M. and Hodgson, N. (2012) 'Learned Voices of European Citizens: from governmental to political subjectivation', *Teoría de la Educación*, 24(1), 19–40.

Simons, M. and Masschelein, J. (2008) 'From schools to learning environments: The dark side of being exceptional', *Journal of Philosophy of Education*, 42(3–4) pp. 687–704.

Simons, M., Olssen, M. and Peters, M. (2009) *Re-Reading Education Policies: A Handbook Studying the Policy Agenda of the 21st Century*, Rotterdam: Sense.

Yeatman, A. (1993) 'Corporate management and the shift from the welfare to the competition state', *Discourse*, 13(2), 3–9.

Part III
Social Inequality

6
Gender, Power and Education

Gabrielle Ivinson

Broadly speaking, feminist activists and scholars within the field of gender and education in the West have theorised power though a central concern with how patriarchy exerts effects within institutions and specifically in schools, colleges and universities. In two thousand years of Western culture there have been moments when equality between men and women was actively espoused and practised, yet these moments have been remarkably short-lived in modernity. Researching gender, as Kim Thomas reminds us, 'requires an examination of the cultural creation of male dominance as well as the creation of female subordination' (1990, p. 2). Carol Pateman (1988) persuasively argues that the social contract theorist instigated a new kind of patriarchy that was predicated on a fraternal bond. Fraternal, in comparison to paternal, patriarchy created not only oppositional roles for women but laid the foundation for the hierarchical valuing of masculinity and femininity that came to accord low status to women's places, social roles, work, knowledge and being. This chapter will outline relationships between gender, power and education by demonstrating how schools as public institutions continue to perpetrate the asymmetrical valuing of masculinity and femininity that was re-inscribed in the social contract theories of the seventeenth and eighteenth centuries. It will argue that schools were created through patriarchal structures, and that the division of social life into public and private domains leave legacies which still impact our current agencies, perceptions, attitudes and evaluations as well as the way teachers, boys and girls interact and conduct themselves in schools.

The chapter starts with a brief introduction to fraternal patriarchy from Pateman's illuminating perspective. The next two sections deal with how women gained access to educational institutions and how once inside these institutions gender division were perpetuated through less visible means. As feminists have developed theoretical lenses to explore how power operates in education, they have placed the emphasis on structures, dominant discourses and more recently on matter. A brief overview of theoretical developments is followed by illustrations from ethnographic work to demonstrate how gender emerges in everyday classroom practice. The examples draw on work that Patricia Murphy and I carried out in secondary schools in England, and have been re-analysed in order to gesture towards some of the potential of new 'third wave' material feminisms to theorise power, gender and education.

Patriarchal power

The history of patriarchy has been at the centre of feminists theorising of power in the West. In relation to patriarchy, Carole Pateman (1988) claims that 'the most influential political story of modern times' is the story told by seventeenth and eighteenth century social contract theorists, Hobbes, Locke and Rousseau. This story centres on the Western European Enlightenment philosophers and therefore applies to a limited range of social and political contexts and does not address the conditions of subordination for women in many parts of the globe, a limitation that feminists are increasingly concerned about. Nevertheless, Pateman's account is helpful because it illustrates how a particular political story effectively reframed the basis of social organisation and instigated a powerful asymmetry between public and private life, and thus between the social status of men and women as citizens. It allows us to trace the way women were excluded from the scientific endeavours undertaken in public institutions, and so were generally unrecognised as scientists and academics right up until relatively recently. Vestiges of this historical legacy haunt institutional life today, and the asymmetric values attached to masculinity and femininity can be detected, even in contemporary school and classroom life, as will become apparent later in the chapter.

Pateman (1988) tells how the social theorists of the late seventeenth and early eighteenth century, such as Hobbes, Locke and Rousseau, successfully disconnected civic society from the rule of 'God the Father', and replaced it with arguments derived from rationality. The crux of the argument was freedom. The social contract theorists treated society as if it was founded on an original contract entered into freely by people. The argument aimed to persuade people that it was in their own best interests to submit themselves to the authority of the state and be bound by civil law in exchange for the securities, benefits and the rights of social life.

A great deal of the persuasive impetus came from telling stories about pre-social human existence, for example, Hobbes invoked 'man's' sinful nature, his separation from God, personified by disobedience, wilfulness and selfishness after the Fall, to scare people into accepting the social contract. Locke, on the other hand, described the pre-social state 'as one of 'peace, goodwill, mutual assistance and co-operation' (Macnaughten and Urry, 2001, p. 11), reminiscent of the Garden of Eden. It followed, Locke suggested, that humanity should organise itself around 'natural laws'. By introducing the notion of social contract, Hobbes, Locke and Rousseau broke the chain of association based on the Divine Rule that had previously justified people's differential place in society. Pateman pointed out that since the social contract developed in the seventeenth century, public space has been constructed around a new form of patriarchy, not based on kinship but on brotherhood; men banded with men to retain political power through a fraternal bond. As a reward for undertaking duties in the public domain as soldiers, civil servants and rulers, men were offered freedom (dominion) within the private realm of family life. To guarantee men's dominion in the private realm, and maintain women's low status with respect to men, the social contract theorists separated public and private life and argued that private domain was not subject to the same rules as the public domain. Pateman goes so far as to suggest that the social contract was a sexual contract that positioned women in a similar position to Greek and Roman slaves. She argued that the social theorists introduced an entirely new form of patriarchy. Men's fraternal bound was predicated on women's lack of freedom enshrined in the marriage contract. Women were increasingly defined according to the limited roles afforded by the private realm, which amounted to domestic duties, child-care and attending to their husbands' needs. The differentiation of sex groups is intimately tied up with the creation of the Church state and the social state (Pateman, 1988). Thus, fraternal patriarchy reframed political membership and men came, once again, to enjoy superior rights to women within society purely by an accident of birth.

This story underpins the formation of social institutions and especially those, which built the modern educational system in the UK between 1840s and 1970s (Arnot and Dillabough, 2000, p.5). The institutions, and specifically schools and universities, were created to maintain the separation of the sexes. The political construction of a distinction between public and private, which became increasingly secured though legal structures, perpetuated the cultural creation of male dominance as well as the creation of female subordination. Yet, we often confuse paternal and fraternal patriarchy. Oftentimes people appeal to natural law, as if somehow women are essentially or genetically different to men, to justify the different treatment of men and women in society and in schools. What happens as people make these assertions is that they invoke a gender hierarchy, such that women's roles are given inferior status, without acknowledging that this inferiority grew from structural rather than natural origins. Separating the sexes was built into the very fabric of public life including the formation of institutions, architecture, discourses, ritual and routines. In effect, the social contract theorists legitimated structural inequalities in political and social life, which women have been opposing ever since and which came to find a political voice with the women's suffrage movements of the nineteenth century (de Beauvoir, 1952 [1974]).

Gaining access to educational institutions

Gaining access to schools and universities has been fundamental to women's struggle for emancipation and access to the public domain. Women gained access to universities in the UK only in the late nineteenth century. Initially, women gained access by creating separate women's colleges, such as Girton, in 1869 and Newnham Hall in 1875, both in Cambridge, and Lady Margaret Hall and (Mary) Somerville College in Oxford sponsored, as the names suggest, by wealthy women (Dyhouse, 1995). Yet, initially, even when women took degrees the respective universities did not validate them. It was not until the 1920s that women gained the right to full university membership. Women's right to vote remained restricted in Oxford and Cambridge Universities until the 1970s. This struggle illustrates the way that women were not legitimated as those who produce academic knowledge. For example, Hetha Ayrton (1854–1923), who was an English engineer, mathematician, physicist and inventor, was nominated for fellowship of the Royal Society in 1902. She was turned down because, as a married woman, she was judged to have no standing in law (Mason, 1991.) According to the Royal Society's records even today, of the 1,600 living fellows, only 5% are women. As women gained access to the physical buildings of schools and universities, so exclusion has continued in less visible forms.

The story of education in the UK is also a story of class. Arnot and Dillabough (2000) point out that schools and universities were created within a patriarchal culture, and only elite men were expected to be educated to fulfil roles in the public realm. The first grammar schools in the UK were built for boys in the fourteenth century, and up until the nineteenth century there was little institutional educational provision for girls (Purvis, cited in Ivinson and Murphy, 2007, 17). Upper class girls were educated by governesses in their homes and were taught subjects such as music, dancing and embroidery in preparation for marriage (Purvis, 1991). Working-class girls learned to spin, cook and sew at home. In the mid-eighteenth century, upper-class women with substantial capital, as well as the middle classes and managerial workers, sought their right to an education as a means of accessing the public domain of professional work (Delamont, 1978). Feminists such as Margaret Cavendish (1623–1673), Mary Astell (1666–1731) and Mary Wollstonecraft (1759–1797) campaigned for girls to gain access to education, paving the way for the first girls' public school, Cheltenham Ladies College in 1853, which was run by Miss Dorothea Beale, and taught the daughters of gentlemen (Purvis, 1991). While some feminists wanted girls to study the same curriculum as boys, considerable pressure from parents wishing to guarantee their daughters' capital in the marriage endorsed the study of music, painting and conversational French. Girls in elementary schools were given lessons on domestic economy along with needlework and laundry work instead of science (ibid.). In the first half of the nineteenth century, the education deemed appropriate for girls reflected societal views about sex differences. As Purvis (1991) pointed out, working-class girls were schooled for domestic labour and to become good wives and mothers. A popular belief that education endangered woman's health was used to support the view that women's vital energies should be channelled towards reproduction. Curricula for girls reflected the division into public and private realms such that the education of the working class and the moneyed upper-classes followed distinctly different trajectories. These gender and class patterns can still be found in post 16 education, evidenced by statistics on examination results reported by subject.

Invisible divisions

Having gained access to the right to education following the Education Acts of the late nineteenth century, the majority of girls in the UK continued to experience subordination through the differential treatment they received in co-educational public schools in comparison to boys. Following the sex discrimination acts of the 1970s, institutional practices that maintained boundaries between the sexes became less visible yet continued to work though practices that operate below the radar of conscious awareness.

In the section above on the history of schooling, we saw that the range of subjects available to girls in schools has been different to those available to boys. However, once inside subject classrooms, gender divisions continue to operate through cultures in which girls tend to be treated differently to boys. Feminist studies of classrooms in the 70s and 80s found that girls in general were quiet, compliant and displayed a lack of belief in their own abilities in comparison to boys who took up more of a teacher's time, demanded more attention and were more boisterous and seemingly more self-confident than girls (Spender, 1982, Stanworth, 1983; Clarricoates, 1980; Walkden and Walkerdine, 1985, cited in Skelton, 2001). Recent ethnographic studies suggest that these patterns persist in school classrooms today (Jackson, 2006, Paechter, 2006; Ivinson and Murphy, 2007; Allan, 2009, Skelton, 2010). Specific kinds of cultures emerge in classrooms through practices that are made up of a wider variety of elements such as a teacher's instructional discourse, the subject being taught, and the student mix as well as school routines. Furthermore teachers' instructional and regulative discourses have all been identified as gendered (Arnot, 1983; Arnot et al., 1987; 1999; Singh, 1995; Weiner, 1994; Weiner et al., 1984; 1997).

During the 1980s feminists launched initiatives[1] that encouraged girls to study and achieve in science and technology, in part by recovering the history of women in science and presenting scientific principles through examples that aimed to capture girls' interests. Feminist teachers tried to provide messages that girls too could be scientists, explorers and architects. The statistical patterning was partially reversed in Western countries in the 1990s when girls started to outperform boys in science (Arnot et al., 1998; Younger et al., 1999; Skelton, 2001). This led to a moral panic about the so-called 'gender gap' and arguments arose in the popular press and among some politicians that the teaching profession had become overly feminised, creating school cultures that disadvantaged boys (for example, Hoff Sommers, 2000). Scholars have demonstrated that the statistical analysis of the so-called gender gap, did not appear across all science, technology, engineering and mathematics (STEM) subjects, and further, that neither working-class girls nor boys achieved well in science and mathematics (Gorard et al., 1999; 2000; Murphy and Whitelegg, 2006).

There are personal, national and international costs resulting from girls and working-class boys failing to become professional scientists and engineers. Like many other countries, the UK needs to double the number of recruits to engineering to meet demand, yet nearly half of all co-educational secondary schools had no girls studying physics in 2011.

A recent report by the Women's Engineering Society (WES) in 2014[2] reported that companies that had 'more women on their boards were found to outperform their rivals with a 42% higher return in sales, 66% higher return on investment and 53% higher return on equity'.[3] The sections above suggests that the creation of public institutions, structures such as the law, curricula, pedagogy and school cultures set up different roles, possibilities and imaginaries for women as citizens and as scholars. A matrix of patriarchal forces (Walby, 1990) or 'interlocking systems of oppression' (Hill Collins, 2000, 82) still marginalise groups according to gender, class and race (Pateman and Mills, 2007). Next we turn to the way feminist scholars developed poststructuralist approaches to theorise gender and power within education.

Post structuralist theorising of power and gender in education

Despite the strong advances girls and women made by gaining access to education institutions, schools continue to perpetuate boundaries between the sexes. Like Pateman, Foucault argued that regulative structures such as the Law shifted in the eighteenth century. Regulation came to operate through indirect means; for example, registry offices, law courts, hospitals and social work institutions all developed bureaucratic mechanisms or forms of governmentality to classify, count and label people. Schools and academies introduced tests, labelling children and young people as successes or failures according to their performances in public examinations. Foucault's term bio-power captures the sense that there is no one source of power (God or the Monarchy) and that instead, human bodies became regulated and produced through multiple and complex layers of regulation. For example, juridical systems of power *produce* subjects that they subsequently come to represent. Following Foucault, Judith Butler argued that 'the feminist subject turns out to be discursively constituted by the very political system that is supposed to facilitate its emancipation' (Butler, 1990, 2).

Thus, processes of subjectification were said to constitute and reconstitute people through the discourse and the practices they have access to (Davies, 2003; Blackman et al., 2008). Social norms of masculinity or femininity were said to circulate as 'truths' or hegemonic norms (Butler, 1990; Connell, 1987). Studies suggested that girls police themselves for fear that others would judge their talk, gestures, dress or forms of embodiment as abnormal (Gordon et al., 2001). In the struggle to appear feminine, empirical studies have shown that girls down play their ability and wit (Kramer, 1985; Sadker and Sadker, 1994; Measor and Sikes, 1992; Francis et al., 2009, cited in Skelton, 2001). Feminists came to see gender as performativity. Walkerdine et al. (2002) pointed to the psychological effort required by girls to conform to institutional 'truths' that privilege masculinity in school. She showed how girls are often left to fulfil complementary and subordinate roles to boys and are to undertake the emotional work of caring, containing and nurturing boys. As girls conform to these practices so they inadvertently recreate the historical public-private division. Foucault's (1972) disciplinary matrix of truth and power, as it is applied to schooling, becomes a very gloomy story of how regulative systems perpetuate legacies from the past. Connell (1987) pointed out that school practices can either reinforce or disrupt gendered legacies, yet much current empirical work suggests that the past weighs heavily on the present and, for example, boys still tend to conform to, or feel pressure to conform to, hegemonic masculinity (for example, Jackson, 2006; Skelton, 2001; Ivinson and Murphy, 2007). Instead of women and girls being excluded from public institutions, they become excluded once inside schools and academies, through less visible systems.

Some contemporary Marxist scholars have argued that poststructural feminist analysis of power as discourse, influenced by Foucault's work, has increasing placed the theoretical weight on the individual and rather than social structures (for example, Bourne, 2002). New feminist theory is beginning to shift the way in which power is theorised within education, by paying closer attention to the role of matter and materiality and by further emphasising dynamic process, emergence and contingency.

New material feminism, schooling and power

New material feminists are developing innovative ways to re-interrogate gender, inequality, discrimination and violence in education (Taylor and Ivinson, 2013). Hughes and Lury (2013) argue that material feminism has shifted away from a politics of identity and back towards an engagement with power and ethics. Specifically, such approaches allow us to interrogate knowledge as 'event' rather than as static categories or curricular content, and to view persons in processes of becoming. After a brief introduction to material feminism, three illustrative examples will be presented to demonstrate how gender emerges through the force of matter in the on-going flow of classroom life.

Material feminists critically reject pictures of social life as progressing according to the principles of unity and the linearity of Euclidean physics

(Alaimo and Hekman, 2008). Influenced by the philosophy of quantum physics, feminists such as Karen Barad (2007; 2012) have drawn attention to the role of matter, and specifically experimental apparatus in the way phenomena come into view. Barad is a quantum physicist as well as a philosopher and she re-examined the experimental apparatus described by the physicist and philosopher Niels Bohr. Bohr demonstrated that when a beam of light was shone through one kind of scientific apparatus, it emerged as particles and through another as waves. Matter appears to change form depending on the configuration of the scientific apparatus. Instead of imagining scientific experiments as neutral, they appear to be part of the phenomena that come into view.

> The object (of scientific investigation)…is not free floating body located inside a technomaterial environment; rather, this identification is the result of particular historically and culturally specific intra-actions of material-discursive apparatuses. (Barad, 2007, 217)

Accordingly, the scientist does not create knowledge, and instead knowledge emerges from within an inter-acting assemblage of elements including the machines and tools used to count, name and manipulate matter. In effect, Barad questions the boundaries created through words and concepts, and more profoundly she suggests that 'the primary ontological units are not "things" but phenomena' (2007, 141). Boundaries shift according to dominant discourses but also according to minute and on-going realignments among elements such as matter (human and non-human) and space that are unfolding all the time in the dynamic processes of life.

> The world is an ongoing process of mattering through which mattering itself acquires meaning and form through the realization of different agential possibilities. Temporality and spatiality emerge in this processual historicity. Relations of exteriority, connectivity, and exclusion are reconfigured. (Barad 2007, 141)

Within this new quantum landscape, feminists are seeking to recognise that we live in a more-than-human world in which many physical, energetic, material as well as social, economic and cultural forces have effects. Within the 'cross cutting interdisciplinary vectors' (Hughes and Lury, 2013) of social life, feminists are paying attention to neo-vitalism (Deleuze and Guattari, 1987), the vibratory force of the material world (Bennett, 2010) affective practices (Walkerdine and Jimenez 2012) and forces of life as multiplicities and becomings (Braidotti, 2013; Coleman, 2011; Fraser et al., 2006; Grosz, 2008, 2011; Manning 2013, cited in Hughes and Lury, 2013, 791). Thus, whichever phenomena come into view for researchers and actors depends on the lenses, apparatus, coding machines and discourse that are invoked at specific moments.

Furthermore Barad rejects the bird's eye view claimed by some scientists and instead insists that scientists are entangled with the apparatus and so constitute part of the phenomena that come into view through experiments. To capture this entanglement, she refers to the emergent phenomena as processes of 'worlding'. Her reasoning is based on a fundamental recognition, shared with standpoint theorists (for example, Hartstock, 1983), that knowledge is power. Thus, gender emerges in the process of worlding, and as such, the past weighs heavily on what comes into view in the present. She insists that to appreciate what comes into view in processes of 'worlding', we need to follow Derrida in recognising the need to learn the ghosts of history. I want to take up this notion of ghosting in the example below, which suggests how gender emerges in classroom life, by placing a special emphasis on matter.

In the next section, I return to a study Patricia Murphy and I (Ivinson and Murphy, 2007) carried out in a secondary school that taught boys and girls in separate classes from year 7 to year 9 (young people, aged 11–14). The following account was created by referring to ethnographic field notes and by recognising how my biography growing up in a shipbuilding town attuned me to some industrial machinery that lay dormant at the back of the Design and Technology (D&T) workshop. As a girl, I grew up in a town dominated by heavy industry yet I had been barred from studying woodwork, metal work and engineering at the secondary school I attended. The experience of being brought up so close to heavy industry and yet having been excluded from studying the subject associated with it, left a legacy that was revitalised when I entered the D&T workshop in the secondary school.

The ghosting of gender in the D&T school workshop

On entering the D&T workshop, I saw how the room seemed to be divided in two. At the far end, rows of large industrial machines lumbered like dormant ghosts from the past. Eight-feet long, faded metallic blue lathes were tacky with a sticky film of oil. Men attending evening classes would have lubricated the machines, while undertaking apprenticeships. The lathes were a marvel of complex engineering incorporating turning and drilling applications, four-way tool posts mounted on compound slide-mechanisms and powered by electric motors with six-speed, gearboxes. Elsewhere, the workshop was dotted with upright band saws that stood six-feet tall like sentries in serried rows. Some of the punching, turning and filing machines looked as though they were still used. As I walked through the room, among the lathes positioned in the ample backspace of the workshop, there came a foreboding sense of being back at secondary school that evoked a visceral feeling of exclusion, loss and nostalgia.

Some of my early adolescent memories are of hordes of men filing down the wide streets that led to the shipbuilding yards of the Clyde. In the evening, men swarmed out of the yard gates into the street, stopping the traffic. The machines must have come from the era when shipbuilding had reached its zenith. As I stood in the workshop, masculinity emerged through the materiality of the machines: a fleeting phenomenon yet an aura that still haunts me today.

In the next illustration Sophie's corporeal presence and overly zealous engagement with the scientific apparatus tested Mr White's tolerance to the limits.[4] In the lesson described below, the girls' class undertook a series of lessons to exact and examine factions of crude oil through a process called factional distillation.

The corporeal emergence of femininity in Mr White's school science lab

On entering the chemistry laboratory, the girls moved in an orderly fashion and arranged themselves behind the long wooden benches to wait for Mr White's instruction. In the previous lesson the girls had worked in groups to build the scientific apparatus required for a chemistry experiment called factional distillation. A glass container had been suspended by a tripod above the flame of the Bunsen burner to heat crude oil. As the oil heated, the liquid evaporated and the vapour rose up through the container and dropped down through an outlet into a glass jar positioned below. The oil continued to be heated and a second distillation was captured in a second, third and sometime a fourth jar provided for faction. The girls had assigned themselves roles, such as the one who collected the equipment form the front bench, the one who assembled the apparatus and the one who recorded the results, such as the temperature at which each distillation was effected. Mr White had been at pains to ask the girls to be very careful not to burn themselves and to call him if they needed help. He cautioned them numerous times to walk carefully around the laboratory. During the second lesson, the girls were to 'test' each faction for qualities such as viscosity, smell and colour. Part of this involved heating a small sample of each faction by soaking a piece of cotton with the liquid and setting it alight – so the girls could smell the vapour. All the girls worked carefully and quietly. One girl, Sophie, lit a wooden splint and some of the cotton buds and proceeded to melt her plastic pen over the flame. Mr White noticed immediately, called her out and excluded her from the science lesson.

This incident might have been unremarkable had it not been for the way Mr White treated similar incidents in the boys' class. In the boys' lessons, the boys hurried onto the laboratory, grabbed equipment from the front bench and did not wait for Mr White's instructions before getting started. Huddled around the Bunsen burners, they made piles of wooden splints and small fires were lit and relit on every bench as boys delighted in melting pens and other objects over the flames. Mr White seemed to be fairly oblivious of the boys' actions, however, as he kept himself from going around the groups. No boy was sent out even though equipment was broken and pyromania spread all around the laboratory. In the interview after the lessons we tried to confront the science teachers with the difference in the way the boys and girls had behaved in the laboratory. The phrase 'boys will be boys' cropped up a number of times. When we asked Mr White why he had sent Sophie out of the laboratory, he said he 'did not want that funny business to spread'.

We might say that gender and science emerged as ongoing reconfig-urings of space/apparatus/movement as boys and girls touched, sensed and played or worked differently. The boys, in their lessons, took control of, touched and momentarily owned artefacts such as test tubes, splits, cotton wool and Bunsen burners, and through their agentive and autonomous actions they played with fire, whereas the girls' agency was highly regulated by Mr White. When one girl, Sophie, played like a boy, she quickly drew Mr White's attention and was excluded from the science laboratory to prevent the 'funny business' from spreading. Thus, girls' corporeal presence entangled with scientific apparatus emerged as something uncanny; not quite normal. The haunting of the patriarchal matrix evoked a division between the sexes, both in terms of how the boys and girls behaved, and how they were regulated within the science laboratory. Gender emerged through matter in the Art room in the same school in a different way[5].

Queer matter emerges in the Art classroom

The art room was adorned with multi-coloured paintings, swathes of textured fabrics and cluttered with *objet d'arte*, pieces of pottery, racks of half-finished drawings, paints, water jars, brushes and pallets, and announced an aesthetic haunted by femininity. As the boys worked on the paintings, they chatted and the main topic of conversation was football. The boys had been instructed to focus on using only three colours, and to focus on shading as they painted scenes based on pictures of jazz cafes. At one point, while painting a musician, a boy asked how to mix flesh-coloured paint. Mr Fellows carefully explained to him that he needed to mix red, white and yellow. As the teacher mixed the coloured paint on his pallet for all to see, the colour pink emerged. Just at this moment, the underlying peer group banter shifted from football and boys started accusing each other of being 'queer'. As one boy accused another, so he turned to the next boy and accused him projecting the accusation outward and onward. The homosexual banter spread furiously around the classroom as boys passed the 'insult' from one to the other like a contagion (Joffe 1999). The emergence of pink paint seemed to introduce a ubiquitous femininity into the classroom setting. This visible manifestation of femininity in an already precarious male space seemed to provide the boys and Mr Fellows with an almost intolerable threat. The boys' name-calling and accusations can be seen as a bid to expel any femininity, based on a collective fear that it would pollute them and the space. To stem the flow, Mr Fellows quickly reminded the boys of the football trip that he had recently organised for the following weekend. On inspecting the boys' paintings after the lesson, we noticed that hardly any boys had used pink colours for flesh and instead had chosen black or dark brown for skin colours.

In each of these examples, gender emerged as phenomenal in a fleeting moment or clung here and there in specific material configurations of space-time. The emphasis that new material feminists have placed on process heightens awareness of the importance of *difference* to detect patterns. It was only in comparison to the boys' science lesson that Sophie's treatment and Mr White's otherwise reasonable behaviour became identifiable as gendered. In this way, we can imagine gender not as a structure so much as a force or ghost of a patriarchal matrix strongly rooted in history. Mr White felt Sophie's playfulness as a visceral kind of 'funny business' that should not be legitimated in the school science laboratory. All the science teachers in that school felt comfortable in accepting the boys' playfulness in the science laboratory. It seemed that boys were extended the science domain as a birth right.

Conclusions

It seems that the influential story of the patriarchy born and bred in the seventeenth and eighteenth centuries still haunts education today but in more complex ways. Schools and universities were founded on a division between public and private life. Mr White's reaction to Sophie suggests that scientific and formal knowledge is still to some extent gendered. Despite a long and steady improvement in the numbers of girls studying physics, for example, they are still vastly underrepresented on university courses in the UK (Murphy and Whitelegg, 2006). Historical legacies of the patriarchal matrix can be seen to still haunt educational institutions maintaining a ubiquitous sense that girls are not quite scientists, explorers or discoverers in the way that middle-class boys are imagined to be.

As my description of entering a secondary school D&T workshop suggests, gender can emerge as a phenomena within an assemblage (Deleuze and Guattari, 1987) of machines-workshop-person, where imagination and materiality have a visceral force. As I walked around the workshop, I felt excluded from engineering. My biography entangled with the machines, and the school context all contributed to that feeling. Such *feelings* of exclusion can result in a girl or women backing out of a science laboratory, a boardroom or a public office. In a similar way, *feelings of exclusion* can prevent a father from walking into a primary school playground. Just as the boys in Mr Fellow's art class *felt* the need to defend themselves against the imagined invasion of femininity into their classroom space, so the very materiality (small chairs, drapes of fabric, bright colours) of a primary school might feel threatening to a father. To enter the primary school classroom might *feel* like a threat to a man's masculinity.

We can imagine schools as sites with multiple strata and practices (Deleuze and Guattari, 1987), some of which are contradictory. However, within schools there are also spaces for agency, negotiations, avoidance, opposition, and resistance. 'These spaces are limited but significant, in the context.' (Gordon et al., 2000, 187). In general we found that girls did not enact 'agentic embodiment' in the same ways as boys, and when one girl, Sophie, acted 'like a boy' her behaviour was not tolerated (Ivinson and Murphy, 2007).

New material feminism(s) and queer scholarship on neo-materialism is encouraging us to think with new ontologies of the decentered subject: this is a posthuman version of a non-unitary, impersonal and post-identitarian subject (Hughes and Lury, 2013). This scholarship is being taken up within the field of education to think critically and creatively about subjectivity more as a residue, an effect, of over-coding by which the flows of the social body or 'life force' are organised, captured and repressed. Power enters into Deleuze and Guattari's (1987) theorising, for example, as 'territorialisation'. In this way persons are taken over, or invaded by forces. In the examples above, these forces were 'industrial masculinity', 'pinkness' or 'funny business'. In each example, these invisible forces were felt as threatening or in some way not quite right.

The renewed focus on matter is yielding insights into how knowledge, gender and power emerge within entanglements of persons, in time and space, and with all manner of matter. New material feminists are drawing on onto-epistemological methodologies (Barad, 2007) to interrogate local classroom cultures as glocal, complex, rhyzomatic, intra-active, ecological, human, and more that human places (see Hughes and Lury, 2013). By paying attention to the dynamic unfolding of life in its diversity, it becomes possible to recognise how patterning, boundary making and contingency all work together and how gender emerges as a phenomena that cannot always be articulated through language, recognised more as effect rather than as discourse, yet at least as powerful.

Notes

1. *Girls Into Science and Technology* (GIST) and *Women in Science and Engineering* (WISE).
2. Available from: http://www.wes.org.uk/sites/default/files/Women%20in%20 Engineering%20Statistics%20February%202014.pdf [Accessed 4 February 2015].
3. Quoted from Women on Boards, BIS, February 2011. Available from: http:// www.wes.org.uk/sites/default/files/Women%20in%20Engineering%20 Statistics%20February%202014.pdf [Accessed 4 February 2015].
4. (A full account of this incident can be found in Ivinson and Murphy, 2007, pp. 90–99).
5. (A full account can be found in Ivinson and Murphy, 2007, 138–140).

References

Alaimo, S. and Hekman, S. (eds) (2008) *Material Feminisms*, Bloomington: Indiana University Press.
Allan, J. (2009) 'Provocations: Putting Philosophy to Work on Inclusion', in K. Quinlivan, B. Kaur, R. Boyask (eds), Educational Enactments in a Globalised World: Intercultural Conversations, Rotterdam, Sense, 1–12.
Arnot, M. (1983) A Cloud over Co-Education: An Analysis of the Forms of Transmission of Class and Gender Relations. In: S. Walker, and L. Barton, (eds) *Gender, Class and Education*, London: Falmer Press.
Arnot, M. and Dillabough, J. (eds) (2000) *Challenging Democracy? International Perspectives on Gender, Education and Citizenship*, London: RoutledgeFalmer.
Arnot, M. and Weiner, G. (1987) *Gender Under Scrutiny: New Inquiries In Education*, London: Hutchinson in association with the Open University.

Arnot, M., Gray, J., James, M., Rudduck, J. and Duveen, G. (1998) *Recent Research On Gender And Educational Performance*, London: Office for Standards in Education (Ofsted).

Arnot, M., David, M. and Weiner, G. (1999) *Closing the Gender Gap, Postwar Education and Social Change*, London: Polity Press.

Barad, K. (2007) *Meeting The Universe Halfway: Quantum Physics And The Entanglement Of Matter And Meaning* (Durham and London, Duke University Press).

Barad, K. (2012) 'Quantum Entanglements and Hauntological Relations of Inheritance: Dis/continuities, SpaceTimeEnfoldings, and Justice-to-Come', *Derrida Today*, 3(2), 240–268. DOI: 10.3366/E1754850010000813

Bennett, J. (2010) *Vibrant Matter: A Political Ecology Of Things*, Durham and London: Duke University Press.

Blackman, L., Cromby, J., Hook, D., Papadopoulous, D. and Walkerdine, V. (2008) Editorial: Creating Subjectivities, *Subjectivity*, 22, 1–27.

Bourne, J. (2002) 'Racism, Postmodernism and the Flight form Class', in Hall, D. McLaren, P. Cole, M. and Rikowski, G. (eds) *Marxism Against Postmodernism in Educational Theory*, Lanham, Boulder, New York, Oxford: Lexington Books.

Butler, J. (1990) *Gender Trouble*, New York: Routledge.

Collins, Hill, P. (2000) *Black Feminist Thought: Knowledge, Consciousness, and the Politics of Empowerment*, New York: Routledge.

Connell, R. W. (1987) *Gender And Power: Society, The Person And Sexual Politics*, Cambridge: Polity Press.

de Beauvoir, S. (1952 [1974]) *The Second Sex*, Harmondsworth: Penguin.

Delamont, S. (1978) 'The Contradiction in Ladies' Education' in Delamont, S. and Duffin, L. (eds) *Nineteenth-Century Woman*, London: Croom Helm.

Deleuze, G. and Guattari, F. (1987) *A Thousand Plateaus: Capitalism and Schizophrenia*, (trans.) B. Massumi, Minneapolis: University of Minnesota Press.

Dyhouse, C. (1995) *No Distinction Of Sex? Women In British Universities, 1870–1939*, (Women's History), London: Routledge.

Foucault, M. (1972) *The Archaeology Of Knowledge* (trans.) A. M. Sheridan Smith, New York: Pantheon Books.

Gorard, S., Rees, G. and Salisbury, J. (1999) 'Reappraising the apparent underachievement of boys at School', *Gender and Education*, 11(4), 441–454.

Gorard, S. (2000) *Education And Social Justice: The Changing Composition Of Schools And Its Implication*, Cardiff: University of Wales Press.

Gordon, T., Holland, J. and Lahelma, E. (2000) *Making Spaces: Citizenship and Difference in Schools*, Basingstoke: Palgrave Macmillan.

Gordon, T., Holland, J. and Lahelma, E. (2001) 'Ethnographic Research in Educational Settings', in Atkinson, P., Coffey, A., Delamont, S. and Lofland, J.(eds) *Handbook of Ethnography*, London: Sage.

Hartsock, N. (1983): 'The Feminist Standpoint' in Harding, S. and Hintikka, M. B. (eds) *Discovering Reality*, Holland, Boston, London: D. Riedel Publishing Company, pp. 283–310. Available from: http://www.parliament.uk/business/publications/parliamentary-archives/archives-highlights/archives-the-suffragettes/archives-the-first-women-in-parliament-1919–1945/ [Accessed 29 April 2014].

Hoff Sommers, C. (2001) *The War Against Boys: How Misguided Feminism is Harming Our Young Men*, Simon & Schuster, New York.

Hughes, C. and Lury, C. (2013) 'Re-turning feminist methodologies: from a social to an ecological epistemology', *Gender and Education* 25(6), 786–799.

Ivinson, G.and Murphy, P. (2007) *Rethinking Single-Sex Teaching: Gender, School Subjects And Learning*, Berkshire: Open University Press, McGraw Hill.

Jackson, C. (2006) Lads and Laddettes in Education, Berkshire: McGraw Hill.

Joffe, H. *Risk and the Other*, Cambridge: Cambridge University Press.

Macnaughten, P. and Urry, J. (2001) *Bodies of Nature*, London: Sage.

Mahony, P. (1985) *Schools for the Boys? Co-education Reassessed*. London: Hutchinson.

Mason, J. (1991) 'HerthaAyrton (1845–1923) and the admission of women to the Royal Society of London', *Notes and Records of the Royal Society of London*, 45(2), 201–220.

Murphy, P. and Whitelegg, E. (2006) *Girls in the Physics Classroom: A Review of the Research into the Participation of Girls in Physics*, London: Institute of Physics Publishing.

Paechter, C. (2006) 'Reconceptualizingthe Gendered Body: Learning and Constructing Masculinities Andfeminities in School,' Gender and Education, 18(2), 121–135.

Pateman, C. (1988) *The Sexual Contract*, Cambridge: Polity Press.

Pateman, C. and Mills, C. (2007) *Contract and Domination*, Cambridge Polity Press.

Purvis, J. (1991) *A History of Women's Education in England*, Milton Keynes: Open University Press.

Singh, P. (1995) 'Discourses of computing competence, evaluation and gender: the case of computer use in the primary classroom', *Discourse: Studies In The Cultural Politics In Education*, 16(1), 81–110.

Skelton, C. (2001) *Schooling the Boys: Masculinities and Primary School Education*, Buckingham: Open University Press.

Taylor, C. A. and Ivinson, G. (2013) Editorial in Special Issue: 'Material Feminisms: new directions for education', *Gender and Education*, 25(6) 665–670.

Thomas, K. (1990) *Gender and Subject in Higher Education*, Bristol: Taylor and Francis.

Walby, S. (1990) 'Theorizing Patriarchy', Basil Blackwell.

Walkerdine, V. and Jimenez, L. (2012) *Gender, Work and Community After De-Industrialisation. A Psychosocial Approach to Affect*, Basingstoke, Palgrave Macmillan.

Walkerdine, V., Lucey, H. and Melody, J. (2002) *Growing Up Girl: Psychosocial explorations of Gender & Class*, London: Palgrave; New York: University Press, New York.

Weiner, G. (1994) *Feminisms in Education and Introduction*, Buckingham: Open University Press.

Weiner, G., Arnot, M. and David, M. (1997) 'Is the future female? Female success, male disadvantage and changing patterns in education', in: Halsey, A. H., Lauder, H., Brown, P. and Wells, A. (eds) *Education, Economy, Culture and Society*, Oxford: Oxford University Press.

Weiner, G. and Arnot, M. (1984) *Gender Under Scrutiny: New Inquiries In Education*, London, Melbourne: Hutchinson in association with The Open University.

Younger, M. Warrington, M. and Williams, J. (1999) 'The gender gap and class-room interactions, reality and rhetoric', *British Journal of Sociology of Education*, 20(3) 325–341.

7

UK Secondary Schools Under Surveillance: What are the Implications for Race? A Critical Race and Butlerian Analysis

Charlotte Chadderton

The 'war on terror' and surveillance

Since 11 September 2001, and the London bombings of July 2005, the 'war on terror' has led to the subjection of populations to new regimes of control and reinforced state sovereignty. This involves, in countries such as the UK and the US, the limiting of personal freedoms, increased regulation of immigration and constant surveillance, as a response to the perceived increased risk of terrorist attacks. In this paper, I argue that the counter-terrorism agenda is one of the reasons schools have invested to such an extent in new technologies of surveillance, and explore the implications such surveillance has for the way in which students are raced.

Recent years have seen an explosive expansion of new technologies of surveillance installed not just in the wider community, but also in UK secondary schools. Although there has been much discussion devoted to these new technologies and their impact in general, as an educational phenomenon, surveillance in schools is only just beginning to receive media and academic attention (for example, Hope, 2009; McCahill and Finn, 2010; Taylor, 2013). Schools have installed closed circuit television cameras (CCTV), metal detectors, alcohol and drug testing, chipped identity cards and electronic registers, biometric tools such as iris and fingerprint recognition, and cyberspace surveillance including webcams and websites hosting student data for parental access, among others (Hope, 2009). There have been reports of systems to log what a pupil chooses for lunch so parents can check their child's diet (UK Press Association, 2009) and of CCTV cameras being installed in school toilets (Chadderton, 2009).

The installation of surveillance devices tends to be justified on grounds of security (see for example Marx and Steeves, 2010). Protection from both external and internal threats of 'dangerous others' provides the ostensible impetus for the installation of CCTV in schools in the UK. This move followed incidents such as the stabbing of head teacher Phillip Lawrence at the school gate in 1995, and the massacre in a Dunblane Primary School in 1996 in which an outsider shot and killed 16 children and their teacher, as a response to fears around allegedly increasing knife crime, and also school and college shootings in the US at Columbine in 2001 and Virginia Tech in 2007. Reasons of health and personal safety are also cited for the introduction of these new technologies, including the reduction of bullying, theft, smoking, junk food consumption and truancy.

However, there is much evidence to suggest that surveillance systems do not ensure security – indeed there was both an armed guard and video surveillance system at Columbine. This begs the question of why there has been such an increase in new surveillance technologies in recent years. There are of course, as with any phenomenon, many reasons, which are inevitably interconnected. These include a 'culture of fear' (Furedi, 2005), and a commercial enterprise for security device businesses (Casella, 2010). Alternatively as Ragnedda (2010) argues,

[s]urveillance is much more than simply monitoring, watching and recording individuals and their data. [...] Surveillance is an interaction of power that creates and advances relations of domination. In practice, surveillance is a mode of governance, one that controls access and opportunities. (p. 356)

There is therefore more to surveillance regimes than monitoring and security.

It should be emphasised that there is still a real lack of empirical data on new technologies of surveillance in schools in the UK, and the data that is available has not focussed on race (see for example, Taylor, 2013). My arguments in this paper therefore, are based on small studies, newspaper reports and other, relevant literature, mostly from the US. There is no data, for example, on what is done with the CCTV tapes, or on who watches them, nor whether they are watched at all. There is no data on whether the students or teachers perceive there to be a race aspect to the surveillance. I have submitted two applications for funding for large projects which would explore these issues in more depth, but both have been turned down. Taylor (2013) has conducted a rare empirical study of the perspectives of both students and staff from three secondary schools in northern England. She draws our attention to the lack of legal regulation around what she terms *surveillance schools*, pointing out that, for example, in the UK, the Data Protection Act 1998 is 'inappropriate in a school setting. Head teachers are vested with the autonomy to implement any technology they desire, and they are not legally obliged to gain the consent of the parents, or even inform them' (p. 100).

Reading the work of Judith Butler through the lens of Critical Race Theory

In this article I use insights from Critical Race Theory (CRT) as well as the work of Judith Butler (2004a; 2004b; 2010) to consider the possible racial implications of the extensive use of new technologies of surveillance in UK secondary schools. Whilst acknowledging that there are tensions in combining CRT – generally considered a structuralist approach – and the work of Judith Butler – generally located in the poststructuralist tradition although more recently shifting towards a more critical perspective – I argue that using insights from both allows us a more in-depth study of the production of race and racial identities and the implications of this for policy-making in the UK (see Chadderton, 2013). I draw parallels between the two theories in order to consider the way in which some lives are recognised as fully human lives, and others are not.

CRT provides an explicit structural framework for investigating racism and the way racism operates. It considers all institutional and social arrangements to be based on the interests of those politically designated 'white', which is referred to as a system of white supremacy. White supremacy in this context does not refer specifically to extreme forms of oppression such as slavery or apartheid, nor to the actions of white right-wing extremists (although these are also taken seriously), but to a system of everyday oppression and exploitation which benefits the interests of whites as a political collective (Allen, 2001). In my reading of CRT, race does not *replace* class as a determiner of educational experience, the more traditional unit of analysis in the UK, rather it foregrounds race as *a* key determiner, and some situations cannot be explained without an understanding of race.

The term white supremacy does not necessarily refer to skin colour, rather to structures of subordination and domination, something which tends to be misunderstood by CRT's critics (for example, Cole, 2009). Despite the official acknowledgement of structural and possibly unwitting racism in the term 'institutional racism', which identified covert racism in the police force in 1999, racism in the UK still tends to be understood in terms of extreme, violent acts, or the openly racist rhetoric of the British National Party or Neo-Nazi groups (Moschel, 2007). This structural framework is thus very useful as an analytical tool for understanding covert racism. Importantly, critical race theorists argue that white supremacy is a system so deeply engrained in western cultures that it frequently goes unnoticed, perceived simply as normal or natural (Ladson-Billings, 1998). The question in this analysis is not whether white supremacy can be identified, but how it is manifested.

As my own racial positioning is 'so-called white', I do not pretend that my use of CRT is not to some extent problematic. However, I engage with CRT as a theory and analytical tool whilst explicitly rejecting those tendencies in whiteness studies for whites to dwell self-indulgently on their own whiteness, hoping that in some way this piece, even coming from a white author, has some legitimacy, operating both within and against whiteness (Ignatiev, 1997).

Critical Race theorists have examined the role of the war on terror in shaping racial discourses and racial oppression. Ladson-Billings (2003) explores the way in which, since the attack on 11 September 2001 ('9/11'), discourses around US identities have become polarised into those who are with the US, and those who are against it. Oztas (2011) argues that there has been a similar response in the UK, rendered more potent through the London bombings on 7 July 2005 ('7/7'). The population is perceived as split into two groups: a group which is to be protected from threat, and a group which is threatening (Oztas, 2011). In this case, the 'allegedly suspect' terrorists are Muslims, pre-defined as belonging to a culture that does not share the values of the west. This concept builds on longstanding discourses of Islam as an under-developed culture which condones, even encourages violence. Oztas argues that the image of Muslims in the UK is also confused with notions of a visible immigrant, the Other who threatens the west with a presumed lack of civilised values. The notion of terrorism is perceived as essentially linked to this 'incompatibility' with western life, which in effect implicates all Muslims. Thus, links with violence and threat are seen as integral to Islam, and by association, to all Muslims. As Ladson-Billings (2003) argues, the division of populations in this way has implications for who can be considered a citizen of a given nation, and who, by implication, cannot.

In this article, I read the work of Judith Butler through a CRT lens. Her work is useful for scholars exploring the way in which subjectivities are constituted, allowing a critical, in-depth study of the way in which identities are produced and re-produced through political frames which tend to favour white-western, male and middle-class identities. While dealing with inequalities, her work tends to be associated with gender discrimination rather than race. However, her more recent work does have a racial focus, dealing with the way in which 'recognisability' as a human is racially framed, and the implications this has for counter-terrorism measures (Butler, 2004a; 2010).

For Butler, identity categories do not reflect essential or innate subjectivities. Rather, identities are discursively constituted, by which is meant that all identities are actually produced by discourse. Butler's recent work considers the way lives are divided into those who are fully 'recognisable' as human, and those who are not. By recognisable, she means conceivable as lives on an equal level as other lives:

> The terms by which we are recognised as human are socially articulated and changeable. And sometimes the very terms that confer 'humanness' on some individuals are those that deprive certain other individuals of the possibility of achieving that status, producing a differential between the human and the less-than-human. These norms have far-reaching consequences for how we understand the model of the human entitled to rights or included in the participatory sphere of political deliberation. The human is understood differently depending on its race, the legibility of that race, its morphology, the legibility of that morphology, its sex, the perceptual verifiability of that sex, its ethnicity, the categorical understanding of that ethnicity. Certain humans are recognised as less than human. (Butler 2004b, p. 2)

Thus, lives and bodies are understood, 'recognised', according to social norms, and will have different entitlements to rights. Those with fewer rights, she argues, will be recognised as 'less-than-human'. These lives, which do not fully count as lives, are actually regarded as a threat to life. This perception therefore justifies a defence in cases where recognisable lives are perceived to be under threat. Lives, then, in a Butlerian framework, are produced through specific mechanisms of power,

> These categories, conventions and norms that prepare or establish a subject for recognition [...] precede and make possible the act of

recognition itself. In this sense, recognisability precedes recognition. (Butler, 2010, p. 5)

As the discourses that constitute the subject pre-date that subject, an individual subject is perceived as the embodiment of the discourse. This understanding is very relevant for the differentiation of bodies through the counter-terrorism agenda. Racial frames 'differentiate [...] in advance who will count as a life, and who will not' (Butler, 2010, p. xxix). A 'frame' in Butlerian terms, is a collection of discourses that shapes perception. Contrary to the early critiques of Butler's work, here she argues that these frames, whilst discursive, are not 'merely' perceptual or cultural: they have material effects on real lives and interaction (see for example, Butler, 1998). I use the notion of material here, not in the historical Marxist sense, but in a critical realist sense, to refer to the 'real'. Butler, particularly her more recent work, which has shifted away from what could be termed a more extreme poststructuralist stance, can be read materially through the use of 'frames' of reference and CRT can be read through a Butlerian-materialist frame.

In this way, Butler's work has parallels with CRT. Perceived racial heritage defines whether an individual belongs to the group that threatens the West, or that which is under threat. As Ladson-Billings (2003) argues, those who are perceived as a threat are viewed simplistically as evil and irrational and even non-human. Oztas (2011) argues that those of (perceived) Arab, North African or Middle Eastern origin find themselves outside the law, as it is individuals from these groups whose citizenship rights are most likely to be suspended both under English (Prevention of Terrorism Act 2005; Civil Contingencies Act 2004) and US law (USA Patriot Act 2001). These racial groups, then, have become the (imagined, nevertheless, with real consequences) embodiment of threat. In being beyond the law, their position as (perceived) non-human is reified – without the rights of a citizen, it could be argued they are rendered a non-human subject. Thus, in counter-terrorism discourses, (perceived) racial groups who are likely to be Muslims are recognised (in Butlerian terms) as non-human.

There are further similarities between Butler's work and CRT. Some critiques of CRT consider that, despite its emphasis on racial formation, CRT is essentialist and '...the essentialism inherent in the original epistemological intent of "race" is preserved' (Darder and Torres, 2004). Hill (2009) has argued that the concept of white supremacy is 'too blunt' (p. 3). However, the potential instability of the fixity of race to bodies presumed by Butler is, it could be argued, inherent in understanding the ways in which CRT comprehends the significance of white supremacy in making oppressive racial identifications. The fixidity of race requires the everyday and ongoing exercise of white supremacy. Theorising white supremacy is therefore necessary to understanding how race is not only recognised as embodied but also how this constitutes, and is constituted by, a form of power. Ignatiev (1995), for example, demonstrates how the Irish in the US have not always been considered white, rather they actually chose to *become* white. White supremacy, understood through a Butlerian lens, is therefore a fluid notion and is historically located.

The return to sovereignty and the 'state of exception'

Butler (2004a) has argued that the 'war on terror' and its implications for citizens in western democracies is illustrative of a return from what Foucault termed governmentality – a system of governmental control in which power is de-centred and exerted, instead, by shaping the behaviour, attitudes and subjectivities of citizens in order to effect self-regulation – towards sovereignty and the more overt exercise of state power. Importantly, she argues that sovereignty was never completely replaced by governmentality, rather, it could be reintroduced by those in positions of power whenever they felt it necessary. She links this shift to sovereignty to the notion of the 'state of exception', based on the work of Agamben (1998; 2005) who argues that western democracies have reintroduced a permanent state of exception, in which the so-called democratic state can suspend laws and engage in actions for which public consent is not sought. Agamben uses the situation of the Jewish people under the Nazis to exemplify the state of exception, suggesting that the Nazi terror was not necessarily exceptional, but rather an extreme form of sovereignty which can be reintroduced in a democracy by the powerful at any time. Whenever they choose, he argues, the powerful can reduce groups of citizens to what he refers as bare life, or mere physical existence, thus exercising sovereignty and removing from these groups the protection of law. He equates these dispossessed groups with the *homo sacer*, a paradoxical figure from Roman law, who may not be used for sacrifice, but may be killed by anyone without this being considered a crime. This paradox illustrates the dual nature of the *homo sacer*: this is a figure that does not enjoy the rights of a citizen, and therefore may not live a political life, yet s/he leads a life defined by politics. Colatrella (2011) argues that Agamben exaggerates our present situation, which cannot be compared to that of the Holocaust. However, it is perhaps worth recognising that there are common features: Butler

(2004a) takes up the notion of the state of exception to consider the implications of the war on terror for western democracies, in particular the US. She argues that an indefinite, all-pervasive 'state of emergency' has been introduced in which laws can be suspended at the will of those in power, giving as an example the indefinite detention of the detainees at Guantanamo Bay, suggesting that such measures are 'the means by which the exceptional becomes established as a naturalised norm' (p. 67). As Douglas (2009, p. 37) argues, 'in the state of exception, what needs to be emphasised is that it is not a power relation of pure violence, but rather, of *potential violence'*.

Butler argues that there is a racial frame through which certain groups are viewed such that they are deemed less than human, a condition she equates with the *homo sacer* – a group who are deprived of their rights as citizens, it is this condition that can be seen as a power relation of potential violence. In the case of the war on terror, the frame through which the less than human are viewed is Islam. Like the critical race theorists cited above, Butler argues that Islam is regarded as beyond the hegemonic norms of the West, which positions Muslims as suspicious or threatening. It is the fact that all Muslims, or those taken to be Muslim, Arabs, or Middle Eastern are viewed through a racial frame defining them as threatening and non-western, which means that these citizens are considered to embody the threat of terror, which they are seen to carry as an essential part of their subjectivity, and which therefore allows them to be 'recognised' as non-citizens. As non-citizens, they do not enjoy the same entitlement to rights as citizens, and deprived of legal protection, Muslims become recognised as 'humans who are not humans', or the potential *homo sacer*. As such, sovereignty differentiates between humans on grounds of (perceived) race and ethnicity. Thus Butler (2004a) argues that managing a population does not only produce subjects, 'it is also the process of their de-subjectivation, one with enormous political and legal consequences' (p. 98). This process is justified to the population, where justification is required, on grounds of the necessity of a 'state of emergency', requiring sometimes extreme political responses to the alleged terrorist threat.

Linking school surveillance, counter-terrorism and race

Some might argue that the link between surveillance in schools and the counter-terrorism agenda is quite tenuous. However, research has shown that the counter-terrorism agenda is changing the face of our cities in particular, creating new borders, restrictions and regulations (see for example Coaffee and Rogers, 2008). The link between school surveil-lance and counter-terrorism in the UK has been made explicit through government policy and documentation allocating education staff a role in monitoring extremism: The Prevent Strategy (re-launched 2011) and The Channel Project both aim to prevent young people from becoming radicalised (Home Office, 2011). Although counter-terrorism agendas in the last decade have focused on various groups and ideologies, including the far right, animal rights groups, student protestors, anarchists, Irish nationalists and Islamic extremism, the present UK government has focused primarily on the Islamic threat, stating on the Prevent website, '[c]urrently, the greatest threat comes from Al Qa'ida, its affiliates and like-minded groups'. The Department for Education and Schools (2005) produced guidance for schools after 7/7 focusing on the schools' capacity to tackle terrorism directly and called for teachers to be involved 'more explicitly in national security issues than at any time in British history' (Preston, 2009: 196). The Department for Children Schools and Families (2008) introduced an 'extremism toolkit' for schools, 'Learning together to be safe: a toolkit to help schools contribute to the prevention of violent extremism', also tying schools into surveillance and counter-terrorism agendas. Higher education providers are expected to engage with Special Branch (a unit of the British police responsible for national security and criminal intelligence) to monitor students for signs of radicalism. In the US, in the wake of 9/11 and the Beslan school hostage crisis in which Chechen Islamic militants took 1100 people hostage at a North Ossetia school, the Department of Homeland Security made grants available for the purchase of security systems in schools (Casella, 2006, in Monahan and Torres, 2010, p. 4).

Of course, schools have long engaged in surveillance practices such as physical observation, attendance registers, dress codes and behav-iour policies, exams, tests and publishing of League Tables (cf. Foucault, 1991). However, more recently, school children are subject to much more rigid regimes – indeed, some would argue they are criminalised by such practices (Giroux, 2009). Any deviations from the norm are punished very severely: levels of exclusion from secondary schools have risen to unprecedented levels in the UK, and schools more frequently resort to punishments involving the police for misdemeanours that would previously have been dealt with by staff, parents and governors. We have also seen the introduction of on-site police officers (more common in the US, but still present at least part-time in some, particu-larly inner-city UK schools), the presence of whom, it could be argued, links the school and criminal justice system. Although it would be unrealistic to argue that the only reason for these shifts towards more rigid regimes of control is the war on terror, as we can see from the policies mentioned above, and following Judith Butler, it makes sense to assume that the counter-terror agenda is impacting on and feeding into education policy.

It is often presumed that surveillance is neutral and 'democratic', that is, it affects all sectors of society equally, as we are all under surveillance (Monahan and Torres, 2010). Normally, the work of Foucault and his writing on the Panopticon are used when theorising surveillance. Foucault's work certainly allows us to understand how the modern, western world is governed by biopolitical power which functions by disciplining subjects so they internalise the discipline and creating 'docile bodies' (Foucault, 1991). However, Foucault did not differentiate between these docile bodies in terms of race. Viewed through a CRT lens however, surveillance cannot be considered racially neutral. The racial aspect of new technologies of school surveillance has rarely been made explicit. A small amount of work has been done in the US (Monahan and Torres, 2010; Simmons, 2010), but nothing in the UK. A recent project on the 'surveilled' (McCahill and Finn, 2010) examined the social impact of new surveillance technologies on the lives of school children living in a northern English city, which included looking at 13 to 16 year-old children in three schools. The project found that children's experiences differed across social class and gender, but it did not examine the implications for race. Recent work on surveillance in general has identified 'social sorting' (see Lyon, 2003) which 'indicates the tendency for surveillance systems to operate as mechanisms for societal differentiation' (Monahan and Fisher, 2008, p. 219). Therefore, existing inequalities are likely to be reproduced by surveillance regimes (Monahan and Fisher, 2008; Simmons, 2010).

As we have seen, the counter-terror agenda is shaped by a racial frame. Since the discourses that shape the frame tend to be implicit rather than explicit, I draw on CRT to render the racial aspects of school surveillance visible. In the counter-terrorism context, as I argue above, racial minorities, particularly those who are perceived to be Muslims, are already positioned as embodying threat, and are thus in need of control and surveillance. Minority ethnic individuals are already disproportionately subjected to more surveillance outside school, such as police 'stop and search' practices on the streets, airport controls and police profiling 'which continue to rely upon racial markers of "risk"' (Monahan and Fisher, 2008, p. 217). Black, Asian or Minority Ethnic groups (BAME) are seven times more likely to be stopped and searched than white people. The number of arrests for the white group decreased during 2010–2011, however arrests of Black persons rose by 5%, and arrests of Asian people by 13%. Some 26% of the prison population comes from BAME groups. In 2010, the highest average custodial sentence length (ACSL) for those given determinate sentences for indictable offences was recorded for the Black ethnic group, at 20.8 months, followed by the Asian and Other groups with averages of 19.9 months and 19.7 months respectively. The lowest ACSL was recorded for the white group at 14.9 months (all data, Justice, 2011). Equally, in a school context, research has shown that minority ethnic young people are more likely to be excluded from school than white young people (Gillborn, 2006). It has been suggested that one reason for this is the perception of teachers, many of whom view minority ethnic children as a challenge or threat, their perceptions shaped by dominant discourses (for example, Gillborn, 1990; Mirza, 1992; Basit, 1997).

As yet there is a lack of empirical research linking new technologies of surveillance in schools and race, and we can only assume the impact on young people's subjectivities and racial inequalities. Other research has argued that those who are perceived to be in need of surveillance are positioned as suspects (Monahan and Torres, 2010). McCahill and Finn (2010) suggested that the females in their study were more acutely aware of being under surveillance because women's bodies already tend to be more scrutinised than men's. As racial minorities are already frequently positioned as threatening or suspects, and are already more scrutinised than whites, it makes sense to assume that school surveillance is likely to impact more harshly on racial minorities than their white counterparts, and these discourses are likely to build on longstanding notions of perceived essentialised links between minority ethnic bodies and criminality and threat (Oztas, 2011). Research on surveillance technologies in general has pointed to the importance of the interpretation of the body in the way in which surveillance devices are employed. In his study of young working-class males, Nayak (2006, p. 64) showed how they are excluded from clubs and bars because of their dress and the way they move. Equally, a study by Norris and Armstrong showed that '[t]hose responsible for operating open-street CCTV surveillance cameras use them to target young working-class males who have their "head up, back straight, upper body moving too much", or those who were "swaggering, looking hard"' (Norris and Armstrong, 1999, p. 122, cited in McCahill and Finn, 2010, p. 286). These examples suggest that the way in which different bodies and their behaviours are 'recognised' (in Butlerian terms) is dependent on dominant discourses of race, class and gender. It therefore seems likely that new technologies of surveillance will regulate and control bodies accordingly, and that the existing raced dynamic in schools will be reinforced by increased surveillance.

Reproducing white supremacy and the *homo sacer*

A CRT analysis of schooling allows us to theorise the links between school surveillance, counter-terrorism and race, and to see schools as sites where the counter-terrorism agenda will be played out. Critical race theorists have extended the analysis of others (for example Bourdieu and Passeron, 1990; Durkheim, 1956) to argue that not only does formal education have a specific function to teach loyalty to the state and to ensure the maintenance of the social status quo, it ensures the maintenance of white supremacy (Ladson-Billings, 1998; Gillborn, 2006). Thus we see that white supremacy is not a fixed structure, rather it requires continual maintenance work, to which this new surveillance regime potentially contributes. Following Butler, it can be argued that through the framing of specific bodies as threat, these bodies become a legitimate target. Taking the example of photography, she writes that photographs both allocate positions to those on camera, the target, and those behind the camera, the viewer, and remove the wider context in which these photographs are taken, playing a key role in producing the subject,

> cameras [...] both frame and form the human and non-human target [...] In a way, that focussing on the target produces a position for the soldier, the reporter, and the public audience, structuring the visual field that makes each position possible. The frame not only orchestrates such positions, but also delimits the visual field itself. (Butler, 2010, pp. x–xi)

Surveillance can be seen as creating a similar process: the fact that bodies already 'recognised' as threat are under surveillance, actually reproduces their subject position as threat. In the context of the war on terror, Muslim lives are not fully recognisable as lives, but rather are viewed as threat to life. They are, indeed, already recognised as a terrorist threat, and as 'recognisability precedes recognition' (Butler, 2010, p. 5), increased surveillance and monitoring will ensure that young people who are Muslims are the embodiment of the threat. As Butler explains, this 'recognition' of threat further justifies the increase in surveillance.

Once Muslim citizens are recognised as a threat to life, and their surveillance is justified, they become the less-than-human, as they are recognised as the embodiment of the threat to Britishness, and therefore they are vulnerable to the potential violence of the position of non-citizen, non-human, whose entitlement to rights is very much reduced – potentially the *homo sacer*. For a group already frequently positioned as unbritish, as explained above, Muslims, or those perceived as Muslims, their vulnerability is only compounded.

When a population appears as a direct threat to my life, they do not appear as 'lives', but as the threat to life (a living figure that figures the threat to life). Consider how this is compounded under those conditions in which Islam is seen as barbaric or pre- modern, as not yet having conformed to those norms that make the human recognisable. (Butler, 2010, p. 42)

Moreover, those bodies that are caught in the background of the CCTV images, those that are not understood to be directly under surveillance, are reconfirmed in their 'innocence' – indeed, recognised as full lives – in this case, those whose lives are perceived as under threat, the white British. Thus, surveillance is actively producing those divided populations identified by critical race theorists. The CCTV camera, then, creates and re-creates the frame so that, '[t]he frame does not simply exhibit reality, but actively participates in a strategy of containment, selectively producing and enforcing what will count as reality' (Butler, 2010, p. xiii). Also, we can observe at a micro-level the process of desubjectivation identified by Butler, in which a group of citizens, Muslims, already defined as threat, come to be recognised as the non-citizen, described as the less-than-human or the *homo sacer*; the group whose perceived need for surveillance justifies their continued and increased surveillance, which in turn reproduces their subject position as beyond human, or indeed, de-subjectivates.

Drawing on both Judith Butler and CRT, then, I argue that the surveillance and monitoring procedures for allegedly ensuring the security of young people at school in the UK are actually reproducing structures of white supremacy and both the discourse and the materiality of race. The installation of new surveillance technologies can be seen, at least partly, as a response to counter-terrorism discourses, and in addition, feed into and re-produce these discourses. Surveillance procedures actually produce the recognisability of white bodies as lives, and minority ethnic bodies as threat, therefore maintaining the structures of white supremacy. As subjectivities are seen as discursively constituted, this is likely to have a very real effect on the way in which young people are perceived and perceive themselves.

Moreover, whilst the process may not yet be complete, it could be argued that the state of exception is creeping into the liberal democracy of the UK. The state of exception, then, is characterised by the suspension of 'normal' law to protect the interest of the sovereign, and the removal from the political realm of a specific group, which is treated as bare life, in that must be 'constantly monitored and exposed to the potentiality of violence' (Douglas, 2009, p. 33). It cannot be overlooked that the demands on educational institutions to monitor young people are made in the wider context of provisions for the temporary suspension of citizenship rights. These laws, as Douglas argues, 'essentially nullify the application of normal laws protecting human rights, while still holding them technically "in force"' (Douglas, 2009, p. 33). It is these 'exceptional' laws which justify the increased surveillance, and it is in this way that the state of exception is becoming 'normal'. Douglas (2009) argues that,

> [m]aking people suspects is equivalent to making people bare life [...] Electronic and biometric surveillance are the tactics through which the government is creating a space in which the exception is routine practice. The biopolitical implication of surveillance is the universalisation of bare life: 'History teaches us how practices first reserved for foreigners find themselves applied later to the rest of the citizenry' (Agamben, 2004). These new control measures have created a situation in which not only is there no clear distinction between private and political life, but there is no fundamental claim, or right, to a political life as such – not even for citizens from birth; thus, the originary biopolitical act that inscribes life as political from birth is more and more a potential depoliticization and ban from the political realm. (p. 37)

Those young people 'recognised' as threatening in the counter-terrorism context fulfil the criteria of the *homo sacer* – they are constantly monitored, their rights to privacy suspended (Taylor, 2013), potentially vulnerable to the complete withdrawal of their citizenship rights, and depoliticised whilst being hyperpolitically defined. Therefore although to some the notion of an encroaching state of exception in democratic Europe may be extreme, if we take the example of new regimes and technologies of surveillance in many UK schools, it could be argued that many features of a permanent state of emergency, thus the state of exception, are increasingly defining our lives as extreme measures are resorted to, in response to a perceived threat of terrorism.

Conclusion

In this paper, I have argued that new regimes of surveillance in UK secondary schools are partially linked to the government's counter-terrorism agenda, and have implications for the ways in which popula-tions are divided along lines of race. Using a framework that draws on both the work of critical race theorists and Judith Butler, I have shown how the war on terror is both fed by, and reinforces and reproduces an existing regime of white supremacy. I have also suggested that the war on terror has ushered in an era of increased sovereignty, which is the key to understanding how this regime of surveillance is justified:

> Sovereignty becomes that instrument of power by which law is either used tacitly or suspended, populations are monitored, detained, regu-lated, inspected, interrogated, rendered uniform in their actions, fully ritualised and exposed to control and regulation in their daily lives. (Butler, 2004a, p. 97)

I have suggested that racial frames differentiate who will be 'recognis-able' (in Butlerian terms) as human and less-than-human, and have equated this to Agamben's (1998) notion of *homo sacer* and bare life, which, although it may seem extreme to some, appears to describe well the encroaching state of exception in the liberally democratic UK. Thus we see a shift from the decentred power of governmentality towards the more overt power of sovereignty, in which existing laws can be suspended whist still being in effect, and certain groups are marginalised to the extent of being beyond the protection of law – in the case of the war on terror, it is Muslims or those who appear to be of Arab or Middle Eastern heritage who are 'recognised' as less-than-human.

I conclude by calling for more empirical research on the extent, meaning, and implications of the explosion of new technologies of surveillance in UK schools, including further work to explore the perceptions and resistances of those implicated in this surveillance, as we cannot presume that young people are passive receivers of these regimes of surveillance (Hope, 2005). Equally, my study illustrates that more research is needed on the implications of the counter-terrorism agenda for educational spaces, and the social consequences for young people and education of this shift to sovereignty and the encroachment of the state of exception.

Acknowledgements

My thanks to John Preston, John Schostak and Helen Colley for fruitful discussions and for reading earlier versions of this paper.

References

Agamben, G. (1998) *Homo Sacer: Sovereign Power And Bare Life*, Stanford, CA: Stanford University Press.

Agamben, G. (2005) *State Of Exception*. Chicago, London: University of Chicago Press.

Allen, R. (2001) 'The globalization of white supremacy: towards a critical discourse on the racialization of the world', *Educational Theory*, 51(4), 467–486.

Basit, T. (1997) *Eastern Values, Western Milieu*, Aldershot, Brookfield, Singapore, Sydney: Ashgate.

Bourdieu, P. and Passeron, J. (1990) *Reproduction In Education, Society And Culture* [La Reproduction], (trans.) R. Nice, London: Sage. (Original work published in 1977.)

Butler, J. (1998) 'Merely Cultural', *New Left Review*, I(227).

Butler, J. (2004a) *Precarious Life. The Powers Of Mourning And Violence*, London, New York: Verso.

Butler, J. (2004b) *Undoing Gender*, New York, Abingdon: Routledge.

Butler, J. (2010) *Frames Of War. When Is Life Grievable?* London, New York: Verso.

Casella, R. (2010) Safety or social control? The security fortification of schools in a capitalist society, in Monahan, T. and Torres, R. D. (eds) *Schools Under Surveillance. Cultures Of Control In Public Education*, New Brunswick, New Jersey, London: Rutgers University Press, pp. 73–86.

Chadderton, C. (2009) *Discourses Of Britishness, Race And Difference. Minority Ethnic Students' Shifting Perspectives Of Their School Experience*, unpublished PhD thesis: Manchester Metropolitan University.

Chadderton, C. (2013) 'Towards a research framework for race in education: Critical Race Theory and Judith Butler', *International Journal of Qualitative Studies in Education*, 26(1), 39–55.

Coaffee, J. and Rogers, P. (2008) 'Rebordering the city for new security challenges: from counter-terrorism to community resilience', *Space and Polity*, 12(1), 101–118.

Colatrella, S. (2011) 'Nothing exceptional: Against Agamben', *Journal for Critical Education Policy Studies*, 9(1).

Cole, M. (2009) *Critical Race Theory and Education. A Marxist Response*, Basingstoke, Palgrave Macmillan.

Darder, A. and Torres, R. (2004) *After Race: Racism after Multiculturalism*, New York: New York University Press.

Department for Children Schools and Families (2008) *Learning To Be Safe: A Toolkit To Help Schools Contribute To The Prevention Of Violent Extremism*, London: DCSF.

Department for Education and Schools (2005) *Moving On From 7/7: Advice To Schools*, London: DfES.

Douglas, J. (2009) Disappearing Citizenship: surveillance and the state of exception. *Surveillance & Society*, 6(1), 32–42.

Durkheim, E. (1956) *Education and Sociology*, The Free Press.

Foucault, M. (1991) *Discipline And Punish: The Birth Of The Prison* [Surveiller et punir] (trans.) A. Sheridan, London: Penguin. (Original work published 1977.)

Furedi, F. (2005) *Politics Of Fear*, London: Bloomsbury academic.

Gillborn, D. (1990) *'Race', Ethnicity And Education*, London: Unwin Hyman.

Gillborn, D. (2006) Rethinking white supremacy: who counts in 'WhiteWorld'. *Ethnicities*, 6(3), 318–340.

Giroux, H. A. (2009) *Youth In A Suspect Society. Democracy Or Disposability?* New York: Palgrave Macmillan.

Hill, D. (2009) 'Race and class in Britain: a critique of the statistical basis for Critical Race Theory in Britain: and some political implications', *Journal for Critical Education Policy Studies*, 7(2).

Home Office (2011) *The Prevent Strategy*. Available from: http://www.homeoffice. gov.uk/counter-terrorism/review-of-prevent-strategy/ [Accessed 27 June 2011].

Hope, A. (2005) 'Panopticism, play and the resistance of surveillance: case studies of the observation of student internet use in UK schools', *British Journal of Sociology of Education*, 26(3) 359–373.

Hope, A. (2009). 'CCTV, school surveillance and social control', *British Educational Research Journal*, 35(6), 891–907.

Ignatiev, N. (1995) *How The Irish Became White*, New York and London: Routledge.

Ignatiev, N. (1997) 'How to be a race traitor: six ways to fight being white' in Delgado, R. and Stefancic, J., *Critical White Studies. Looking Behind The Mirror*, Philadelphia: Temple University Press.

Justice (2011) *Race And The Criminal Justice System*. Available from: http://www. justice.gov.uk/publications/statistics-and-data/criminal-justice/race.htm [Accessed 7 February 2012].

Ladson-Billings, G. (1998) 'Just what is critical race theory and what's it doing in a *nice* field like education?' *Qualitative Studies in Education*, 11(1), 7–24.

Ladson-Billings, G. (2003) 'It's your world, I'm just trying to explain it: understanding our epistemological and methodological challenges', *Qualitative Inquiry*, 9(1), 5–12.

Lyon, D. (2003) 'Introduction', in Lyon, D. (ed.) *Surveillance As Social Sorting. Privacy, Risk And Digital Discrimination*, London, New York: Routledge.

McCahill, M. and Finn, R. (2010) 'The Social impact of Surveillance in Three UK Schools: "Angels", "Devils" and "Teen Mums"', *Surveillance & Society*, 7(3–4), 273–289.

Marx, G. and Steeves, V. (2010) 'From the Beginning: Children as Subjects and Agents of Surveillance', *Surveillance & Society*, 7(3–4), 192–230.

Mirza, H. S. (1992) *Young, Female And Black*, London and New York: Routledge.

Monahan, T. and Fisher, J. A. (2008) Editorial: 'Surveillance and Inequality', *Surveillance & Society*, 5(3), 217–226.

Monahan, T. and Torres, R. D. (2010) 'Introduction', in Monahan, T. and Torres, R. D. (eds) *Schools Under Surveillance. Cultures Of Control In Public Education*, New Brunswick, New Jersey, London: Rutgers University Press, pp. 1–18.

Moschel, M. (2007) 'Color-blindness or total blindness? The absence of CRT in Europe', *Rutgers Race And The Law Review*, 9(1), 57–128.

Nayak, A. (2006) 'Displaced Masculinities: Chavs, Youth and Class in the Post-Industrial City', *Sociology*, 40(5), 813–831.

Oztas, C. (2011) 'The march of the Mehteran. Rethinking the human rights critiques of counter-terrorism', *Utrecht Law Review*, 7(2), 180–191.

Preston, J. (2009) 'Preparing for emergencies: citizenship education, "whiteness" and pedagogies of security', *Citizenship Studies*, 13(2), 187–200.

Ragnedda, M. (2010) Review of Monahan and Torres (eds) *Schools Under Surveillance. Surveillance & Society*, 7(3–4), 356–357.

Simmons, L. (2010) 'The docile body in school space', in Monahan, T. and Torres, R. D. (eds) *Schools Under Surveillance. Cultures Of Control In Public Education*, New Brunswick, New Jersey, London: Rutgers University Press, pp. 55–72.

Taylor, E. (2013) *Surveillance Schools. Security, Discipline And Control In Contemporary Education*, Basingstoke, New York: Palgrave Macmillan.

UK Press Association (2009) *School Dinners Spy Website Launched*. Available from: http://latestnews.virginmedia.com/news/tech/2009/10/08/school_dinners_spy_website_launched. [Accessed 27 September 2009].

8
Naming and Blaming Early School Leavers: An Analysis of Education Policies, Discourses and Practices in Spain

Aina Tarabini

Introduction

Early school leaving (ESL) is one of the main challenges facing the Spanish education system. With 24, 9% of the population made up by 18–24 year olds who have not completed compulsory secondary schooling or pursued further or higher education,[1] Spain thereby doubles the ESL percentage regarding the EU-27 (12. 8%), and is far from the European Benchmark set for 10% ESL across the EU and 15% for Spain by the year 2020.

Reflecting the importance of this phenomenon, several discourses, policies and practices at both the national and regional levels are evidence that combating ESL has become a priority. At first glance, there appears to be general consensus on this issue that goes beyond specific policy policies and specific territorial contexts. As Escudero and Martínez (2012) observed, however, this general consensus vanishes when it comes to details, even in such fundamental questions as who the early school leavers are, why they leave school and how to solve the 'problem'. ESL is a phenomenon designated with certain words and meanings, interpreted and valued according to different perspectives and discourses. 'The concepts to define or sanction it entail different meanings for different involved actors, sometimes ambiguous and even arbitraries' (Escudero, 2005, p. 1). In this context, the aim of the paper is to explore 'what is taken for granted' in the policies, discourses and practices in the fight against ESL, and to respond to the following questions:

How is the risk of early school leaving defined? What are the profiles of students at risk of ESL? What are the main factors causing ESL? What are considered to be the main solutions to this 'problem'? The initial hypothesis is that the answers to these questions are not neutral. On the contrary, they involve important technologies of power linked to the normalisation, psychologisation and self-responsibilisation of the risk of dropping out of school, and they ignore the class relations, class identities and class subjectivities hidden behind this phenomenon.

To carry out the analysis, certain analytical tools from the work of Michael Foucault (1977; 1979; 1980; 1981; 1983) are used; in particular, the paper illustrates the way in which 'regimes of truth' are constructed in relation to both the 'problem' of ESL and its 'solution'. In addition, the paper explores the construction of 'common sense' regarding what a 'good' or 'bad' student is, and the role of the school in both cases. As a result, the analysis not only focuses on education policy, but also on schools, and in particular on the discourses and practices of teachers and other school staff regarding students at risk of dropping out. As authors such as Rumberger (2011) and Enguita et al. (2010) point out: it is essential to study the role of the school and the teachers in the 'decisions' students make to continue or drop out of school, as it is often not a question of deciding to leave school but of being 'pushed out'. Obviously, schools and teachers act within a broad structural, political and institutional framework that conditions their actions. However, it does not reduce their importance as active agents in the production and reproduction of inequalities in education. Educational disadvantages can be constructed and reconstructed through pedagogy, the curriculum, evaluation processes and daily relations within the classroom (Bernstein, 1985). As a result, it is fundamental to study micro-processes within the school, where education inequalities are produced and reproduced, placing the focus on the practices and expectations of teachers and other school staff members.

The paper is organised into the following sections: the first section analyses the 'regimes of truth' that are hidden behind the current policies to respond to ESL in Spain and Catalonia.[2] The second section explores how school staff members explain ESL, and identifies three major explanatory factors in their discourses: students' lack of commitment, family deficiencies and the pathologisation of diversity. The third section reflects, as a conclusion, on the importance of identifying the power relations hidden beneath current policies, practices and discourses regarding ESL. The analysis is based on current research that is part of the ABJOVES Project (Early School Leaving in Spain: An Analysis of

Young People's Educational Expectations, Decisions and Strategies]. This project has carried out a rigorous analysis of policies to combat ESL at different levels of policy-making, involving interviews with teachers, school principals and academic coordinators in secondary schools. The project also includes interviews with students at risk of dropping out of school, and others who have already done so. Due to space limitations, however, the perspective of these students has not been included in this paper.

The construction of regimes of truth in policies to combat early school leaving

In December 2013, Spain passed the Organic Act for the Improvement of the Quality of Education (LOMCE), the country's seventh education reform since the establishment of democracy. The law was passed with only the votes of the governing Partido Popular (PP) (Conservatives), as it was opposed by all the other political parties in the parliament. In fact, the LOMCE has been widely criticised, not only for its content, but also for a process that failed to take the views of the education community into account and for a lack of political and social consensus regarding its measures.

As explicitly stated in wording of the Act, 'the main objectives of the reform are to reduce the rate of early school leaving, improve educational [*sic*] results based on international criteria and improve the employability of students and stimulate their entrepreneurial spirit' (Ministry of Education, 2013, p. 97862). Given the importance attached to reducing ESL, and according to the objectives of the LOMCE, it is essential to explore how this 'problem' is constructed and framed. In other words, what are considered to be the causes of the high level of ESL in Spain? How was this new education Act justified? How are the reforms of the education system required by this law legitimated?

According to the text of the Act, the education reform is based on five principles: 'increasing the autonomy of schools, strengthening the management capacity of school administration, introducing external evaluations at the end of each educational [*sic*] stage, rationalising the educational [*sic*] offer and the flexibilisation of the educational [*sic*] trajectories' (Ministry of Education, 2013, p. 97862). Supporters of the reform believe that these measures will increase the quality of education and permit Spain to achieve the European benchmarks for ESL.

In fact, both the adoption of these specific measures and the need to reform the education system itself are presented as purely technical and rational issues having nothing to do with political ideologies. Educational reform is presented as the best way to improve students' knowledge and skills and, thus, to face the challenges of the so called 'knowledge society'. In turn, specific policy options are presented as if they are in the national interest and for the development of the country. As stated by Spain's Minister of Education, José Ignacio Wert, in the context of the publication of the first draft of the law: 'This is a reform that looks outward, that is sensible, gradual, instrumental (it will improve employment), and in no way ideological' (Grau, 2012, pp. 1–2). Following the same logic, the text justifies the necessity of reform based on 'the objectivity of comparative international studies', 'recommendations of the OECD' (Organisation for Economic Co-operation and Development) and 'the practices of education systems with the best results' (Ministry of Education, 2013, pp. 97861–97862), framing the reforms in exclusively technical and rational terms, and avoiding the political dimensions involved in its design and implementation (Bonal and Tarabini, 2013). Moreover, following Steiner-Khamsi (2004), we would argue that in a context of globalisation, national education reforms have increasingly relied on external forms of legitimation. In this case, results of other European countries in international rankings are used to legitimate specific Spanish education reforms and to present them in a non-controversial way, representing a clear power shift in education policy-setting.

In what follows, the analysis explores how one of the specific principles of the law is explained and justified: the flexibilisation of education trajectories. The reason to focus on this principle is because, according to the law, it is the most directly related to the expected reduction of ESL. In fact, one of the main objectives of the LOMCE is to end the 'demonstrated failure of the educational [*sic*] structure and the principles established by the LOGSE the Educational Reform Act (ERA) approved by the Socialist Party in 1990]'. According to the PP, the previous education reforms passed by the Socialist Party consolidated a mediocre education system with low levels of excellence. In this sense, the new law is intended to change one of the main principles of the LOGSE: the model of comprehensive compulsory secondary education until 16 years of age. With this aim, the LOMCE develops programmes to improve performance in the second and third year of compulsory secondary education, introduces basic vocational training starting at 15 years old, advances the choice of pathways in both the baccalaureate and vocational training and consolidates two clearly differentiated trajectories in the last year of compulsory secondary education. This 'diversification' of trajectories 'will permit students to receive personalised attention to guide them toward the education path that best suits their needs and aspirations' (Ministry of Education, 2013: 97864). In fact, the new law is based on the following premise regarding the needs, aspirations and talents of students:

> All students have talent, but the nature of this talent differs among them. As a result, the education system must have the necessary mechanisms to recognise and foster this talent. The recognition of this diversity among students in their abilities and expectations is the first step toward developing an education structure that contemplates different trajectories. The logic of this reform is based on the evolution toward a system capable of steering students toward the trajectories most suited to their capabilities. (Ministry of Education, 2013, p. 97858)

As can be seen, this clearly omits the role of social class hidden behind both the development of 'talents' and the choice of certain education itineraries. Everything is reduced to a question of individual preferences, capabilities and abilities. The diversity among students (and the consequent levels of inequality in their academic results and education trajectories) is explained by their talents and abilities – conceived as purely natural and biological – and not in relation to their opportunities.

Consequently, discourses regarding the inequality of opportunities that students from different backgrounds experience are relegated to the 'domains of validity, normativity and actuality' (Foucault, cited by Ball, 2013, p. 23). In addition, all research that demonstrates how social class continues to be the variable with the most explanatory power in understanding students' different education itineraries is ignored (Shavit and Blossfeld, 1993). Also ignored is research that shows how separating students in academic versus vocational tracks does not necessarily lead to an improvement in education quality, and much less to reducing inequality (Van Houtte, 2004). Hence, what we find is a strategic selection of research to legitimise certain political choices and to make invisible or ignore other research that points in a different direction than the planned reform model.

In the case of Catalonia, a framework document is available that brings together all the policies and actions taken to combat ESL: *Ofensiva de país a favor de l'èxit escolar* (National drive to increase school success) presented by the Catalan Minister of Education (Convergència i Unió –CIU, conservative/nationalist party) Irene Rigau, in the Catalan

Parliament in June 2012, represents a broad plan. It aims to increase the school success of the population, and contemplates nine areas of action including elements as diverse as the professionalisation of teaching and school management, measures of academic support for students with difficulties and fostering reading in the classroom (Catalan Department of Education, 2012).

In fact, the starting point of the Catalan Education Department is the replacement of the concept of school failure with that of school success. As explicitly mentioned in the document, school failure implies social exclusion and puts the focus entirely on students' final results. In contrast, the concept of success 'allows emphasize on the aspects of the educational [*sic*] process that refer to the development of student potential, promoting a change in the outlook toward education' (Departament d'Ensenyament, 2012, p. 4). In addition, the document argues that the focus on success involves a proactive perspective, which, far from being a fact-finding mission, attempts to directly intervene in the education process. In this sense, the Education Department argues that in order to foster school success it is essential to intervene in the education process and not only in the results. However, in deciding which factors to intervene in, we can clearly see the choice of certain elements over others. These choices are clearly political and ideological, but that again is presented in purely technical, objective and neutral terms (Tarabini et al., 2015).

Actually, some of the factors that the Department considers key to achieving success in education are 'the professionalisation of the teaching staff and school management, teaching and learning strategies, guidance, early detection of educational [*sic*] needs and the involvement of families' (Departament, 2012, p. 4). As can be seen, intervention is focused almost entirely on the school and, in particular, on the organisational and pedagogical aspects of the school. In addition, a central role is given to the family in school success. The school and the family are clearly key agents for reducing ESL. It is also known that pedagogical strategies can contribute to increasing students' opportunities for success and that teachers are key to fostering students' commitment to their education. And there is no doubt that families have a significant role in determining the education trajectories of their children. However, what is the context that makes these relationships possible? This broader context is missing. Thus, in *Ofensiva de País*, such central issues as school segregation and the effects of cutbacks on teaching are ignored, as are the broader questions of equity and quality in education. We fully agree with Bonal and

Verger (2013, p. 349) when they argue that 'it does not make sense to focus solely on the school and the family and to ignore the environment as a space containing educational agents that are essential for combating school failure'.

In addition, it is clear that the Department's strategy is framed within the specific perspective on success that Albaigès and Martinez (2012) identify as 'focused on performance'. This perspective sees school success as intimately tied to academic results and the annual promotion of students, attributing great importance to two factors: the subjects taught at school and the individual effort and merits of students. In fact, it assumes a direct and linear relationship between better performance and lower rates of ESL, ignoring that – as national and international research has shown (Enguita and Riviere, 2010; Rumberger, 2011) – leaving school is not only linked to instrumental issues of learning, but fundamentally to expressive issues[3] and in particular to students' lack of connection and commitment to what the education system is offering.

As can be seen, success in education is not a straightforward or universal concept, but it is subject to specific political and ideological views. And the same occurs with the policies planned to achieve success. As a result, understanding ESL from a purely instrumental perspective linked to performance, and assuming that the solution to this 'problem' will essentially come from family involvement and the organisational and pedagogical improvement of schools, is to ignore other significant explanatory factors, such as social inequalities or exclusionary practices (streaming, labelling, etc.)[4] among others, within schools.

In short, the analysis of the LOMCE and the *Ofensiva de País* (Offensive of the Country) allows us to identify the existence of 'regimes of truth' hidden under the definition of the 'problem' of ESL and its potential solutions; problems and solutions that are understood to be the only possible, plausible and even thinkable ones. Presenting political options as merely technical and objective questions – as made both by LOMCE and the *Ofensiva de País* – denies all possibilities of arguing, discussing or disagreeing, and omits that what counts as 'the truth' is always a product of power. That is the power to produce discourses, to create realities, to settle the agenda; the power to produce knowledge as the legitimated version, to distinguish between 'true' and 'false', between priority and non-priority 'problems', between 'right and wrong' solutions.

According to Foucault, the organisation of the discourse itself is an exercise of power, controlling and preventing what can be said and who has the right to speak. As Foucault asserts: 'in every society the production of discourse is at once controlled, selected, organised and redistributed by a number of procedures' (Foucault, 1981, p. 52). Consequently, the discursive rules are inseparable from the exercise of power. 'Discourse itself is both constituted by, and ensures the reproduction of, the social system, through forms of selection, exclusion and domination' (Young, cited in Hook, 2001, p. 2).

In fact, in the foucauldian proposal, knowledge and power are indissoluble: all forms of power are embedded within knowledge and all knowledge domains are infused by power relations. Power and knowledge are then two aspects of the same process.

> Perhaps we should abandon a whole tradition that allows us to imagine that knowledge can exist only where the power relations are suspended and that knowledge can develop only outside its injections, its demands, its interests. We should admit rather that power produces knowledge; that power and knowledge directly imply one another; that there is no power relation without the correlative constitution of a field of knowledge, nor any knowledge that does not presuppose and constitute at the same time power relations. (Foucault, 1979, p. 27)

Following this approach, it is essential to problematise the very construction of the concepts of school 'failure', 'abandonment' and 'success', bringing to light that which is invisible, naturalised and taken for granted. Why is it expected that greater flexibility of education trajectories will lead to less ESL? According to what evidences is it argued that streaming would lead to greater success in education? Why is the focus on school performance instead of, or together with, school support and the related policies? What does success in education really mean? Success for who and how? The answers to these questions are far from being neutral or merely technical, but the political connotations are mainly avoided in the public debate.

The analysis conducted leads to the same conclusion made by Escudero and Martínez (2012), who argue that the hegemonic logic behind Spanish policies to combat ESL continue to see success and failure as questions mainly related to individual merit, leaving aside other broader education and social factors. In this way, far from being neutral, objective and impartial, the framing of the issue of ESL and its possible solutions forms part of specific political and ideological frameworks, which respond to a clearly conservative logic, as can be seen in the case of both the LOMCE and the analysis in *Ofensiva de País*.

Teachers' discursive practices regarding potential ESLer students

The theoretical tools that Foucault offers us are of great use in analysing the way in which teachers' discourses and practices bring into play power strategies that normalise, legitimise and/or punish certain practices and attitudes among students. Which students are teachers thinking of when they design pedagogical strategies? What types of behaviours do they encourage or repress? How do they explain the emergence of different attitudes toward school among the students? The answers to these questions are not independent from the analysis of power and knowledge stated by Foucault and, in particular, from teachers' belief systems regarding what it means to be a 'good' or 'bad' student and what is a 'correct/normal' or 'deviant' attitude toward education.

In fact, one of the characteristics of the disciplinary penalty is the definition of behaviour and performance on the basis of the two opposed values of 'good' and 'evil'. Consequently, all behaviour falls into the field between 'good' or 'bad' marks, 'good' or 'bad' attitude, etc. As Foucault declared, 'school justice carried this system very far' (Foucault, 1979, p. 180), organising a whole micro-economy of privileges and impositions. Teachers and the other school staff are key agents in defining and systematising these power mechanisms.

Specifically, the analysis conducted in the paper attributes crucial importance to teachers' expectations as the basis upon which boundaries are set regarding what a 'good student' should be and should do; as a fundamental starting point for exploring teachers' discourses and practices related to the risk of ESL. As Rist (2000) demonstrated in the 1970s, teachers' initial expectations are key in explaining students' opportunities of success at school because of the effects of these expectations on students' performance and experience of school. In addition, Rist's study shows that the teachers' image of the 'ideal student' was closely linked to social class criteria. Thus, the characteristics of middle-class students were those that determined the 'pattern of normality' that other students had to fit into, in order to be successful at school.

Based on this classic study by Rist, numerous studies have revealed how students from families with low socio-economic status are over-represented as *targets* of teachers' low expectations. As Dunne and Gazeley (2008) argue, teachers' identification of students with 'problems or learning difficulties' tends to overlap with their implicit conception of the students' social class. Auwarker and Aruguete (2008) came to the same conclusion, adding that teachers' negative expectations regarding students from lower socio-economic classes were especially strong in the case of male students.[5] Thus, the lower academic expectations of teachers regarding students of lower socio-economic status often generate a 'naturalisation' and 'normalisation' of their possible academic difficulties and even their failure and possible school dropout. In contrast, it is expected that middle-class students, with greater family education capital, will have better attitudes, greater abilities and better academic results. In addition, as Grant (2006) has shown, for young white middle-class male students, it is easier to conceive themselves as 'good students' because the characteristics of their social position fits better with the hegemonic image of the 'ideal student'.

The following analysis focuses on three important discursive practices among teachers regarding students at risk from dropping out of school: lack of commitment, family deficit and the psychologisation and/or pathologisation of learning difficulties and behaviour. Obviously, these are not the only discursive practices among teachers. These practices are connected with different teachers' ethical and political attitudes. They are also connected both to the school culture and the social composition of other education institutions. However, beyond these factors, these three discursive practices have great importance – both quantitatively (for the frequency with which they appear) and qualitatively (for the impact on students' education opportunities) – in the discourses of the teachers interviewed.[6]

Lack of commitment as a cause of ESL

One of the principal techniques of power described by Foucault is responsibilisation, in other words, attributing ultimate responsibility to individuals for their own situation at the same time as de-responsibilising other social agents (Foucault, 2008). This assumption assumes that individuals are free and rational in deciding on their own actions, eliminating the effect of structural conditions on individual practices, strategies and decision-making. The student, therefore, constructed as an autonomous, competitive and rational individual, is the primary agent responsible for his/her school success or failure.

This type of discursive practice is clearly revealed when the school staff members are asked about what they believe are the causes of the academic and/or behavioural difficulties of certain students. Thus, lack of motivation, effort and commitment appear as central factors in their explanations of the education results and trajectories of these students.

It is very difficult with some of them [students]. They begin missing classes and when they are old enough [16 years of age] they leave school ... Others don't take advantage of the time because they simply refuse, refuse ... There is no way to get them to see that in the short-term or the long-term it will be beneficial for them to continue in school, to get a diploma or for whatever. They choose to leave and that's it. (Academic coordinator of a publicly subsidised private school with a student body of working-class origins)

What do you think is hidden, that explains this student profile? Okay, first it is their attitude. That's clear, isn't it? It's very difficult to change their attitude. First, because they have no interest, none. But of them, no interest of any type. Then, it is very complicated because they arrive from primary school with this attitude. (Academic coordinator of a public high school with a very heterogeneous student body)

As can be seen in these comments, and as had been expressed by most of the school staff throughout the interviews, the student's interest in what school offers is presented as merely a question of personal decision. The assumption is that the content and methodology of the education are correct and that, therefore, it is the student who must adapt to them. Thus, it is exclusively an issue of a student wanting an education or not; the effect of social origin on students' attitudes, dispositions and education practices is ignored. In addition, discursive practices based on lack of commitment tend to hide the strict separation between the instrumental and expressive dimensions of attitudes towards education, considering that although the former is not only the responsibility of the individual, the latter is perfectly manageable and controllable. In other words, it is understood that students consciously, freely and rationally 'decide' to behave well or badly in school, while having good or bad grades is more than just a matter of choice. In that sense, the whole indefinite domain of the 'non-conforming', or the 'non-adapting', to the established 'good attitudes and rules' become punishable. In Foucault's own words: 'a pupil's offence is not only a minor infraction, but also an inability to carry out his tasks' (Foucault, 1979, p. 177).

Based on this strict separation between 'good' and 'bad', 'performance' and 'attitude', an image is constructed of students 'deserving and undeserving' of specific interventions in education. Those who are considered as 'deserving' are those 'who make an effort', 'who try', who behave as expected. They are, in short, those who do not doubt or question the school order. The 'others', those that do not behave according to the established pattern of the 'ideal student', are not considered worthy of receiving certain education resources.

The policies of behaviour then hierarchise the 'good' and the 'bad' subjects, not only in relation to one abstract, ideal, supposed 'normal' pattern, but also in relation to one another. Moreover, differentiation between 'good' and 'bad' students, between 'deserving' and 'non deserving ones' is not only linked to students' acts and attitudes but above all to the individuals, to the subjects themselves; to their nature and their potentialities (Foucault, 1979, p. 181).

We will never propose a group with an adapted curriculum for students with behavioural problems. The idea is to give an opportunity to the student that we really see can and wants to take advantage of it. The student that has learning difficulties, but not the one with behavioural problems (...) to be in this group, students must prove their commitment and dedication because the school invests its time in them, it is an opportunity for them, so in this contract we make it very clear: if the student does not take advantage of this resource he/she returns to the regular group. (Principal of a public high school with a social body mostly from the lower middle-class.)

If a student behaves very badly, he or she won't go to 3rd A or 4th A [adapted groups]. Students are in these groups because of their grades. It is for students that, for whatever reason, have a poor base or lack ability. It is for people that want to be in the normal group but cannot be (...) If there is someone that disrupts class and doesn't let others work, we don't let them join [the adapted group]. The commitment is clear: going to the adapted group is an advantage for the student, because having a teacher for 10 students is a luxury, because it is adjusted to their level, they [the teachers] help them [the students] to pass, but then [the student] has to commit to controlling himself, to behaving well, if not he has to go to a normal group. (Teacher in a public high school with a social body mostly from the lower middle-class)

In this way, specific attention for students with difficulties is conceived as a reward and not as a right that all students should have. As a result, from this perspective, it is assumed that devoting specific resources (in the form of teaching staff, organisation of the timetable, etc.) to respond to the various levels of ability in the student body is an exception and not the basis upon which to organise the day-to-day activities in schools. In addition, as Escudero and Martínez (2012) have shown, the dominant focus in Spain to deal with school failure has been to design special programmes for at-risk students, partial and non-systemic programmes, practices and mechanisms parallel to the 'standard' structure and functioning of schools that serve to manage the school day of the students with the most difficulties.

According to the Foucauldian perspective, this process has a double effect: on the one hand, it distributes students according to the proximity of their aptitudes and conducts to the established pattern of 'normality'; on the other hand, it places on the students a constant pressure to conform to the same model, so that 'they might all be subjected to subordination and docility...they might all be like one another' (Foucault, 1979, p. 182).

Lastly, it is highly significant that many of the school staff members who were interviewed ignored the responsibility of schools and teachers in explaining students' attitudes toward school, above all, those students that were the most difficult. As Auwarker and Aruguete (2008) showed in their study, student failure is often perceived as outside of teachers' control.

> We are secondary school teachers, we have university degrees, we know our subjects, but we are not psychologists. I can explain whatever you want in my field, but I studied psychology and pedagogy, so I do what I can with the students. I try to understand what I can, but you can't ask the impossible. (Academic coordinator in a public high school with a very heterogeneous student body)

Family deficit as an explanation for ESL

The lack of commitment attributed to the students as another cause of their academic difficulties extends to the family sphere as well. Referring to a 'lack of interest', 'lack of involvement' or 'lack of support' from families becomes common in explaining why some families do not behave as expected by the school. Thus, working-class families with lower socio-economic and education status are often blamed for delegating the education of their children to the schools, without questioning what their real opportunities are for carrying out the educative tasks that teachers expect. To what extent do families understand and share the demands of the school? What are the education expectations of families regarding their children? And in relation to the school? To what extent is the school perceived as a space that is 'ours', a space where families have a right to make decisions and express an opinion? The concept of 'family otherness' regarding the school, used by Bonal (2003), is of great usefulness in responding to these questions, as it puts the focus on the distance that some families feel, perceive and experience in relation to the demands and expectations of the school. Social origin shapes different models and ways of relating with the school, so that what is 'normal' for some is absolutely 'impossible' for others. As a result, it is essential to consider the effect of social class on families' education practices. This is an issue that is not always considered when teachers discuss the education situation of their students.

> What do you think is behind, explains, this student profile? Okay, first is their (students') attitude. And second is the parents. Collaboration with the parents is basic. That parents think what we do here is important, that parents value teachers, that they take seriously what is said, what has to be done. If the parents don't do this...it's very complicated. (Academic coordinator in a public high school with a very heterogeneous student body)

> It's happening more and more, the students with the most social and academic problems come from families with problems. At the beginning of the school year we have a meeting with the parents; they only have to come for an hour in the afternoon. But in one class maybe 7 come, in the other, maybe 12. There's a lack of interest. Not always, but there is a very clear cause and effect relationship between dysfunctional families and learning. (Academic coordinator of a publicly subsidised private school with a student body of working-class origin)

Clearly, the image of the ideal student that we referred to previously has its parallel in an ideal family. This ideal family is middle class with a high level of cultural capital and is capable of collaborating with the school in the education process. In addition, family models that are far from this 'norm' tend to be perceived from the logic of deficit. In other words, the norms of the western middle-class tend to be considered universal and, therefore, variations from them are considered to be deficits, rather than differences resulting from social inequality. As Gay (2002) states, 'these presumptions of universality and deficiency are some of the major causes of inequities in the educational opportunities provided to students from diverse ethnic, racial, cultural [and socioeconomic] backgrounds (Gay, 2002, p. 617).

Moreover, this is not just a question of school staff omitting and/or ignoring the influence of social class on families' education practices, but rather of the adoption of practices, perceptions and biased education expectations based on stereotypes and stigmas. Stigma, as Goffman has pointed out, is not directly associated with the possession of specific attributes in themselves, but rather in the social conceptions linked to those attributes, with the social construction of concepts of 'normal' and 'abnormal'. In this way, it is presumed that certain family 'problems' explain the education difficulties of the student, although the specific characteristics of these families are often not known. The assumption is that certain families, those with lower socio-economic and cultural status, do not have the necessary resources to guarantee the educational development of their children. It would seem that without realising it, teachers adopt the classic thesis of the 'culture of poverty', based on which they presume that all poor people share a series of values, norms and practices that are different from the ideals and requirements of education.

> [Regarding student behavioural problems] This is closely related to family situations. There are even studies that say that on many occasions school phobia is related to single parenthood, to that lack of authority, from a father figure. (Principal in a public high school with a high proportion of students from households with socio-economic difficulties)

> Well, behind absenteeism and dropping out, there tend to be very dysfunctional families, extreme family situations, alcoholism, even violence (...) it's the parents who allow this situation. (Principal of a publicly subsidised private school with a student body of working-class origin)

The psychologisation and pathologisation of ESL

According to Foucault, norms in contemporary society are grounded in medical notions, and 'infractors' of these norms and 'deviants' need to be cured. In fact, on Foucault's account the transition to modernity entailed the replacement of the law by the norm as the primary instrument of social control. That means that, apart from punish or sanction the 'deviant' behaviour has to be increasingly controlled through standards of 'normality'. Penalty becomes about correcting deviations from the norm, organising people into ranks and classifications according to their 'normality'.

This is opposed to a judicial penalty whose essential function is to refer, not to a set of observable phenomena, but to a corpus of laws and texts that must be remembered (...) The disciplinary mechanisms created a 'penalty of the norm' which is irreducible in its principles and functioning to the traditional penalty of the law (...) Like surveillance and with it, normalization becomes one of the great instruments of power at the end of the classical age. Privilege and affiliation were increasingly replaced by a whole range of degrees of normality. (Foucault, 1979, pp. 183–184)

The power of 'normalisation' is, then, not only to impose homogeneity among people, but also to measure the differences between individuals; to hierarchise these differences according to the very 'nature' of the individuals. Based on this perspective, students' learning and behavioural 'problems' are not necessarily explained by questions of attitude but are directly associated with innate and biological factors. These kinds of discourses can be clearly observed in some of the interviews conducted with the school staff. Essentially, students that do not meet expectations regarding behaviour or performance (the 'normal' and expected behaviour or performance, the one that marks the 'correct homogeneous rule') end up being the target of medical-psychological diagnoses and interventions, under the assumption that the 'unsuitability' of the school context can be explained by a mental disorder. In this way, the practices, behaviour and attitudes that do not fit in the school culture are defined as pathological, are psychiatrised, and consequently, the possibility of changing them is externalised. If the lack of commitment to school is an issue linked to psychological problems, there is little that teachers can do to reverse the situation. The solution is shifted to the medical-psychological sphere, whether through the use of medications or psychological therapy to modify the behaviour of students.

There is a significant group of students, the most unmotivated there are. I would say it is not so much a problem of being unmotivated as much as a problem of attention deficit, more a psychiatric issue, you know. They are students that have very low abilities to respond, to be able to focus, to...to have the optimal conditions so they can learn, no? But of course, here you/we are a little bit lost because it is more a medical problem, I think. (Teacher in a public high school with a student body mostly from the upper middle-class.)

Given this understanding, it is essential to question the proliferation of diagnoses of mental health problems among children and adolescents. It must not be forgotten that the classification of mental disorders is extremely sensitive to socio-historical valorisations and conceptualisations. In other words, it is related to the construction of 'normality' and 'abnormality' in different historical, temporal, social and territorial contexts. Thus, as Foucault argued, the pathologisation of certain behaviours is a response to a demand for disciplinary and social control, which, despite being presented as 'natural' or 'normal', is based on specific political, valuative and ideological assumptions. The psychologisation of social problems is a key mechanism within this logic:

> Hidden behind the behavioural problems of some students are mental problems, school phobias, depression, Asperger's, psychosis...What we have noted in recent years, with the crisis...with all the social problems, families without work, there are so many problems and so much anxiety at home...the behaviour of the students we are getting is worsening. There is a relationship with these families that are stressed out, without work...all of this results in unhealthy behaviour in the students...with kids that suddenly refuse to go to school, that are seriously psychologically impaired. They can't come. It is beyond them. They can't even make it to the door...(Principal in a public high school with a high proportion of students from households that have socio-economic difficulties)

The psycho-pathologisation of certain attitudes toward school is, in short, a powerful mechanism for exerting power and the grounds for exempting schools, 'ordinary' pedagogical mechanisms and teachers themselves from responsibility for the risk of certain students leaving school. When a clinical discourse is constructed on the lack of student commitment to education, when diversity is pathologised, only medical responses to a 'problem' of a clearly social nature appear adequate.

Conclusions

The analysis conducted in this paper demonstrates the inseparable relation between power relations and the production of knowledges in contemporary societies, as well as the role that education policies and practices play. As Foucault stated: 'power produces knowledge (...) Power and knowledge directly imply one another (...) There is no power relation without the correlative constitution of a field of knowledge, nor any knowledge that does not presuppose and constitutes at the same time, power relations' (Foucault, 1979, p. 93). In this way, the power-knowledge couplet allows distinguishing between 'true' and 'false' statements, defining the techniques and procedures which are valorised for obtaining the truth, setting the status of those who are charged with saying what counts as true or establishing the mechanisms for sanctioning (Foucault, 1977, pp. 112–113).

The field of education is one of the privileged areas in the production of scientific knowledge that is embedded with the creation of 'truths', as it was analysed in the case of the policies addressed to reduce ESL in Catalonia and Spain. In this sense, the very meaning of failure or success in education is presented as a merely objective question, not related to specific political and ideological options. And the same happens with the 'solutions' proposed to solve the defined 'problem'. The regimes of truth created around ESL, are thus clearly related with the propagation and selective dissemination of specific discourses by political actors representing particular ideological interests. Undoubtedly, ESL is a 'problem', especially for those who suffer it, since it clearly reduces their present and future opportunities. It is also a 'problem' in terms of equity and social cohesion of the whole system. It is so even in terms of efficiency and efficacy. But the definition and solutions to this 'problem' are not neutral at all.

At the same time, the Foucauldian perspective proposed in the analysis allows understanding power in everyday life, in the mundane practices and in the social relationships embedded in the field of education. According to this conception, the paper has attributed key importance to the micro-processes where inequalities in education are produced and reproduced and according to teachers' practices and expectations. Teachers are not neutral actors in dealing with inequality and in providing opportunities in education for their students. Their practices and discourses shape pupil's experiences, identities and opportunities. As has been analysed, the power of teachers lies in its enormous capacity to decide who is a 'good' or a 'bad' student and to create different rewards for each of them. The pattern of 'normality' within a specific classroom or school is created by the school staff, and has the capacity (the 'pedagogic authority' or 'school authority' as Bourdieu and Passeron would say) to define distinctive types of intelligences and abilities with different values; which can create disparate curricula and forms of pedagogical organisation for the specific groups of students established. As Ball indicates: 'the use of testing, examining, profiling, and streaming in education...are all examples of such dividing practices (...) through the creation of remedial and advanced groups, and the separation of the educationally subnormal or those with special education needs, abilities are stigmatized and normalized' (Ball, 1990, p. 8).

Finally, the analysis seeks to demonstrate the widespread 'advent of individualisation' seen in contemporary policies, practices and discourses related to ESL. That is the effect of power technologies: to omit the effect of the social class relationships, identities and subjectivities hidden under the process of ESL; to put the focus on the individual as the sole person and the ultimate responsible of their risk and even failure in education. The three main causes attributed to ESL by the school staff interviewed for this paper – lack of commitment, family deficit and pyschologisation or pathologisation of learning difficulties – are with no doubt clear examples of this process.

Notes

This paper has been produced within the project ABJOVES (*Early School Leaving in Spain: An Analysis of Young People's Educational Expectations, Decisions and Strategies*) (Spanish Ministry of Economy 2012–2015). Available from: http://www.abjoves. es. [Accessed 20 July 2015].

1. The official formulation of the European Strategy 2020 is the: 'percentage of the population aged 18–24 with lower secondary education at the most, and not in further education or training'.
2. It is important to mention that Spain is composed of seventeen regions ('Comunidades Autónomas') with full competencies in the education sector. Catalonia, in particular, was one of the first regions in completing the legal transfer of education competencies from the central state. Analysing education policies in Spain thus involves the regional-autonomic level of governance as well as the national one.
3. According to Bernstein (1977), the instrumental order is concerned with the transmission of formal school knowledge (learners are intended to acquire knowledge and specific vocational skills) while the expressive order is concerned with the transmission of values and norms (learners are intended to develop particular kinds of conduct and character).
4. For more information about school exclusion practices and processes see, for example, Gazeley (2010).
5. Although the focus of this chapter is on social class, it is important to point out that class is clearly articulated with gender and ethnicity (Reay, 1998). Thus, the negative expectations of teachers regarding students of low socioeconomic status are especially strong in the case of male students and those of immigrant origin.
6. Our analysis is based on the results of interviews carried out with teachers, principals, counsellors, and academic coordinators as part of the previously cited ABJOVES project, as well as from a complementary project carried out during the 2012–2013 and 2013–2014 academic years on the situation of

secondary school students in an average size municipality in the province of Barcelona (Catalonia).

References

Auwarker, A. E., Aruguete, M. S. (2008) 'Effects of Student Gender and Socioeconomic Status on Teacher Perceptions', *Journal of Educational Research*, 101, 243–246.

Ball, S. (1990) (ed.) *Foucault And Education. Discipline And Knowledges*, London: Routledge.

Ball, S. (2013) *Foucault, Power And Education*, New York and London: Routledge.

Bernstein, B. (1977) *Class, Codes and Control Volume* 3 (2nd edn), London: Routledge and Kegan Paul.

Bernstein, B. (1985) 'Clasificación y enmarcación del conocimiento educativo' [Classification and framing of education knowledge], *Revista Colombiana de Educación*, p. 15.

Bonal, X., Tarabini, A. (2013) 'The Role of PISA in Shaping Hegemonic Educational Discourses, Policies and Practices: the case of Spain', *Research in Comparative and International Education*, 8(3), 333–339.

Bonal X., Verger, A. (2013) *L'agenda de la política educativa: una anàlisi de les opcions de govern*, Fundació Jaume Bofill: Barcelona.

Catalan Department of Education (2012) *A favor de l'èxit escolar. Pla per a la reducció del fracàs escolar a Catalunya 2012–2018*, Generalitat de Catalunya: Barcelona.

Dunne, M., Gazeley, M. (2008) 'Teachers, social class and underachievement', *British Journal of Sociology of Education*, 29(5), 451–463.

Enguita, M., Mena, L, Riviere, J. (2010) *Fracaso y abandono escolar en España*, La caixa, Colección Estudios Sociales, p. 29.

Escudero, J. M (2005) 'Fracaso escolar, exclusión educativa. ¿De qué se excluye y cómo?' [Failure in school, education exclusion: what is the student excluded from and how], *Profesorado, revista de currículum y formación del profesorado*, 1(1).

Escudero, J. M, Martínez, B. (2012) 'Las políticas de lucha contra el fracaso escolar ¿Programas especiales o cambios profundos del sistema y la educación?' *Revista de Educación*, 174–193.

Foucault, M. (1977) 'The political function of the intellectual', *Radical Philosophy*, 17.

Foucault, M. (1979) *Discipline And Punish. The Birth Of The Prison*. London: Peregrine.

Foucault (1980) *Power/Knowledge: Selected Interviews Ans Other Writings*. New York: Pantheon.

Foucault, M. (1981) 'The order of discourse', in Young, R. (ed.) *Untying The Text: A Post-Structural Anthology*, Boston: Routledge & Kegan Paul, pp. 48–78.

Foucault M. (1983) 'Why study power: the question of the subject', in: Dreyfus, H. and Rabinow, P. (eds) *Michael Foucault: Beyonf Structuralism And Hermeneutics*, Chicago, IL: University Chicago Press.

Foucault M. (2008) *The Birth of Biopolitics: Lectures at the College de France 1978–1979*, Basingstoke: Palgrave.

Gay, G. (2002) 'Culturally responsive teaching in special education for ethically diverse students: setting the stage', *Qualitative Studies in Education*, 15(6), 613–629.

Gazeley, L. (2010) 'The Role of School Exclusion Processes in the Re-Production of Social and Educational Disadvantage', *British Journal of Educational Studies*, 58(3), 293–309.

Grant, B. (2006) 'Disciplining Students: the construction of student subjectivities', *British Journal of Sociology of Education*, 18(1), 101–114.

Grau, J. (2012) Wert Afirma que la Reforma Educativa es Práctica, no Ideológica, y no Recentraliza [Wert declares that the new education reform is practical, not ideological nor recentralizing], ABC, 21 September http://www.abc.es/20120921/sociedad/abci-educacion-reforma-moncloa-wert- 201209211315.html

Hook, D. (2001) 'Discourse, knowledge, materiality, history: Foucault and discourse analysis', *Theory And Psychology*, 11(4), 521–547.

Ministry of Education of Spain (2013) *Ley Orgánica para la Mejora de la Calidad Educativa* (LOMCE), MEC: Madrid.

Reay, D. (1998) 'Rethinking social class. Qualitative perspectives on class and gender' *Sociology*, 32(2), 259–275.

Rist, R, (2000) [1970] 'Student Social Class and Teacher Expectations: The self-fullfilling prophecy in ghetto education', *Harvard Educational Review*, 70(3), 257–301.

Rumberger, R. (2011) *Dropping Out. Why Students Drop Out Of High School And What Can Be Done About It*, Harvard: Harvard University Press.

Shavit, Y., Blossfeld, H. P. (1993) 'Persisting Barriers: Changes in Educational Opportunities in Thirteen Countries' in Shavit, Y. and Blossfeld, H. P. (eds) *Persistent Inequality: Changing Educational Attainment in Thirteen Countries*, Boulder, Col.: Westview Press, pp. 1–24.

Steiner-Khamsi, G. (2004) *The Global Politics of Educational Borrowing and Lending*, New York: Teachers' College Press.

Tarabini, A., Curran, M., Montes, A. and Parcerisa, L. l. (2015) 'Las políticas de lucha contra el abandono escolar en Cataluña: un análisis comparada del concepto éxito escolar' [ESL policies in Catalonia: a comparative analysis of the concept of education success], in Tarabini, A. (dir) *Políticas de lucha contra el abandon escolar en España* [Policies to fight ESL in Spain]. Madrid: Síntesis.

Van Houtte, M. (2004) 'Tracking effects on school achievement: A quantitative explanation in terms of the academic culture of school staff', *American Journal of Education*, 110(4), 354–388.

Part IV
Empowerment

9
21st Century Emancipation: Pedagogies in and from the Margins

Sara C. Motta

South American social movements are re-inventing a new emancipatory politics of knowledge in which those invisibilised and excluded by neoliberal globalisation, are emerging as the emancipatory subjects of our times. These subjects develop social relations which disrupt the power of capital in their everyday lives through practices which reconnect people and communities with their own creative capacities and with each other. In this article I conceptualise and reflect on the role of the pedagogical in this reinvention through the development of a theoretical dialogue between Gramsci's Marxian framework, and Black and Decolonial feminisms. I argue that pedagogical practices are central to the geopolitics of neoliberal globalisation and thus, more importantly, to emancipatory epistemologies, as these practices enable the unlearning of dominant social relationships, subjectivities and ways of life, and the learning of new ones. I explore this through engagement with the politics of knowledge of the Brazilian Movimento dos Trabalhadores Rurais Sem Terra (Landless Rural Workers' Movement [MST]), and La Máscara, a feminist theatre collective in Colombia.

Firstly I contextualise my analysis through summarising the geopolitics of knowledge of neoliberal globalisation, with particular focus on its articulation in Colombia and Brazil, to then outline key elements of a counter-hegemonic politics of knowledge as emerging from the margins in South America and beyond. I then move to outline a theoretical dialogue between Gramscian analysis and decolonial feminism as a means of conceptualising and analysing the counter-hegemonic politics of knowledge of the MST and La Máscara, and end with some reflections on what this suggests about the relationship between pedagogies of and from the margins and twenty-first century emancipation.

My contribution engages with Chapter 3, 'Gramsci, Education and Power' by Peter Mayo. It builds on the concepts Mayo introduces of hegemony, the complex and contradictory nature of subaltern consciousness and the figure of the organic intellectual. It does this by framing the organic intellectual as collective, conceptualising the contradictory nature of subaltern consciousness through the categories of common and good sense and embracing multiple literacies that move beyond those of the written word. However, it also moves beyond Gramsci via critical interrogation of the representational political and epistemological assumptions in his work through a dialogue with decolonial and black feminisms.

The geopolitics of knowledge of neoliberal globalisation

The politics of knowledge have taken centre stage in the representations, practices, and prescriptions of neoliberal globalisation. From Tony Blair in the United Kingdom declaring that the modernised Labour Party would put 'education, education, education' at the heart of their Third Way agenda, through to President Alvaro Uribe (2002–2010) in Colombia declaring his intent to implement an 'educational revolution', education (and by implication epistemology, or the politics of knowledge) has become politicised. This project, commodifying education, is an increasingly globalised project that reinforces unequal and uneven relationships between countries, and within countries, between communities and ways of life, deepening the lines of exclusions that characterise neoliberalism.

As part of this commodification, South America is reproduced as the epistemological underside of capitalist coloniality; represented as the passive receiver and consumer of knowledge and research, designed and developed by unelected transnational actors (often of the global North). Contemporary capitalism is thus produced through a particular way of knowing which situates 'the West' and a project of homogenising universalism as the pinnacle of development and progress (Mignolo, 2009, pp. 2–3). Such geopolitics of knowledge is enacted through a violent relation against the 'other', as 'other' forms of knowledge are devalued and denied.

These violent logics are not only epistemological but ontological, for ways of knowing are also ways of inhabiting and creating the world and each other; for example, as the Ada Songor Advocacy Forum of Ghana demonstrate, meaning making and being in the world are constituted through the literacies of symbolism, storytelling and embodied connections with the land and broader cosmos (Langdon et al., 2014). Thus, when communities are dispossessed from their land, their embodied spiritual connection to each other and the land is ruptured and torn apart thus creating epistemic and ontological wounds. Eradicating ways of knowing therefore enacts, not merely a discursive eradication, but an ontological denial of being 'otherwise'. As Lugones (2010, p. 745) describes in relation to the generic dynamics of capitalist coloniality but eminently relevant here,

> The civilizing transformation justified the colonization of memory and thus of people's sense of self, of intersubjective relation, of their relation to the spirit world, to land, to the very fabric of their conception of reality, identity and social, ecological and cosmological organisation.

Within these epistemological geopolitics, the oppressed subject becomes as Lugones (2006, p. 78) also states, 'invisible, not within the bounds of normalcy ... as inferior, or as threatening because not ruled from within by modern rationality'. Thus the neoliberal project fosters practices, policies, and rationalities that seek to deepen a monological and inherently antidemocratic closure of epistemological and ontological possibility constitutive of capitalist coloniality.

Importantly, this process involves a restructuring of the state in deeply anti-popular and disciplinary ways. As Rose (1993, pp. 294–295) explains, 'We are dealing with a new form of governmentality' that has two distinct kinds of control; the first being quasi-market mechanisms epitomised as competition, localised entrepreneurial initiatives, delivery of value for money, and competitive tendering; the second being direct state controls in the form of imposed targets, outputs, efficiency gains, and performance criteria. As Coté et al., argue (2007, p. 319), 'These [controls] allow populations to be divided and managed, and our daily lives to be more intensely immersed in capitalist exploitation and state-based rational-bureaucratic control.'

In education, externally implemented systems of ranking and evaluation are imposed to create disciplinary mechanisms and self-disciplining subjects that devalue indigenous traditions of pedagogy, education, epistemology and ways of life. Capitalist coloniality is exercised by international centres of power such as the IMF, World Bank, European Union and by transnational capital, determining the meanings of quality, professionalism and modernisation in this culture of neoliberal education reform. In the Colombian case, these types of epistemological logics and power relationships became institutionalised during the Uribe governments through inclusion of private entities and organisations in the evaluation of education quality. Thus the demands of the private sector became key in the development of pedagogy and curricula, as evidenced in the Estrategia de Gestión del Recurso Humano en Colombia (EGERH). As Pinilla (2012, p. 7) argues, this situation moves the framework underlying Colombian education reform in a direction in which,

> It is the private sector that should define and evaluate education of workers, in line with the work positions available, orientating students to labour demand and determining the conditions of training offered in a way that results in the total correspondence in the training given and the work to be performed, without recourse to the emblematic frameworks of integral education.

As Libâneo (2008) demonstrates in the case of the Workers' Party's educational reforms in Brazil, these reforms are framed within a logic of measurable results, external evaluation, competition for funding, a productivist orientation of education and the increasing growth of the private sector as a provider and organiser of education. Similarly, educational restructuring has come from above, and particularly from the guidance and prescription of international experts and technocrats to the detriment of nationally-orientated and designed programmes.

These epistemologial politics in which education is viewed as a commodity to be accessed by consumer-students so that they can become globally competitive workers, becomes embedded into teacher-training programs, school curricula and university strategic plans. As Light et al. (2009, p. 5) describe in relation to Colombia,

> Colombia's leaders believe that education is key to addressing two of the country's biggest challenges: a) the concern for social peace, inclusion and social integration; and b) the need for economic development in an era of competitiveness and globalisation.

Yet this type of education is primarily to create workers to reproduce uncritically neo-liberal capitalist logics and to satisfy financial and business interests. Education is conceptualised as a commodity that is consumed in order to obtain particular measurable skills and competencies that will ensure successful entrance into the job market. As Meija (2002, pp. 7–8) argues, there is a clear subject of knowledge that such epistemological logics aim at creating; which is a docile and competent worker who 'sees education only as the obtainment of technical skills, and is the subject of homo econmicus, only interested in their salary' and capacity to consume.

In this paradigm, the educator, particularly acute in the global South, is de-intellectualised, de-professionalised, and de-politicised, presented as a mere transmitter of skills. The Colombian 2006–2016 Education Plan is a paradigmatic example of such logics. In the area of curricula reform and teacher development, the plan built on the first national evaluation of teachers' and school principals' performance undertaken in 2003. The plan institutionalised a national pedagogic evaluation in which teams of educators visit schools as a means to redefine the curriculum and expected student outcomes, using quantifiable measures. Three broad standards were established: basic competencies in subject areas (mathematics, language, social sciences and natural sciences), citizenship competencies and work-related competences (Light et al, 2009, pp. 13–14).

This proclaimed educational revolution placed heavy rhetorical emphasis on teachers to take the lead in implementing many of these curricula changes. Yet ironically, the top-down technocratic approach to the design of the educational paradigm had shaped its contours and contents in a way that excluded the voices and perspectives of educators (Meade and Gershberg, 2008, pp. 10–12). Teachers were expected to change their practices and improve their content knowledge, with evaluations of their performance implemented as part of school improvement plans, and executed by these new education managers. This approach undermines the professionalism of teachers and their autonomy to make decisions regarding ways to teach or improve their teaching practice. Evaluations were linked to pay and working conditions – clearly a means of creating insecurity and fear in workers, thereby ensuring their compliance with the reforms. Lopes, when analysing teacher training programs in Brazil noted similar logics. As he explains (2004, p. 114), 'training in the name of autonomy and creativity is put at the service of the insertion of this subject into the globalized world maintaining the submission of education to a productivist model', thus disarticulating the intellectual, cultural and epistemological possibilities of counter-hegemonic resistances (Lopes, 2005, p. 112).

As Martinez (cited in Salcedo, 2013, p. 127) describes such restructuring of teacher training and teacher-subjectivities produces a

subject of knowledge that becomes the subject of normalisation...enabling the multiplication of institutional mechanisms and juridical controls that enclose, surveil and punish, which are socially accepted and in which the educator becomes trapped in the role of a functionary worker.

The resulting mechanisms of evaluation and standardisation discipline the teacher-subject in pernicious ways, including devaluation of their expertise, deterioration of working conditions, and increasing precariousness cumulating as the threat of loss of employment. As Ernandi Mendes described to me, in relation to the conditions facing teachers at school and university levels in Ceará, Brazil,

> Micro-management practices of evaluation have been implemented which increase the anxieties and fears of teachers and disempower them in the making of decisions in relation to pedagogy and [the] curriculum. They also depoliticise the teacher-subject reproducing hegemonic forms of teacher subjectivity. On top of this resources are being cut and more responsibilities delegated to us, as tenured positions become rarer and rarer.

Indeed in some cases, those educators that are viewed as dissenting to this neoliberal paradigm can suffer death threats and the actual loss of life as teacher-unionists are targeted (Motta, 2014b). As Mario Novelli demonstrates in the case of Colombia, critical teachers have been at the forefront of struggles for social justice and democracy in education; developing (2010, p. 272) 'popular education, education for democracy and human rights, justice in education, raising awareness of processes of marginalisation and non-violent activism'. This struggle has led these teachers to be targets of the government, which actively vilified all those in opposition as terrorist guerrillas threatening the democratic stability agenda, and therefore, Colombia's entrance into the globalised world. Such processes attempt to eradicate the subjective, social, and cultural conditions for the emergence of critical educators and pedagogical-political projects committed to fostering the self-emancipation of oppressed communities.

This educational and epistemological project also seeks to produce certain student subjectivities. The ideal neoliberal student is a consumer-student prepared to become indebted (through private finance) to ensure their access to education and, by implication, success and inclusion as a worker and consumer. Such a process of subjectification is embedded in instrumental rationalities that produce social and cultural terrains of competition and separation. In this situation, the individual (student, student's family and/or teacher) is represented as primarily responsible for social and economic success or failure. This process acts to mystify the structural nature of such exclusion, particularly the consequences of standardised curricula that speak over local needs, combined with reduced public funding for education and an economic model that produces structural unemployment.

This discourse is often internalised into poor student subjectivities fostering a structure of emotions in which happiness, self-worth and success become focused on access to educational services. Failure is often experienced as self-failure and internalised in processes of blaming, shaming, and devaluation. As Salcedo (2013) and Meija (2002) demonstrate in the Colombian case, such a framing of the importance of education in the possibility of success, inclusion and modernity enters into the very desires and affective attachments of Colombia's poor. Access to education becomes a route to dignity and inclusion in consumer society. The desire for such a good becomes a motor force of the individual's activities, horizons and choices. Such neoliberalisation of desire augments the inequalities and exclusion of neoliberal development as the wealthy are able to access the internationally renowned and ranked public universities, whilst the poor are relegated to the poor quality private institutions which offer diplomas based on short, online and technical courses. As Salcedo (2013, p. 123) describes it, the impact of this,

> is to expand educational hope into the intimacy of society...stimulating cultural consumerism free from the right to education, making this seem like the immediate and obvious answer for the individual...Bringing this into relationships, affectivity, citizenship and politics...this brings the mark of modernity into the everyday in which to improve life chances; one must learn to educate oneself.

Not only does this link in the oppressed to the parasitic processes of global financialisation of capital but it also culturally and subjectively fragments and individualises poor communities. Such logics of disarticulation of political possibility and critical imagination within the subaltern are a pernicious, dehumanising form of enacting the politics of knowledge of neoliberal globalisation. These processes attempt to deny the subaltern the cultural, intellectual, and affective knowledges and wisdoms through which to transform their realities of exclusion and oppression.

Yet processes of privatisation and marketisation, in which access to education for many remains a myth that can result in indebtedness with no guarantee of decent employment, has created fractures in the epistemological politics of neoliberal globalisation. As Campo and Giraldo (2009, p. 115) argue in relation to Colombia,

[I]n this way the poor student, with poor quality basic education, as opposed to having better opportunities to public education, is obliged to finance their private education through educative credit, which creates a situation of extreme inequity; they are unable to compete for the few places at public universities... Access is a mechanism to privatise the costs of higher education on the shoulders of the poorest students.

And as Mancebo (2004b, p. 86) argues in relation to educational reform in Brazil,

[F]ar from resolving or correcting the unequal distribution of educational goods, privatization promoted by the policy has tended to deepen the historic discrimination and denial of the right to higher education for the popular sectors. The allocation of poor students to private institutions crystallizes even more the dynamics of segmentation and differentiation in the school system, resulting in the strongest academic schools for those that enter public institutions and the weaker academic schools, save exceptions, for the poor.

As the promises of inclusion, choice, and development remain unmet, fault lines have become cracks of political possibility out of which have emerged movements that politicise the pedagogical and pedagogise the political.

Emancipatory epistemologies: politicising the pedagogical and pedagogising the political

Such epistemological and educational alternatives have most viscerally and forcefully emerged in Latin America. Here the neoliberal attempt to disarticulate alternative epistemological and ontological horizons of the political has been resisted. This is manifest in the election to power of various governments falling under the broad rubric of the 'pinktide'. Examples include those of Luiz Ignácio (Lula) da Silva of the Workers' Party (PT) in Brazil, Hugo Chávez in Venezuela, and Evo Morales in Bolivia. These alternatives have also emerged in social movement and community struggles – for example, the recovered factories movement in Argentina, the MST in Brazil, water movements in Uruguay, indigenous movements in Ecuador and Bolivia, the urban land committees in Venezuela, and feminist nonviolent movements in Colombia.

Arguably, within this multiplicity of experiences are the contours and practices of a reinvention of emancipatory politics for the twenty-first century. Such emancipatory horizons and practices are deeply democratic, plural and decentralised fostering processes in which communities learn to govern themselves, This foregrounds the multiplicity that is at the heart of this reinvention and the necessity, therefore, to speak and theorise in the plural. There is no overarching model of transformation as is common in twentieth-century conceptualisations of emancipation, rather a series of practices, experiences and struggles that enable the asking of questions, and open experimentation from which emerge processes of political and social emancipation.

At the heart of this reinvention is an epistemological politics in which the pedagogical takes centre stage. The term 'pedagogical' is used broadly to refer to an articulation of learning aims and processes in social, ethical, spiritual, and affective as well as cognitive relationships. Pedagogical practices constitute the processes of unlearning dominant subjectivities, social relations and ways of life and in learning new ones. More concretely, they enable the conditions of emergence of a reinvented emancipatory politics, the immanent development of emancipatory visions, and can offer fruitful ways to overcome movements' difficulties and contradictions to foster their sustainability and flourishing (Motta, 2014a).

Such a politics of knowledge builds upon heritages of radical and subaltern educational traditions and cultural practices such as indigenous cosmologies, liberation theology and popular education. These practices are the descendants of Simon Rodriguez's project of epistemological emancipation. Escobar elaborates on this project (cited in Cendales et al., 2013, p. 7),

> [Rodriguez] wanted all – blacks, indigenous poor, direct descendants of the coloniser – to be equals; he intuited that education could fulfil this task because he had no doubt of the intellectual capacities of anyone, and believed conversely, that the people should be the basis from (which) popular democracy is constructed.

This project also builds upon the heritage of critical educators such as Paulo Freire. For Freire, knowledge does not exist as a fixed object of facts (a bank) from which individuals might make withdrawals. Rather, knowledge is constructed through the dialogical process of engagement between the self and the other, mediated by the world (Freire 2006, p. 25). The understanding of knowledge as an abstract object which constructs its subjects is critiqued as a stagnant, degenerate knowledge by which 'words are emptied of their concreteness and become a hollow, alienated verbosity' (Freire, 2006 p. 52). As Jonathan Mansell (2013, p. 18) explains,

> In such circumstances, knowledge becomes the master of people; people become mere vassals to be filled with knowledge. Knowledge is in this context anti-democratic: distant, remote, imperial grammar, to be recited without innovation, without questioning, in this context knowledge disembodies people, turns them into mere repeaters, imitators rather than allowing them to develop their radical person-hood as unique creators of meaning.

These subaltern educational heritages, traditions, philosophies and practices dethrone the knowing subject of patriarchal capitalist colo-niality from his claimed position of universal superiority, which (emphasises) *his* mastery of others and production of the word as separate from the world. In contrast, emancipatory pedagogy fosters processes of mass intellectuality and creativity. These processes enable communities to re-author themselves through the power of the word which, as Freire argues, is the power to name, to be a subject in the world and thus change the world (1996, p. 69). This politics embraces multiple forms of knowledge, including the affective, embodied, oral, cognitive and cultural. It experiments with collective and horizontal pedagogies that enable communities to author themselves and their worlds.

This politics of knowledge and the politicisation of the pedagogical occur in formal educational settings, often on the margins of dominant processes of neoliberal restructuring (see Motta, 2014a). This politicisa-tion also occurs in the messy spaces where subjects, bodies, epistemolo-gies and spatialities meet in movement politics, community organising and informal educational processes. Within this, the school is reimag-ined as a site for the development of thinking, autonomous and innova-tive subjects, able to collectively produce their self-liberation. Teacher training is reconnected to a pedagogical-political project in which educa-tors make an ethical commitment to the oppressed. These practices transgress the borders of an education separated from life, and learning dissociated from ethical and political commitments. Instead it seeks to co-create pedagogical projects with communities in struggle.

To conceptualise and analyse this emancipatory politics of knowl-edge, I develop a neo-Gramscian inspired framework that is deepened to include gender and epistemological politics through engagement with Black and Decolonial feminisms. I choose these frameworks as the move-ments discussed use them and because these they also emerge(d) from the epistemological margins out of practices of struggle and commitments to emancipation.

Theorising from the epistemological margins

Gramsci develops the concept of hegemony to conceptualise the most stable reproduction of capitalism. Hegemony is premised on the construction of consent (termed common-sense) to domination within the subaltern. To become hegemonic, a conception of the world, reflective of the particular interests of the dominant, must 'incorporate itself into everyday life as if it were an expression of it, and to act as an actual and active guiding force, giving direction to how people act and react'(Gramsci, 1971, p. 268). The construction of hegemony is inherently pedagogical as it involves the learning of ways of being, social relationships, and subjectivities. As Gramsci (1971, p. 350) states, 'Every relationship of hegemony is necessarily a pedagogical relationship.' This learning can occur in the formal arena of schooling and education and in the informal spheres of everyday life.

Hegemony is not closed or determinant, however, because the subaltern are historical subjects with histories of struggle, cultural practices and moral economies. The residues of such histories infuse everyday consciousness and are conceptualised in Gramsci as good-sense, which 'rough and jagged though they always are, are better than the passing away of the world in its death-throes and the swan-song that it produces' (Gramsci, 1971, p. 343). Therefore everyday consciousness is contradictory and fragmented even when hegemonic, leaving the immanent possibility of the articulation of counter-hegemonic moral economies and political practices.

For Gramsci, it is the organic intellectual who can play a role in politicising the tensions between common and good-sense. As he argues (1971, p. 10), 'The mode of being of the new intellectual can no longer consist in eloquence which is an exterior and momentary mover of feelings and passions, but in active participation in practical life as constructor, organizer, permanent persuader.' The bridge that enables the intellectual to become such a permanent persuader is a pedagogical one in which (s)he takes on the role of teacher to unite theory and practice, the universal and concrete, by being embedded in subaltern struggle (Fischman and McLaren, 2005, p. 435).Gramsci frames the knowledge of the organic intellectual as conceptual and argues that this intellectual practice can guide the masses to revolutionary truth.

In sum, Gramsci's framework allows a conceptualisation of the political struggle that enables the reproduction of everyday life, demonstrating how this struggle is inherently pedagogical. This implies that the subaltern are not merely acted upon but are active political agents, whose subjectivity can both be normalised as part of the status quo and/or implicitly and explicitly challenge these processes of hegemonic subjectification. It thereby helps to unravel the concrete epistemological and pedagogical mechanisms through which dominant social relationships, subjectivities, and rationalities are reproduced. Importantly, it can also enable a conceptualisation of the inherently pedagogical role of decolonial subjectivities, social relationships, and ways of life through the figure of the organic intellectual.

However, there are certain shortcomings in Gramsci's conceptualisation of the organic intellectual and of the nature of hegemony and hegemonic subjectivities, particularly in regard to the epistemological and patriarchal logics of capitalist coloniality. Despite critiquing the separation of the word from the world, Gramsci's conceptualisation of revolutionary knowledge reifies representational logics of knowledge creation and the knower, and fails to problematise the processes of gendered subjectification that produce embodied and affective alienations and separations (Schugurensky, 2000, p. 501). As Coté et al., argue (2007, p. 322),

> Although the organic intellectual is oriented against capitalist hegemony, this figure's ethical commitments, pedagogic methods, and political vision remain governed by a logic that is itself hegemonic; that is, it is a logic that endeavours 'to assimilate and to conquer' a 'social group,' and that seeks 'dominance' over an entire social formation.

Therefore, as a means to build on his conceptualisation of hegemony, counter-hegemony, and organic intellectuals and their pedagogical practice, it is important to combine the works of Decolonial and Black feminists.

Decolonial and Black feminists demonstrate how the epistemological politics of colonial patriarchal capitalism posits 'the thinker' as the pinnacle of the knowing subject. This individualised and 'Europeanised' subject has particular embodied attributes and affective practices. His detached, masculinised 'rationality' is able to control the unruly and irrational emotions and bodily desires and the irrationalities of all others named as disorderly and underdeveloped (Hooks, 2001; 2003; Lorde, 2000). The result is to situate the European epistemological, monological, and individualised subject as the centre through which all other contents and forms of epistemological practice would be judged – and ultimately devalued.

Therefore, for Decolonial and Black feminists, enlightenment modernity enacts a monological closure and the silencing of all others. Emotional, embodied, oral, popular, and spiritual knowledges are delegitimised, invisibilised, and denied. Such a conceptualisation creates relationships of 'power-over' between the knower and the known subject. A particular form of knowing, knowledge generation, and knowledge is transformed into the universal epistemology (Agathangelou and Ling, 2004). Such a politics of knowledge reproduces a representational praxis of epistemology (and politics) in which there is a division of labour and hierarchy between doers and thinkers, and intellectual and practical labour.

These feminist traditions therefore suggest that emancipation involves not merely changing rationalities or dominant understandings and practices but also decolonising our subjectivities in their embodied, affective, and spiritual realms, thus overcoming the dualisms between emotional/rational, public/private, and scientific/non-scientific of capitalist coloniality. Such emancipation moves the analysis of the hegemonic construction of subjectivities and social relationships, concomitant with the processes of construction of counterhegemonic subjectivities and social relationships, beyond the conceptual and material focus of Gramscian analysis. It suggests including in our analysis the pedagogies of producing and transforming affective and embodied hierarchies, attachments, and practices, the epistemologies of cosmological and cultural formations, and of politicising pedagogically the realm of the private and gendered subjectivities.

These scholars (Lugones, 2010; Hooks, 2001; Anzaldúa, 1987; Motta, 2014a and 2014f) also suggest that deconstruction of the hegemonic contours of neoliberal capitalism involves a critique of the knowing-subject of capitalist coloniality. Arguably, Gramsci partially achieves this deconstruction through his focus on the cultural realm and the contradictory elements of consciousness in common- and good-sense. However, the conceptualisation of organic intellectuality posited predominantly values conceptual and written knowledge as the objectives of revolutionary educational work, thereby reinscribing the logics of othering of other forms of knowledge such as the spiritual, cultural, oral, and embodied. The organic intellectual is also often posited as the individual educator in a way that also reinscribes the logics of separation and representation in epistemological and political construction of strategic and theoretical knowledges for transformation.

Through these feminisms from the margins we can deconstruct colonial paradigms of knowing, the knower, knowledge, and knowledge construction within 20th century critical theory. Subsequently, multiple knowledges, multiple and collective forms of knowledge creation, and multiple sites and subjects of knowledge creation can be embraced. Ultimately, what is suggested and conceptualised are pedagogies, knowledges, and ways of creating knowledge that enable the unlearning of dominant rationalities, ways of life, as well as social relationships and the learning of new ones.

With this conceptual framework I move to map and conceptualise the emancipatory politics of knowledge in two movements; the MST of Brazil and La Máscara feminist theatre collective of Colombia.

Formal education: 'other' schools, 'other' teachers

The MST and Educaçãodo Campo

> They defend....a different education; an education of the subject people of the countryside; an education associated with emotions, symbols, ways of life, struggle, resistance, dreams, an education associated with a dignified life impossible within the contours of capitalist society. (Pingas, 2007, p. 41, cited in de Almeida et al., 2008, p. 103)

The understanding of agrarian reform developed over three decades by the MST, one of the largest social movements in the region, involves much more than a legal redistribution of land and legalisation of occupations of unused privately-owned land. The MST seeks the democratisation of Brazilian society at the political, economic, and cultural levels through the self-organisation of the popular classes. As Conte (2006, p. 43) describes,

> We propose is something that doesn't exist, and because of this it is a utopia and thus we must work to create this at the micro-level. We propose a reappropriation of power, of the power that has been stolen from us. They don't only steal our homes, our land, they also steal our power. They steal our power from us when they convince us that we don't have power.

Thus the organisation of MST communities is multidimensional, involving the development of sustainable community agricultural production, the collective organisation of social reproduction, and the development and honouring of cultural and spiritual traditions.

At the heart of the emergence and consolidation of these processes are autonomous forms of education. Like Gramsci's conceptualisation of hegemony and counter-hegemony, the MST view these practices as deeply embedded in the everyday realities and experiences of subaltern communities. As the MST describe,

> Through our work we produce knowledges, we develop capabilities and forms of consciousness. In itself work has a pedagogical potential, and the school can develop this potentiality, as it supports people to become aware of its connections with other dimensions of human life; its culture, values, political positions. Because of this our schools need to be connected with the world of work and work with education. (MST, 2001, pp. 8–9)

The MST has achieved recognition of this strategy of transformatory education at the state level through PRONERA (Programa Nacional de Educação na Reforma Agrária), which aims to, 'strengthen education for agrarian reform in the MST communities, utilising methodologies that are specific to the countryside that will contribute to sustainable rural development in Brazil' (Pontes Furtado, 2003, p. 200).

The educational philosophy and theory upon which PRONERA projects are founded is *educação do campo*, involving a methodology called *pedagogia da terra*, developed by the MST. *Educação do campo* critiques traditional rural education in which rural communities are presented as ignorant, underdeveloped and conservative, and in which curricula are developed in abstract with no relationship to community members' everyday needs, struggles, and concerns. As de Souza et al., describe (2008, p. 47),

> The rural school…was based on an idea of the social backwardness and precarity of those of the countryside. Education for this population was never in the national debate and much less in public policy. The historical representation of those in the countryside was that 'to work with the land letters are not really necessary.'

Thus, for the MST *educação do campo* is a means of developing a rural education *in* and *for* the rural population. It is therefore connected to the everyday realities of communities and valorises their knowledges and contributions to Brazilian society and history. Through the politicisation and systematisation of their good-sense cultural, spiritual, and experiential ways of knowing, it aims to foster the development of the self-governing capacities and potentials of individuals and communities. This pedagogical practice (re)connects education with life, politicises pedagogy, and is embedded in an ethics of care and commitment for the oppressed (for detailed analysis, see Gonçalves-Fernandes et al., 2008).

Educação do campo is thus a manifestation of an emancipatory educational project that cannot be realised within the confines of capitalist agriculture and schooling, as outlined in the previous section (Caldart, 2000, p. 19). It escapes those confines and instead necessitates the development of 'other' schools and 'other' teachers that work against and beyond the traditional and now neoliberalised schooling system (for further details see Motta, 2014c). Thus, the MST has developed its own schooling network and teacher training programs. *Educação do campo* is therefore a central site of struggle over societal projects and the possibilities of self-organised and deeply democratic emancipatory processes of transformation.

More specifically, if we look to the case of Ceará, the growth of MST settlements, the consolidation of groups of popular educators, and the granting of government funds for education projects has enabled the development of multiple extension projects in adult and youth education, as well as in teacher training; along with the building and equipping of primary and secondary schools in MST communities. Two projects, one of primary-level adult education and the other a teacher-training course in *educação do campo* were developed through collaborative and democratising methodologies of curriculum design (for details of these projects see PRONERA, 2007a; 2007b). The latter involved a participatory process of curriculum development, which included movement representatives and educators dialoguing with a group of popular educators and coordinators from the State University of Ceará. As Sandra Gadelha, one of the coordinators of the teacher-training course, explained to me in April 2010, the group met over several days to discuss the basic contours of the curriculum, including the conceptual, ethical and political orientations that would underpin the course.

Out of these participatory discussions, the guiding principles of the projects were developed. These principles included the valorisation of a multiplicity of knowledges, including those of rural communities; the development of methods that enable a dialogue of these knowledges; responsibility, and commitment to life, social, and human ethics; the recovery of the cultures and identities of social movements in the countryside; and the collective construction of knowledge for transformation of situations of oppression (de Souza et al., 2008, p. 49).

The projects demonstrate a commitment to facilitate emancipatory pedagogical practices in the everyday realities of communities that build upon the good-sense elements of consciousness, understanding, culture, and history. There is therefore a valorisation of the wisdom of peasant communities that directly contests the politics of knowledge of colonial capitalism in which landless peasants are presented as conservative, traditional, and uneducated. There is an active commitment to the production of mass intellectuality and organic intellectuality from and for the popular classes. Thus, there is a counter-politics of knowledge that seeks to decolonise the practices and relationships of rural communities in struggle (Pontes Furtado, 2003).

An example of this can be found in the segment of the curriculum organised around the sociology of education. This segment of the teacher-training explores the empirical and theoretical aspects of the sociology of education; the relationship between education and society; the role of education in social development and transformation; a sociological analysis of schooling; the relationship between education and the state; the social relationships between the countryside and the city; the social and political organisation of MST communities; and the role of education in agrarian reform. The contents of the course combine classical texts in critical sociology of education, Brazilian subaltern thinkers' conceptualisation of the sociology of education, MST texts and reflections, and the participants' experiences in relation to the themes discussed.

The course creates multiple learning spaces, which stretches the narrow definition of schooling beyond its association with classrooms separate from everyday life, reconnecting learning with practice and experiences. As Fonseca et al. (2008, p. 64) describe,

> The school that we seek organises educational processes through their reconciliation with everyday life. Thus, it is necessary to find other spaces, outside of the class room [*sic*]. As spaces of construction, reflection and learning... [s]ocial movements create other spaces, outside of the school, as spaces of potential learning; struggles, marches, occupations, experiences of cooperative production in the countryside and the city which foster relationships of solidarity.

Multiple knowledges are included, and the curriculum is organised around the creation of a dialogical learning space. Multiple pedagogies are also developed, which engage not only with the conceptual but with the spiritual, symbolic, and the embodied realities of communities' struggles and histories. Thus, there is a use of poetry, art, and theatre, including the recovery of histories of struggles and the dignity of communities. This involves practices such as *mistica*, which is an artistic/cultural practice that opens and closes MST events, including workshops, meetings, occupations, and marches. Mistica can take the form of poetry, the re-enactment of popular struggle and history, dance, song, and often ends with all participants touching each other by holding hands or through a collective embrace (for more details, see MST, 2001). Mistica involves pedagogies of the body in which new intimacies and levels of trust are developed between participants in their embodied enactments of their histories of struggle and by embracing each other.

These pedagogies help participants to collectively develop their organisational capacities and understanding of the political role of education and pedagogy. The activities also strengthen participants' political commitments and the connections between different MST communities and other communities in struggle. Such processes involve the resignification of subjects and the development of 'other' educators trained in the distinct pedagogical commitments of *educação do campo*.

For the popular educators involved in the design, development, and implementation of the projects, the process has involved a radicalisation of university praxis through its embedding in the logics of subaltern struggle. This struggle has been particularly fraught in a time of the increasing marketisation of higher education (HE) and the imposition of external ranking and evaluation systems. Thus, for the educators, this work has been pursued on top of their normal working day; the conditions of which have deteriorated in terms of teaching hours, publication demands and wages.

These popular educators have become the border-thinkers who bridge the university and the movement, creating practices that challenge the neoliberal contours of the former and help to foster the emancipatory practices of the latter. In their forging of spaces of possibility within the university environment, they are contesting the logics of competition, ranking, and the de-intellectualisation of neoliberal education. These practices, however, demand extraordinary levels of commitment and energy, can result in burnout and exhaustion, and are not often met with accolades or rewards at the university level.

Thus, working collaboratively as critical educators is a transgressive act of becoming other, of liberating the educator-self from the confines of the individualised and commodified university worker. Pedagogies of possibility such as these are conceptualised by many critical educators that I spoke to, as acts of revolutionary love. As Freire (2006, p. 29) argues, 'As individuals or as peoples, by fighting for the restoration of [our] humanity [we] will be attempting the restoration of true generosity.

And this fight, because of the purpose given it, will actually constitute an act of love.'

In sum, the politics of knowledge of the MST builds on traditions of radical education, cultural practices and the embodied experiences of movement participants. It embraces a multiplicity of knowledges and pedagogies. Within this, the cultural becomes the linkage between the political and the pedagogical, enabling communities to author themselves and their worlds in liberatory ways. This educational project is committed to the creation of 'other' teachers who are ethically committed to the oppressed, and who co-create political-pedagogical projects of emancipation. The project inevitably fosters the creation of 'other' schools in which education is re-connected to life, and learning to struggle. For the critical educators participating in these struggles, the process also means they politicise their pedagogical practices and transgress the separations between the university and community; thereby challenging the authoritarian logics of marketised education. Arguably the politics of knowledge of the MST is a struggle over societal projects, ways of life and forms of being.

Informal movement pedagogies: decolonising everyday life

La Máscara Feminist Theatre Collective

La Máscara Theatre Company is a unique feminist theatre group in Cali, Colombia that works with *theatre of the oppressed* pedagogies and methodologies. Formed in 1972, the collective have produced themselves as integral actors, articulating individual and collective voices of liberation and empowerment linked to key problematics facing women. They have achieved this through developing multiple pedagogies, which are embodied, affective, spiritual, intellectual, imaginative, and include dance, poetry, voice, music, bodywork, and methods of theatrical expression (Restrepo, 1998, pp. 79–81). Importantly in their reweaving of themselves and their world, they do not privilege any particular forms of pedagogy or knowledge. They enact in their practice a dialogue of knowledges that decentre the knowing-subject of capitalist coloniality and the written word produced through abstract conceptualisation as the pinnacle of knowledge.

The group conceptualise feminism as the creation of epistemological, political, cultural, and embodied relationships and practices that are alternatives to the former militarised capitalist patriarchy in Colombia (Restrepo, 1998, p. 120). The group members are committed to an ethical practice of dialogue and listening but also, as Lucy Bolona (interview December 2010) explains,

[T]he need for the oppressed to at times enact monologues, not to silence, but to create the spaces necessary for those who have been without voice and visibility to be heard and seen.

The Collective performs within a theatre setting, as well as presenting street performances, and actively seeks to create ruptures in the hegemonic representations of gendered relationships of power as they interpolate the personal, collective and political. By creating narratives, images, sensations, and representations that enact a discontinuity in the hegemonic narrative of social life, they seek to open up possibilities of critical reflection and practice. They engage with the problematics of gendered violence, motherhood, sex work, infanticide, the family, sexuality and desire (Restrepo, 1998, pp. 148–150). They enact multiple interplays between bodies, spaces, lighting, silence, and sound; developing pedagogies of the sensations and emotions to create the condition of imaginative and conceptual openings to otherness. As Pilar Restrepo describes it,

We need to produce works that develop through humour, irony, the dancing body (and) circus techniques, break the silence, provoke reflection and questions...We open dialogues, inviting others to think, open and transform themselves.

These experiences have also radically transformed the actresses of the Máscara, allowing them to co-create multiple readings of the world and ways of weaving themselves, their relationships, bodies, sexualities, desires, and the broader communities of which they form a part.

For Pilar Restrepo (interview December 2010) this was an intensely uncomfortable and challenging experience despite its leading to joy, creativity, and self-valorisation. As she explains, 'We were used to the men deciding everything, directing, writing the script, managing theatre groups.' These women have embraced the discomfort that accompanies processes of unlearning the subjectivities and relationships of patriarchal colonial capitalism. Such intensely embodied experiences of transformation enable, she continues, 'ways to re-think resentment, anger and bitterness that arise out of multiple experiences of oppression and violence...ways to convert pain into creation.'

La Máscara also develops participatory theatre with excluded and oppressed communities in which members become critical community facilitators that foster the voice, dignity, and agency of oppressed women. Isabella and Elizabeth, two displaced Afro-Colombian women, are participants in Aves de Paraíso (Birds of Paradise) community theatre groups facilitated by La Máscara. After being displaced in 2001 from Nariño and Chocó states on the Pacific coast of Colombia, they left the violence of state-sponsored paramilitary groups and guerrilla groups to arrive into the neoliberal violence of urban poverty and exclusion. Elizabeth is a grandmother, tall and proud with lines of sorrow around her eyes. Isabella is a single mother of five children who has a deep voice and laugh, yet with a well of sadness in her eyes. They have participated in the theatre group since 2006. It is, as Isabella told me (Motta, 2010), 'a space of peace, of escape, of warmth and humanity'.

As both explained, in their *tierra* (land) no one went hungry. There was always food as they lived in the countryside where there was abundance. Neighbours shared and supported each other. The region where Elizabeth is from has been taken over by multinationals, supported by the Colombian government. Egyptian palms are grown for export, which destroys the surrounding land, further undermining *campesino* (peasant) ways of life. To be violently displaced in this way from your land, way of life, and community, and then arrive to more violence and displacement, is a form of long-term trauma. The violence in their lives is multidimensional. It cannot be understood or transformed from the outside or by a model developed in another place and another context. Such violence is intensely placed, subjective, affective, intellectual, and psychological.

It is this multidimensionality of power, its effects, and how one transforms these conditions into liberation and social justice that is one of the major problematics of La Máscara Theatre. Thus the theatre of the oppressed methodology seeks to facilitate processes of collective understanding, representation, and transformation through the development of theatre. Its objective – like popular education – is self-liberation from oppression, facilitating self-liberation from the passive state of spectators to actors that self-determine, not only the theatre but also their everyday lives. As theatre is multidimensional – affective, cultural, psychological, embodied, physical, and intellectual – it has the potential to transform the multidimensional nature of oppression.

For La Máscara, the key elements of their work are that it is dialogical and integral in the types of collective and individual experiences developed and that it facilitates free play that accepts and values people's life experience, diversity, and expressions. Importantly, they seek to facilitate experimental space in which communities have the time and space to reflect upon their realities and experiment with their own transformation. The theatre aims to encourage rebellious thought, promoting ideas, perspectives, and actions that are unconventional and which generate a plurality of options and alternatives (Restrepo, 1998).

La Máscara develops multiple affective pedagogies, for example, using the power of laughter in a way that relativises the power of order and control through the counter-power of uncontrollable laughter. It opposes desperation and bitterness with the power of liberatory laughter. As Elizabeth expressed, 'It would be so easy to be full of bitterness, to become cold-hearted. Here we prevent this and keep it at bay. This doesn't mean we don't continue to suffer but it does mean that it doesn't destroy us.'

Finally, the Collective is dedicated to public work, making visible to the public the self-liberation and determination of otherwise excluded and demonised communities. As Isabella explained, 'We have shown our work in Cali. It creates a bridge between displaced communities and Caleños. Our work really needs to be presented in every barrio (community).' The theatre of the oppressed brings the creative, affective, and intellectual capacities of communities and individuals to the centre of the praxis of social transformation. As Pilar explains,

> Amongst the arts, theatre possesses the privilege of being a live art, which allows us to see the complexity of social relations and interpret reality in an inventive way, which develops an experience of reflection. Theatre becomes an extraordinary instrument for people and community development.

La Máscara is part of the reinvention of counterhegemonic pedagogical-political projects. These contest the violent logics of monologue, authoritarianism, and closure of capitalist coloniality, embracing instead, multiple forms of knowledge, subjects of knowledge production, and collective ways of producing knowledge for social transformation. Not as victims but as survivors, the subjects emerge to transgress these epistemological and ontological violences. This politics of knowledge is a contest over societal projects understood as a struggle over the heart and soul of a people and their rights to self-determination and self-government. Central to these practices is recognition of the pedagogical nature of (counter) hegemony and embracing of alternative pedagogies through which to decolonise mind, body, heart and soul, and produce social relationships in multiple emancipatory ways.

Conclusion: pedagogies in and from the margins

Those subjects invisibilised and denied by patriarchal capitalist coloniality are emerging as the emancipatory subjects of our time. As the examples of the MST and the Máscara forcefully demonstrate, the subjects are authoring a politics of knowledge that pedagogises the political and politicises the pedagogical.

The participants contest and transgress the geopolitics of neoliberalism through an embrace of the placed body of the oppressed as epistemologically privileged. This process dissolves the hierarchies and divisions between mind and body, abstract and concrete and knowing and life constitutive of coloniality. The methodologies, knowledges, and pedagogies crafted open emancipatory pathways as they enable the unlearning of dominant social relationships, subjectivities and ways of life, and the learning of new ones.

It is ethically and politically important to develop our theories in dialogue with the philosophies and theorisations of these movements and subjects. It is imperative that this work of translation is done to facilitate learning from, and the nurturing of, each other's struggles for liberation. Here to privilege the margins, involves critical educators embracing the difficult, yet beautiful journey of becoming 'other' to the dominant authoritarian and violent logics of marketised education.

References

Agathangelou, A. A., and Ling, L. H. M. (2004) 'The House of IR: From Family Power Politics to the *Poisies* of Worldism', *International Studies Review*, 6, 21–49.

Almeida de, L. P.; Pingas, M. R.; Pinto, P. E.; Knijnik, G. (2008) 'Discutindo a cultura camponesa no processo de ensino-aprendizagem em três escolas do sul do Brasil', in Bezerra Machado, C. L.; Soares Campos, C. S. and Paludo C. (eds), *Teoria e práctica da educação do campo: Análises de experiências*, Brasília: MDA, pp. 100–109.

Anzaldua, G. (1987) *Borderlands/La Frontera: The New Mestiza*, San Francisco: Aunt Lute Books.

Caldart, R. S. (2000) *Pedagogia do Movimento Sem Terra: Escola é ais do que escola*, Petrópolis: Vozes.

Campo, V. M.; and Giraldo, J. E. (2009) 'Redito educativo, acciones afirmativas y equidad social en la educación superior en Colombia', *Revista de Estudios Sociales*, 33, 106–117.

Cendales, L.; Mejía, M. R. and Jairo Muñoz, M. (eds.) (2013) *Entretejidos de la educación popular en Colombia, CEAAL*, Bogota: Ediciones desde Abajo.

Conte, I. I. (2006) A educação como proceso de formação de sujeitos. Veranopolis: ITERRA/UERGS MST (2001) 'Pedagogia do Movimento Sem Terra: acompanhamento as escolas,' Boletim de Educação no 8, São Paulo.

Coté, M.; Day, R. and de Peuter, G. (2007) 'Utopian Pedagogy: Creating Radical Alternatives in the Neoliberal Age', *Review of Education, Pedagogy, and Cultural Studies*, 29(4), 317–336.

de Souza, E. J.; Ferreira de Andrade, E.; Mendes de Lima, G. A. and Bezerra Machado, C. L. (2008) 'Limites e possibilidades: Um olhar sobre o projeto politico pedagogico na perspectiva da educação do campo', in Bezerra Machado, C. L.; Soares Campos, C. S. and Paludo, C. (eds) *Teoria e práctica da educaçáo do campo: Análises de experiências*, Brasilia: MDA, pp. 44–58.

Fischman, G. E. and McLaren, P. (2005) 'Intellectuals or Critical Pedagogy, Commitment, and Praxis Rethinking Critical Pedagogy and the Gramscian and Freirean Legacies: From Organic to Committed,' *Cultural Studies – Critical Methodologies*, 5(4) pp. 425–446.

Fonseca, da C.; Lourenço de Souza; Santin L. M.; Rodrigues, T. M. and Mazzini, V. L. (2008) 'A organização do processo educativo', in Bezerra Machado, C. L.; Soares Campos, C. S. and Paludo C. (eds.) *Teoria e práctica da educaçáo do campo: Análises de experiências*, MDA: Brasília, pp. 58–69.

Freire, P. (1993) [2006] *Pedagogy of the Oppressed*, New York: Continuum Books. *Teachers as Cultural Workers: Letters to Those Who Dare Teach* (1998) (trans.) Donaldo Macedo, Dale Koike, and Alexandre Oliveira, Boulder, CO: Westview Press.

Gonçalves-Fernandes, A.; Alves de Sousa, E.; Conte, I. I.; Maggioni, L.; Vanusa de Abreu, M.; and Riberio, M. (2008) 'A Pedagogia e as prácticas educativas na educaçáo do campo', in Bezerra Machado, C. L.; Soares Campos, C. S. and Paludo, C. (eds) *Teoria e práctica da educaçáo do campo: Análises de experiências*, Brasília: MDA, pp. 26–43.

Gramsci, A. (1971) *Selections from the Prison Notebooks of Antonio Gramsci*, ed. and trans. [from the Italian] Hoare, Q. and Nowell Smith, G. London: Lawrence and Wishart.

Hooks, B. (2001) *Salvation: Black People and Love*, New York: Harper Collins.

Hooks, B. (2003) Teaching Community. A Pedagogy of Hope, London: Routledge Chapman& Hall.

Langdon, J., Larweh K. and Cameron S. (2014) 'The Thumbless Hand, the Dog and the Chameleon: Enriching Social Movement Learning Theory through Epistemically Grounded Narratives Emerging from a Participatory Action Research Case Study in Ghana (Peer-Reviewed Article)' *Interface: a journal for and about social movements*, 6:1 (pp. 27–44).

Libâneo, J. C. 2008 'Algunas Aspectos de Politica Educacional do Governo Lula e sua Repercussão no funcionamento das escolas,' Revista HISTEDBR On-Line, Campinas, 32, 168–178.

Light et al. 2009, Light, D., Manso, M., and Noguera, M. (2009) An educational Revolution to Support Change in the Classroom: Colombia and Educational Challenges of the Twenty First Century,' *Policy Futures in Education*, 7: 1: 88–101.

Lorde, A. (2000) *The Uses of the Erotic: The Erotic as Power*, Tucson, AZ: Kore Press.

Lopes, A. C. (2005) 'Politicas de curriculo: Mediação por grupos disciplinares de ensino de Ciências e matemática' in A. C. Lopes and E. Macedo (org.) Currículo de Ciências em debate. Campinas: Papirus.

Lugones, M. (2006)'On Complex Communications', *Hypathia* 21(3), 75–85.

Lugones, M. (2010) 'Toward a Decolonial Feminism', *Hypathia* 25(4), 742–759.

Mancebo, D. (2004). 'Reforma universitária: Reflexões sobre a privatização e a mercantilização do conhecimento [University reform: Reflections on the privatization and commoditization of knowledge]', *Educaçáo Social*, 25(88), 852–853. Available: http://www.scielo.br/pdf/es/v25n88/a10v2588.pdf.

Mansell, J. (2013) 'Naming the World: Situating Freirean Pedagogics in the Philosophical Problematic of Nuestra América', in Motta, Sara C. and Cole, M. (eds) *Education and Social Change in Latin America*, London; New York: Palgrave Macmillan, pp. 17–35.

Meade, B. and Gershberg, A (2008) 'Rerstructuring Towards Equity? Examining Recent Efforts to Better Target Education Resources to the Poor in Colombia,' UNESCO: Education for All Global Monitoring Report pp 10–12.

Meija, R.M., 2002:' La calidad de la educación en tiempos de globalización' Una mirada critica desde la educación popular, Congreso Pedagogico Nacional de Fe y Alegría, Nicarague 21–22 October 2002.

Meija, A.-M. (2002) Power, Prestige and Bilingualism, Clevedon, UK: Multilingual Matters.

Mignolo, W. D. (2009) 'Epistemic Disobedience, Independent Thought, and De-colonial Freedom', *Theory, Culture and Society*, 26(7–8), 1–23.

Motta, S. C. (2010). 'Aves de Paraiso: Theatre of the Oppressed in Cali, Colombia', *Nottingham Critical Pedagogy*. Available from: http://nottinghamcriticalpedagogy.wordpress.com/2010/12/26/aves-de-paraiso-theatre-of-the-oppressed-in-cali-colombia/. [Accessed 20 July 2015].

Motta, S. C. (2014a) 'Politicizing the Pedagogical and Politicizing Pedagogy', in Motta, Sara C. and Cole, Mike, *Constructing 21stCentiry Socialism: The Role of Radical Education*, London; New York: Palgrave Macmillan, pp. 1–16.

Motta, S. C. (2014b) 'Militarized Neoliberalism in Colombia: Disarticulating Dissent and Articulating Consent to Neoliberal Epistemologies, Pedagogies, and Ways of Life', in Motta, Sara C. and Cole, Mike, *Constructing 21st Century Socialism: The Role of Radical Education*, London; New York: Palgrave Macmillan, pp. 19–41.

Motta, S. C. (2014c) 'Epistemological Counterhegemonies from Below: Radical Educators in/and the MST and Solidarity Economy Movements', in Motta, Sara C. and Cole, Mike, *Constructing 21st Century Socialism: The Role of Radical Education*, London; New York: Palgrave Macmillan, pp. 117–141.

Motta, S. C. (2014d) 'Latin America: Reinventing Revolutions, An 'Other' Politics if Practice and Theory' in Stahler-Stolk, R., Vanden, R. E. and Becker, M. (eds) Rethinking Latin American Social Movements: Radical Action from Below'. Rowman and Littlefield: Lanham and London.

Novelli, M. (2010) 'Education, conflict and social', in Justice: insights from Colombia, *Educational Review*, 62(3), 271–285.

Pinilla, P. A. (2012) 'El fin de la educacion y la deificacion de la formacion del capital humano.' http://viva.org.co/escuelas/?p=237 [Accessed 21 July 2015].

Pontes Furtado, E. D. (2003) 'A Educação de Jovens e Adultos no Campo: Uma Análise a Luz do PRONERO', in Lopes de Matos, K. S. (ed.) *Movimentos Sociais, Educaçã0 Popular e Escola: a favour da diversidade*, Fortaleza: Editora UFC, pp. 198–211.

PRONERA (2007a) 'Practica de Ensino: Curso de Formação de Educadores e Educadoras nas Áreas de Assentamentos de Reforma Agrãria no Ceará', Fortaleza: Pronera, UECE.

PRONERA (2007b) 'Metologia do Trabahlo Científico – Modulo 1', Fortaleza: Pronera and UECE.

Restrepo, P. (1998) *La Máscara, la Mariposa y la Metáfora: Creación Teatral de Mujeres*, Santiago de Cali: Teatro La Máscara.

Rose, N. (1993) 'Government, Authority and Expertise in Advanced Liberalism', *Economy and Society*, 22(3), 283–299.

Salcedo, J. R. (2013) 'La forma neoliberal del capital humano y sus efectos en el derecho a la educación' Actual Pedagog, 61 (Jan-Feb 2013) 113.138.

Schugurensky, D. (2000) 'Adult Education and Social Transformation: On Gramsci, Freire, and the Challenge of Comparing Comparisons', *Comparative Education Review*, 44(4), 515–522.

10
Power and Education in the Bolivarian Republic of Venezuela

Mike Cole

In the Introduction to this chapter, I set out the three forms of power that are integral to the Bolivarian Republic of Venezuela: the power of knowledge; political power; and economic power. I go on to discuss the politics and economics of the Bolivarian Revolution, both educational and educative processes in themselves, before turning to education per se. Education in Venezuela manifests itself as revolutionary knowledge and the self-education of the people; and knowledge, mass intellectuality and empowerment in the public sphere, as well as in its more common institutional form. I then discuss the specific characteristics of institutional education in Venezuela, with a consideration of both the formal education system and alternative education. I conclude with some brief thoughts on what we in the global north might learn from the Bolivarian Revolution.

Introduction

In 2010, stressing the prime importance of education, the late President Hugo Chávez identified it as a key form of power in the ongoing Bolivarian Revolution in Venezuela:

> When we talk about power, what are we talking about[?]...The first power that we all have is knowledge. So we've made efforts first in education, against illiteracy, for the development of thinking, studying, analysis. In a way, that has never happened before. Today, Venezuela is a giant school, it's all a school. From children of one-year-old until old age, all of us are studying and learning. And then political power, the capacity to make decisions, the community councils, communes, the people's power, the popular assemblies.

And then there is the economic power. Transferring economic power to the people, the wealth of the people distributed throughout the nation. (Cited in Sheehan, 2010, without page no.)

Of these three forms of power in contemporary Venezuela, the first – knowledge – is *by definition* obviously educational and takes the forms of the revolutionary knowledge, which is a knowledge of why capitalism is an inherently exploitative system, and thus why there is a need for a social revolution to put an end to that system. Additionally, knowledge takes the form of the self-education of the people; of mass intellectuality and of empowerment in the public sphere as well as liberatory processes in educational institutions, both formal and alternative. As we shall see, a specific feature of education in the Bolivarian context is the way in which it permeates the whole society, and is not confined to institutions, as we shall see in Chávez's 'giant school' described below.

The second form of power – political power – is also an educational process that can best be described as a dialectical relationship between *el pueblo* (the people) and the president, both Chávez and the incumbent president Nicolás Maduro, whereby *el pueblo* both inform the president and are informed by him through the revolutionary study, which involves studying the various thinkers that can inform socialism, as discussed below, and the practice of both the people and the president, and for which the synthesis is twenty-first century socialism and anti-(US) imperialism.

Like the power of knowledge and the consolidation of political power in the hands of the people, the transfer of economic power to the people in the Bolivarian Republic of Venezuela is about the transition from capitalism to socialism, in part via the creation of nexuses of power parallel to the state, entailing extensive economic power to the people, a revolutionary project that is profoundly educational, and educative too. All these processes are, of course, counterhegemonic to the dominant global neoliberal and imperialist consensus. Socialist revolutions, as *ongoing* processes, are by their very nature educational in that, for the revolution to move forward, there is a continuous need for a sustained intellectual critique of capitalism, an understanding of the dangers inherent in twentieth-century socialism and Stalinism, *and* the need to learn afresh as the revolution progresses. Some twenty-first socialists (for example, Motta, 2013) invoke Open Marxism which, rather than positing the need for a vanguard to create the revolution, stresses social movements and unpredictability rather than the role of the (communist) party in creating unknown worlds beyond capitalism.

With respect to the distribution of wealth, while mass dispersal of assets from rich to poor, from capital to labour has not occurred, the creation of a massive social democratic infrastructure under Chávez (first elected in 1998) and continuing under President Nicolás Maduro (see, for example, Dominguez, 2013; see also Cole, 2014a) has resulted in a reduction of the poverty rate from 50% in 1998 to 25% in 2015, with extreme poverty down from 20% to 7%. The national budget for 2014 allocated 62% of revenue towards social investment, compared to 'social spending' in the pre- Chávez governments which never exceeded 36% of the budget (The Embassy of the Bolivarian Republic of Venezuela in the UK and Ireland (2013)).

The politics of the Bolivarian revolution

In the 1990s, as a condition for their obtaining international loans; and even by threats (Victor, 2009), a number of policies, based squarely on neoliberal capitalist principles and formulated in the US were foisted on governments in Latin American and the Caribbean. The 'Washington Consensus',[1] as it became known, was most thoroughly applied in Venezuela. In 1998, Maria Paez Victor (2009, without page no.) describes how the Consensus affected the country, 'This oil-rich country's economy was in ruins, schools and hospitals were almost derelict, and almost 80 percent of the population was impoverished.' In that year, Chávez won the presidential elections in Venezuela by a landslide.

Victor (2009, without page no.) concisely summarises Chávez's impact on the racist oligarchy on the one hand, and on the people on the other,

> Immediately the elites and middle classes opposed him as an upstart, an Indian who does not know his place, a Black who is a disgrace to the position. Hugo Chávez established a new Constitution that re-set the rules of a government that had been putty in the hands of the elites. Ratified in overwhelming numbers, the Constitution gave indigenous peoples, for the first time, the constitutional right to their language, religion, culture and lands. It established Human Rights, civil and social, like the right to food, a clean environment, education, jobs, and health care, binding the government to provide them. It declared the country a participatory democracy with direct input of people into political decision-making through their communal councils and it asserted government control of oil revenues: Oil belongs to the people.

However, twenty-first century socialism in the making did not begin with Chávez. To exemplify this point, George Ciccariello-Maher (2013, p. 6) makes a distinction between *el proceso* (the *ongoing* process) and *el presidente* (the president), the former of which he describes as 'the deepening, radicalization, and autonomy of the revolutionary movements that constitute the "base" of the Bolivarian Revolution', which involved individual and collective action by revolutionaries that predated Chávez by several decades. Ciccariello-Maher (2013, p. 274) emphasises that almost everyone he interviewed in *We Created Chávez: A People's History of the Venezuelan Revolution*, as well as all those interviewed in the pathbreaking book *Venezuela Speaks!* (Martinez et al., 2010), spontaneously made this distinction. As one organiser told him, 'Chávez didn't create the movements, *we created him*' (Ciccareiello-Maher, 2013, p. 7).

Dario Azzellini (2013, without page no.) describes the dual process at work in the revolution as follows,

> The particular character of what Hugo Chávez called the Bolivarian process lies in the understanding that social transformation can be constructed from two directions, 'from above' and 'from below'. Bolivarianism...includes among its participants both traditional organizations and new autonomous groups; it encompasses both state-centric and anti-systemic currents. The process thus differs from traditional Leninist or social democratic approaches, both of which see the state as the central agent of change; it differs as well from movement-based approaches that conceive of no role whatsoever for the state in a process of revolutionary change.

As we shall see later in this chapter, Chávez's charisma and intellectual inspiration was a key element in mass intellectuality in the public sphere, as well as in the overall ethos guiding the Bolivarian educational project. It is important to stress at this stage, as noted earlier, that the Bolivarian Republic of Venezuela remains a capitalist society. In 2011, for example, the poorest fifth's share of personal income was less than 6%, while the share of the wealthiest fifth was almost 45% (Instituto Nacional de Estadística, 2011, p. 8). The full socialist economic transformation, envisaged by both Chávez and Maduro has yet to take place. Having said that, it is also crucial to point out that twenty-first century socialism *in the making* is apparent throughout the society, in the communal councils, communes and workplaces, and crucially, in the minds and actions of the people in the *barrios* (large communities attached to major cities where the poor live) (Ciccariello-Maher, 2013; see also Cole, 2014a).

Next, I will explain the politics of the Bolivarian Revolution by pointing to the central political institutions that are crucial for changes in policies.

Communal councils

> We have to go beyond the local. We have to begin creating...a kind of confederation, local, regional and national, of communal councils. We have to head towards the creation of a communal state. And the old bourgeois state, which is still alive and kicking – this we have to progressively dismantle, at the same time as we build up the communal state, the socialist state, the Bolivarian state, a state that is capable of carrying through a revolution. (Hugo Chávez, cited in Socialist Outlook. Editorial, 2007, without page no.)

The communal councils, which discuss and decide on local spending and development plans, are key in the Bolivarian process. As Azzellini (2013) explains, communal councils began forming independently in different parts of Venezuela in 2005 as an initiative 'from below', as rank-and-file organisations promoting forms of local self-administration called 'local government' or 'communitarian governments'. Following Chávez's landslide victory in the 2006 elections, and as the revolution intensified, 'official' communal councils were created, consisting of small self-governing units throughout the country that 'allow the organized people to directly manage public policy and projects oriented toward responding to the needs and aspirations of communities in the construction of a society of equity and social justice' (Article 2 of the 2006 Law on Communal Councils, cited in Ciccariello-Maher, 2013, p. 244).

In urban areas, the councils encompass 150 to400 families; in rural zones, a minimum of 20; and in indigenous zones, at least 10 families. The councils build up a non-representative structure of direct participation that exists parallel to the elected representative bodies of constituted power, and that are financed directly by national state institutions (Azzellini, 2013). Within a year 18,320 councils had been established (Ciccariello-Maher, 2013, p. 244), and in 2013, there were approximately 44,000 (Azzellini, 2013). Their objective is to submit the bureaucracy to the will of the people through direct participation at the local level. Committee members are elected by the community for two-year revocable terms and are unpaid. Ciccariello-Maher (2013, pp. 245–246) concludes, having noted that every council elects a five-person committee to oversee other levels of government at municipal, regional, and national level, that this is a powerful weapon against corrupt state and local bureaucracies that many hope that this form of participatory democracy will replace the bourgeois state and representative democracy. According to the National Plan for Economic and Social Development 2007–2013, 'Since sovereignty resides absolutely in the people, the people can itself direct the state, without needing to delegate its sovereignty as it does in indirect or representative democracy' (cited in Azzellini, 2013). The government also created the Federal Council of the Government (CFG), linking the government and the councils, and allowing the two to jointly decide on budget allocation. This empowerment of ordinary Venezuelans by direct participation constitutes a deep educational experience that is in total contrast to voting in a narrow choice of pro-capitalist politicians, in part based on their personality, every five years or so (traditional representative democracy). In participatory democracy (discussed in more detail later in the chapter) people get to plan for the needs of the community as a whole. In traditional representative democracies, on the other hand, ideological processes of interpellation[2] attempt, largely successfully, to convince the populace that there is no alternative to neoliberal capitalism, a deliberately mystified set of anti-democratic institutions, which benefit the rich at the expense of the poor. Schools and universities in the capitalist heartlands are increasingly playing a central role in this ideological onslaught. In communal councils, people are empowered. In representative neoliberal democracies, they are disempowered.

Communes

At a higher level of self-government, socialist communes are being created. These are formed by combining various communal councils in a specific territory. The councils themselves decide about the geography of these communes. The communes are able to develop medium- and long-term projects of greater impact than the communal councils (although not including education policies), while decisions continue to be made in the assemblies of the communal councils. As of 2013, there were more than two hundred communes being constructed. Communes can, in turn, form communal cities, again with administration and planning from below if the entire territory is organised in communal councils and communes.

Workplace democracy

The most successful attempt at the democratisation of ownership and control of the means of production is the Enterprises of Communal Social

Property (EPSC), which consists of local production units and community service enterprises. The EPSCs are the collective property of the communities, who decide on the organisational structures, the workers employed, and the eventual use of profits. Government enterprises and institutions have promoted the communal enterprises since 2009, and since 2013 several thousand EPSCs have been formed (Azzellini, 2013).

In June 2013, labour movement activists from all over Venezuela met for the country's first 'workers' congress' to discuss workplace democracy and the construction of socialism. The aim of the meeting was to 'promote, strengthen and consolidate the self-organisation of the working class, based on an analysis of its labour and an evaluation of its struggles, to allow for the generation of its unity around a common plan of struggle' (Robertson, 2013). As Ewan Robertson (2013) explains, as part of resistance to factory closures and management lockouts by bosses opposed to Chávez, dozens of workplaces came under worker management in the last decade, either partly or entirely. However, the workers' control movement, which had the support of Chávez, has tended to stagnate because of opposition from management bureaucrats and reformist politicians within the Bolivarian process.

The congress, the result of a year of meetings between workers in different parts of the country, took up the slogan of the Venezuelan radical Left, 'Neither capitalists nor bureaucrats, all power to the working class.' The main themes of the congress were 'the self-organisation of the working class'; 'the class struggle and the state; legality and legitimacy'; 'workers' councils, worker control and management for the transformation of the capitalist economy'; and the 'formation and socialisation of knowledge'. The main goal of the congress was to draft a final declaration on the national political situation and on the labour movement, and to draw up a manifesto and plan of struggle. Again, the educational implications are obvious – the workers taking direct control of their own lives by composing a revolutionary programme, analysing Venezuelan politics from the viewpoint of labour rather than capital, making their own judgements instead of being on the receiving end of decisions made on high by and for the ruling class, as is the case in the UK and other neoliberal democracies.

Education

Revolutionary knowledge and the self-education of the people

Revolutionaries constantly need to relate theory to practice, and this involves serious academic study. For example, former guerrilla commander Douglas Bravo explains the rediscovery of the spiritual and religious matrix of the indigenous and enslaved African populations George (Ciccariello-Maher, 2013). In a similar vein, revolutionary, Isidro Ramírez, tells Ciccariello-Maher of the importance of both liberation theology and the various cultural histories that make up Venezuela's plurality of spiritualities, and that were all but erased by Eurocentrism; a matter that is, of course, quintessentially educational. Similarly, Rafael Uzcátegui, a member of the Party of the Venezuelan Revolution (PRV) in the 1960s, reminds us again of the central place of education in the revolutionary process. Uzcátegui's recollection of how the PRV had a great 'theoretical structure' reads like a university course on socialist thinking and imperialism. PRV's members learned not just Venezuelan history, but a wide spectrum of theory ranging from Maoism, through humanist neo-Marxism and autonomist Marxism, taking on Spartacus League Marxism and *foquismo* to traditional historical Latin American anti-imperialist struggle. If one reads the work by Martinez et al., (2010) and Ciccariello-Maher's (2013) volume, one cannot fail to be aware of the massive self-educative processes at work in Venezuela. What differentiated these educational processes from similar Marxist reading groups popular at about the same time in the UK (I was a member of one) were the real possibilities in Venezuela for putting theory into practice outside of academia.[3]

Knowledge, mass intellectuality and empowerment in the public sphere: Chávez's 'giant school'

Venezuela as 'a giant school' and 'education for socialism' are both exemplified in the Revolutionary Reading Plan launched by Chávez in 2009 (Pearson, 2009). The plan involves the distribution by the government of 2.5 million books to build up the communal libraries. Chávez said that part of the plan was a 'rescuing of our true history for our youth', explaining that many standard textbooks do not acknowledge the European imperialist genocide of the indigenous peoples and their resistance (Pearson, 2009). Chávez went on to recommend that people do collective reading and exchange knowledge, mainly through the communal councils and the popular libraries. He called on communal councils as well as 'factory workers, farmers, and neighbors, to form revolutionary reading squadrons', one of whose tasks is to hold discussions in order to 'unmask the psychological war ... of the oligarchy' (cited in Pearson, 2009, without page no.).

'Read, read and read, that is the task of every day. Reading to form conscious and minds,' Chávez noted, 'every day we must inject the counter revolution a dose of liberation through reading' (cited in MercoPress, 2009, without page no.).

A second example of mass intellectuality and empowerment in the public sphere is the establishment of *Infocentros* by the government for the poor, giving access to modern telecommunications technologies. These centres, numbering some 820, and situated in 86% of Venezuelan municipalities, played a central role between 2006 and 2011 in the eradication of illiteracy (Dominguez, 2013, p. 128). As well as making telecommunication technology available to masses of people, Infocentros also provide free online-training programs. These include text processing, multimedia, the use of calculations and data in excel, surfing the Internet, social networking, computer-generated presentations and a program for the visually impaired. There are also guides to create communicational and photographic products. Help is given for creating websites. It is possible to learn computer-generated drawing, multimedia resources for video forums, and how to look after a computer. In addition, advice is given on how participants in communal councils can learn from their experiences. It is also possible to learn how to generate specialist websites for tourism, communal socialist commercial exchange, and polls, for example. Public speaking and how to improve writing skills are also available (Fundacion Infocentro, Logros del Proyecto Infocentro 2011, Ministerio para Ciencia y Tecnologia, December 14, 2011, pp. 18–22, cited in Dominguez, 2013, p.130).

The total number of visits to Infocentros in 2011 alone was nearly 12.5 million, compared to less than 1.5 million in 2001 (Ministerio para Ciencia y Tecnologia, December 14, 2011, p. 15, cited in Dominguez, 2013, p. 128).

The formal education system[4]

The Bolivarian Government's educational project for schools

As far as more 'formal' education is concerned, after the election of Chávez, there was a massive increase in funding for primary, secondary, and higher education. With respect to the curriculum, the Venezuelan Ministry of Culture stated on its website that there was a need to help school children get rid of 'capitalist thinking' and better understand the ideals and values 'necessary to build a Socialist country and society' (cited in MercoPress, 2009, without page no.). Education is increasingly promoted by the state as a social good that benefits everyone socially, rather than merely a commodity for personal self-advancement. Moreover, education is seen as a social good for its central role in shaping the system of production (Griffiths and Williams, 2009, p. 37).

Tom Griffiths and Jo Williams (2009) outline the essential factors in the Bolivarian Revolution's approach to education that make it truly counterhegemonic. The Venezuelan approach, they argue, draws on concepts of critical and popular education within the framework of a participatory model of endogenous socialist development (Griffiths and Williams, 2009, p. 41). In representative democracies such as the UK and US, political participation is by and large limited to parliamentary politics, which represent the imperatives of capitalism, rather the real needs and interests of people. Nowhere is this more obvious than in the current round of austerity immiseration capitalism where, as the rich get richer and the poor poorer, we are told and many people believe, that 'we are all in it together'. Participatory democracy, a cornerstone of the Bolivarian Revolution on the other hand, involves direct decision making by the people. At the forefront, they note, is 'the struggle to translate policy into practice in ways that are authentically democratic, that promote critical reflection and participation over formalistic and uncritical learning' (Griffiths and Williams, 2009, p. 41).

As in the UK and US, formal school education in Venezuela is based on an explicit, politicised conception of education and its role in society (Griffiths and Williams, 2009, pp. 41 –42). However, whereas in these two countries, the capitalist state increasingly uses formal education merely as a vehicle to promote capitalism (for example, Hill, 2013), in the Bolivarian Republic of Venezuela, 'the political' in education is articulated *against* capitalism and imperialism and *for* socialism. In 2008, a draft national curriculum framework for the Bolivarian Republic was released. It states that the system is 'oriented toward the consolidation of a humanistic, democratic, protagonistic, participatory, multi-ethnic, pluri-cultural, pluri-lingual and intercultural society' (Ministerio del Poder Popular Para la Educación, 2007, p. 11, cited in Griffiths and Williams, 2009, p. 42). The draft went on to critique the former system for reinforcing 'the fundamental values of the capitalist system: individualism, egotism, intolerance, consumerism and ferocious competition ... [which also] promoted the privatisation of education' (Ministerio del Poder Popular Para la Educación, 2007, p. 12, cited in Griffiths and Williams, 2009, p. 42).

It should be stressed at this stage that, in terms of actual practice in the schools and universities, education based on the above revolutionary principles is by no means universal. Indeed, as Griffiths and Williams (2009, p. 44) point out, discussions with education academics and activists during fieldwork in Caracas in 2007, 2008 and 2009, repeatedly raised the challenge of the political and pedagogical conservatism of existing teachers, who are often in opposition to the government's Bolivarian socialist project (see, for example, Griffiths, 2008).

With respect to this project, Tamara Pearson (2011, without page no.) has pointed out that, 'so far such a vision for education is limited to a number of "model" schools and the majority of Venezuelan children continue to be educated in the conventional way.' She goes on to argue that, while education in Venezuela is now accessible to almost everyone, illiteracy has been eradicated, the working conditions and wages of teachers are much improved, and education is more closely linked to the outside world, mainly through community service and the communal councils, 'structural changes in terms of teaching methods and democratic organising of schools and education have been very limited' (Pearson, 2011).

She concludes,

> Building a new education system is an important prong to building a new economic and political system, because the education system is where we form many of our values, where we learn how to relate to people, where we learn our identity and history, and how to participate in society. Hence we need an alternative to the conventional education systems that train us to be workers more than anything else, to be competitive, to operate under almost army-like discipline, to focus only on individual results not collective outcomes, and to not really understand our history, or the more emotional aspects of life...The effort to change Venezuela's education system is intricately connected to its larger political project. (Pearson, 2011, without page no.)

Pearson (2012) has commented on one of the latest government documents. In a generally very positive account of Chávez's 39-page proposed plan for the 2013–2019 period of the Bolivarian Revolution, she notes that, with respect to education, while the plan mentions increasing enrolment, the building of new schools, the introduction or improvement of certain elements of the curriculum content – such as 'the people's and indigenous history of Venezuela', as well as strengthening research into the educative process, there are 'no structural or methodology changes'. There have hardly been any changes, she argues, in the last 12 years. She concludes,

> The achievement of literacy and enrolment of the poorest sectors is important, but the teaching methods are still traditional authoritarian, competitive ones, and while some schools have become more

involved in their community life, many are still merely producers of obedient workers and a source of income for the teachers. More radical change than what has been proposed is needed. (Pearson, 2012, without page no.)

HE in the Bolivarian Republic

Tom Griffiths (2013, p. 92) notes how the massification of HE in Venezuela since Chávez's first election victory is evidenced by frequent references to its now being ranked second in Latin America (behind Cuba) and fifth worldwide in university enrolment rates, as reported by UNESCO in September 2010 (Ramírez, 2010, cited in Griffiths, 2013). This expansion has resulted in a nearly 200 percent increase from 1999 to 2009, from under 900,000 to over 2 million students (Ramírez, 2010, cited in Griffiths, 2013).

Griffiths explains the specific nature of the massification project:

A particular feature of the envisaged transformation is the intent to directly link higher education to the project of national endogenous development, under the banner of reconnecting universities to local communities, and to concrete social problems and their resolution, thus connecting theory with social practice. (Griffiths, 2013, p. 92)

The intending transformation, he points out, following Muhr (2010), seeks to build students' social and political consciousness in order to undertake work in the interests of the local community, the society, and the Bolivarian Republic (Griffiths, 2013, p. 92).

Griffiths and Williams (2009, p. 43) give the example of the UBV. Founded in 2003 as part of a major attempt to extend access to higher education, Universidad Boliviariana de Venezuela (UBV) is free to all students and 'seeks to fundamentally challenge the elitism of many of the traditional universities'. Social justice and equality are 'at the core of all educational content and delivery', and all courses taken there use Participatory Action Research (PAR) methodology, 'described as a multidisciplinary approach linking practice and theory'. PAR methodology bases UBV students in their local communities, working alongside a mentor on a community project, which is a core part of their formal studies (Griffiths and Williams, 2009). Griffiths and Williams (2009, p. 43) give the examples of 'Community Health students working with doctors within the *Barrio Adentro* health mission'; 'legal studies students establishing a community legal centre to advise and support families with civil law issues'; and education students working with a teacher/mentor in schools in their local community, thus empowering the students with the traditional knowledge of the communities, and thereby, empowering communities with the newly-found knowledge of the students.

All UBV students relate theory to their experiences in the project. As Griffiths and Williams (2009, pp. 43–44) explain,

> The approach is designed to place day-to-day decision-making and problem solving in the hands of local communities, as part of the broader societal reconstruction underway, with all participants gaining skills through the process. The intent is that the PAR methodology places researchers in positions of political leadership, but with the projects being democratically controlled and driven by the communities themselves and their own leaders, and aimed at realising the objectives of the community-based organisations.

Griffiths and Williams (2009, p. 44) conclude that while the discussions are interesting, what is most important is *who* is taking part in them. This is not only 'social and economic inclusion' but also *political* inclusion, with educational decision-making in the hands of staff, students, parents/carers, and *the community at large*. I had the privilege of teaching at UBV for a short while in 2006. The course I wrote and taught was titled Introduction to World Systems: Global Imperial Capitalism or International Socialist Equality: Issues and Implications for Education. Standards at UBV, I found, are very high – with seminar discussions and debates comparing more than favourably with universities in which I have taught in the UK and around the world. However, at UBV, as we have seen, advanced theory is very much linked to practice; that is, to improving the lives of people in the communities from where the students come. The students at UBV are almost 100% working class.

Just as with education in schools, in the realms of HE in general, there are serious shortcomings that need addressing. Griffiths (2013, p. 105), for example, cites 'the prevalence of passive, transmission pedagogical practices; top-down and highly centralised governance structures and practices including the appointment (rather than election) of university authorities'. He also refers to 'high levels of casualisation of the academic workforce; and extremely high attrition rates accompanying the expanded enrolments in some universities, caused partly by inadequate funding and resources to support these expanded numbers.'

Alternative education

There is much to learn from alternative schools. The creation of a parallel set of popular educational institutions may be viewed as a process of construction – as part of a longer-term process of anti-capitalist struggle, which can eventually serve as a model and help to free the official state schools from the stranglehold of the long-standing bureaucracy, created in part before the presidency of Chávez.

Myriam Anzola, formerly head of the Universidad Politecnica territorial del Estado Merida 'Kleber Ramirez' (UPTM), and currently the coordinator of the open studies programme at the university, defines Venezuela's alternative schools as,

> informal educative spaces that are guided by the national Bolivarian curriculum, but apply it with a more open and flexible methodology, without prerequisites or ranking students, and allowing them to advance at their own speed. (Anzola and Pearson, 2013, without page no.)

Anzola points out that there are 20 alternative schools in Mérida, the capital of Mérida state in western Venezuela, and one of the country's 23 states. Nestled in a valley formed between the Sierra Nevada de Mérida and the Sierra's Head, two of Venezuela's Andean mountain chains, the city has a population of about 330,000 people. Only seven of the alternative schools, created by the education ministry and the state government, are operating because the ministry has not maintained the necessary technical support. The schools represent a diverse range of projects, including 'an agro-ecological school that encourages children to study and learn within a conservationist and environmentally friendly dynamic'; a science school; a school for artistic development, which stimulates children through creative activity; and one that is 'centred around a project of interpretive systemology [a philosophical theory based on antireductionist thinking, centred around the work of Fuenmayor (1989)] and develops an interest in building meaning through reading.' There is also a school that has children with disabilities, and functions as an example of integration 'in order to increase the sensitivity of the school population towards differences' (Anzola and Pearson, 2013, without page no.).

Finally, there is the school in Barrio Pueblo Neuvo. The Alternative School of Community Organisation and Communicational Development 'promotes an awareness of community surroundings and develops means of social integration in the children' (Anzola and Pearson, 2013, without page no.).[5] Elsewhere Anzola has stated the reason for the other part of the of the school name:

> Since in the activities that they were doing there were many things that had to do with communication, and the radio is here, and also they like theatre, dance and other activities that had to do with communication, we thought we could call it the 'Alternative School for Communicational Development.' (Soundtrack to Fundación CAYAPA, 2011)

The school also encourages participatory democracy. Research conducted in the Alternative School of Community Organisation and Communicational Development on my behalf by Edward Ellis in 2010 revealed that the most important issues as identified by the teachers, known as 'cooperative educational facilitators', were the following: a) creating space: before the Chávez years the teachers would have been considered terrorists and would literally have been hunted down, according to Ellis. In the twenty-first century, socialist praxis socialism means creating a democratic space in the classroom and encouraging people to recognise oppression and overcome it; b) communal, cooperative, and democratic living and learning: no grading or completion, activities are planned and the children decide what they would like to work on; and c) socialism and the community: a dialectical relationship with the community in the barrio, so that the barrio inputs into the school and the school inputs into the barrio, hence by mutual inputs a synthesis is created that is greater than the respective inputs.

Although the experiences in each of the alternative schools are different, what they have in common is a break with routine study and a set curriculum. All pursue an 'environment of freedom and of active participation by the children in their own learning' and the development of school projects. They all prioritise capacities for thinking, rather than memorising and repeating content. This model of education promotes 'the creation of spaces where students are involved in their surrounding reality', which generates social consciousness (Anzola and Pearson, 2013, without page no.).

The schools practice the alternative pedagogy that Anzola defines as centring 'on the empowering of students within their socio-cultural context'. 'It allows them', she goes on, 'to develop their individual talents within a shared project that has a theme that interests all the participants and which responds to the idiosyncrasy of the locality' (Anzola and Pearson, 2013, without page no.).

Bolivarian education: some conclusions

One central message of the Bolivarian Revolution is that a fundamental counterhegemonic shift in the political economy toward socialism, including *universal* free access to education, with a high degree of equity in terms of opportunity and outcomes, can be achieved quite quickly (Griffiths and Williams, 2009, p. 34). As Griffiths and Williams conclude, the Bolivarian system consistently refers these aims back to the underlying project to promote the formation of new republicans with creative and transformational autonomy, with revolutionary ideas and with a positive attitude toward learning, in order to put into practice new and original solutions for the endogenous transformation of the country (Ministerio del Poder Popular Para la Educación 2007, p. 16, cited in Griffiths and Williams, 2009, pp. 42–43).

Another obvious message, as Griffiths (personal correspondence, 2013) points out, is that the expansion reinforces and further promotes the counterhegemonic view of education at all levels as being a human right (and obligation), thus contributing to heightened anticipations among the people. As he puts it, Bolivarian education 'has politicised people and has generated/awoken in the most marginalised a new sense of identity, power and expectation'.

It is sometimes claimed that the making of twenty-first century socialism in Venezuela, with oil reserves the highest in the world at 20% of the global total, is only possible because of this richness of oil. This is a fallacious argument. While oil has, of course, paid for the massive social reforms in that country, the longer term and *basic* issue is how wealth is distributed. As maverick UK *Respect* MP George Galloway has put it with characteristic panache – should he ever be prime minister,

> We would bring all our soldiers home from foreign wars – thus saving billions of pounds. We would scrap the renewal of Trident submarines. And we would pursue what [ConDem business secretary] Vince Cable said was the £100bn-a-year-plus tax avoidance and tax evasion industry. Thus, we'd have no deficit. If you do the maths, if we did those three things we not only would have no deficit, we'd be quids in. We'd be £80bn up. (cited in Aitkenhead, 2012)

This is not to endorse either Galloway or the *Respect* Party. Galloway stood on an anti-war and anti-*austerity* capitalism platform rather than an anti-capitalist or socialist one, when he won the Bradford West by-election by nearly 60% in 2012. Nonetheless, as a short-term solution to the current crisis in capitalism, such measures make sense in the global north, and clearly had credibility to the people of Bradford West.

Longer term, however, such actions would need to be accompanied by a massive distribution of wealth in favour of the working class, along with the implementation of participatory democracy and workers' control. At the time of writing (the run-up to the 2015 UK general election) such a scenario in the UK is in the hearts and minds of only a tiny minority of revolutionary socialists. Jean-Paul Sartre (1960) describes Marxism as a 'living philosophy' continually being adapted and adapting itself 'by means of thousands of new efforts'. To Sartre's observation, Crystal Bartolovich (2002, p. 20) adds, Marxism is not 'simply a discourse nor a body of (academic) knowledge' but a living project. As I have argued, twenty-first century socialism – in the making in the Bolivarian Republic of Venezuela should serve as an example that another world is possible, a world in which education serves the empowerment of the people rather than the hegemony of the ruling class. Thus, Bolivarian education is liberating both at the societal and the personal level.

Notes

1. The Washington Consensus was a set of ten policies formulated in 1989 by the US Government and international capitalist institutions based in the US capital, and encompassing the following:
   - Fiscal discipline – strict criteria for limiting budget deficits
   - Public expenditure priorities – moving them away from subsidies and administration towards previously neglected fields with high economic returns
   - Tax reform – broadening the tax base and cutting marginal tax rates
   - Financial liberalisation – interest rates should ideally be market-determined
   - Exchange rates – should be managed to induce rapid growth in non-traditional exports
   - Trade liberalisation
   - Increasing foreign direct investment (FDI) – by reducing barriers
   - Privatisation – state enterprises should be privatised
   - Deregulation – abolition of regulations that impede the entry of new firms or restrict competition (except in the areas of safety, environment and finance)
   - Secure intellectual property rights (IPR) – without excessive costs, and available to the informal sector
   - Reduced role for the state (World Health Organization, 2014).
2. Interpellation is the *process* by which the legitimation, values, and attitudes required by capitalism are instilled in the populace. Interpellation is the concept Althusser (1971, p. 174) used to describe the way in which ruling class ideology is upheld and the class consciousness of the working class – that class's awareness of its structural location in capitalist society, and how it is

undermined. Interpellation makes us think that ruling-class capitalist values are actually congruent with our values as *individuals*.
3. By reading texts such as Marx's *Capital*, one can become truly aware of the essentially exploitative nature of capitalism; see in particular, Marx's explanation of the Labour Theory of Value explained in Marx, 1887 [1965] (see Cole, 2011, pp. 42–44 for a summary).
4. This section is derived from Cole, 2014a, pp. 81–86.
5. For a full analysis, see Cole, 2014b. Also in Cole, 2014b is a discussion of further research conducted for me by Ellis in 2012; a 2013 interview with one of the teachers, Tamara Pearson, who is also a journalist for venezuelanalysis. com; and a commentary on the video (ADD REF) made by the children at the school in 2011.

References

Aitkenhead, D. (2012) 'George Galloway: "I believe that on judgment day, people have to answer for what they did"' *The Guardian* April 29. http://www. theguardian.com/politics/2012/apr/29/george-galloway-interview-bradford-west

Althusser, L. (1971) 'Ideology and Ideological State Apparatuses,' in *Lenin and Philosophy And Other Essays*, London: New Left Books. Available from: http://www.marx2mao.com/Other/LPOE70NB. https://www.marxists.org/reference/archive/althusser/1970/ideology.htm [Accessed July 30 2015]

Anzola, M. and Pearson, T. (2013 'Alternative Education Can Eliminate Corruption'. Available from: http://venezuelanalysis.com/analysis/9916 [Accessed July 30 2015].

Artz, L. (2012) 'Venezuela: Making a "state for revolution" – the example of community and public media', *Links international journal for socialist renewal*. Available from: http://links.org.au/node/2849. [Accessed July 30 2015].

Azzellini, D. (2013) 'The Communal State: Communal Councils, Communes, and Workplace Democracy, NACLA'. Available from: http://venezuelanalysis.com/analysis/9787. [Accessed July 30 2015].

Bartolovich, C. (2002) 'Introduction,' in C. Bartolovich and N. Lazarus (eds), *Marxism, Modernity and Postcolonial Studies*, Cambridge: Cambridge University Press.

Ciccariello-Maher, G. (2013) *We Created Chávez: A People's History of the Venezuelan Revolution*. Durham, NC, and London: Duke University Press.

Cole, M. (2011) *Racism and Education in the U.K. and the U.S.: Towards a Socialist Alternative*, New York and London: Palgrave Macmillan.

Cole, M. (2014a) The Bolivarian Republic of Venezuela: Education and Twenty-First-Century Socialism in Motta, S. C. and Cole, M. *Constructing Twenty-First-Century Socialism in Latin America The Role of Radical Education*, New York and London: Palgrave Macmillan.

Cole, M. (2014b) 'The Alternative School of Community Organization and Communicational Development, Barrio Pueblo Nuevo, Mérida, Venezuela' in Motta, S. C. and Cole, M. *Constructing Twenty-First-Century Socialism in Latin America: The Role of Radical Education*, New York and London: Palgrave Macmillan.

Dominguez, F. (2013). 'Education for the Creation of a New Venezuela,' in S. C. Motta and M. Cole (eds), *Education and Social Change in Latin America*. New York and London: Palgrave Macmillan, pp. 123–137.

Fuenmayor, R. (1989). *Interpretive Systemology: Its Theoretical and Practical Development in a University School of Systems in Venezuela*. Hull: Department of Management Systems and Sciences, University of Hull.

Fundación CAYAPA (2011). 'La Escuelita: (ENGLISH) The Alternative School of Barrio Pueblo Nuevo.' Mérida, Venezuela, Video, December. http://www.youtube.com/watch?v=mHG89aHxHIo [Accessed July 29, 2015]

Griffiths, T. G. and Williams, J. (2009). 'Mass Schooling for Socialist Transformation in Cuba and Venezuela,' *Journal for Critical Education Policy Studies*, 7(2), 30–50. http://www.jceps.com/index.php?pageID=article&articleID=160 [Accessed July 30 2015]

Hill, D. (ed.) (2013). *Immiseration Capitalism and Education: Austerity, Resistance and Revolt*, Brighton: Institute for Education Policy Studies.

Instituto Nacional de Estadística, (2011). Available from: http://www.ine.gov.ve/documentos/Boletines_Electronicos/Estadisticas_Sociales_y_Amb. [Accessed

Jessop, B. (1990) *State Theory: Putting the Capitalist State in Its Place*, Cambridge: Polity.

Maduro, N. (2014) 'Venezuela: A Call for Peace', *New York Times*. Available from: http://venezuelanalysis.com/analysis/10565.

Martinez, C., Fox, M. and Farrell, J. (2010). *Venezuela Speaks! Voices from the Grassroots*, Oakland, CA: PM Press.

Marx, K. (1887) [1965] *Capital Vol. 1*, Moscow: Progress Publishers.

MercoPress (2009) 'To School for Reading Classes with Karl Marx and Che Guevara', MercoPress, May 17. Available from: http://en.mercopress.com/2009/05/17/to-school-for-reading-classes-with-karl-marx-and-che-guevara. [Accessed July 30 2015].

Ministerio del Poder Popular Para la Educació n (2007). Currículo Nacional Bolivariano: Diseñ o Curricular del Sistema Educativa Bolivariano.'http://www.me.gov.ve/media.eventos/2007/d1_908_69.pdf

Motta, S. (2013) 'We Are the Ones We have Been Waiting For', The Feminization of Resistance in Venezuela, Latin American Perspectives, 40(4): 35–54.

Muhr, T. (2010). 'Counter-hegemonic Regionalism and Higher Education for All: Venezuela and the ALBA,' *Globalisation, Societies and Education*, 8 (1), 39–57.

Pearson, T. (2009) 'Venezuela Opens National Art Gallery and Launches National Reading Plan', Available from: http://venezuelanalysis.com. [Accessed July 30 2015]

Pearson, T. (2011) 'Venezuela's Dreams: Has the Bolivarian Revolution Changed Education?' Available from: http://venezuealanalysis.com/analysis/6072. [Accessed July 30 2015].

Pearson, T. (2012) 'Planning the Next 6 Years of Venezuela's Bolivarian Revolution'. Available from: http://venezuelanalysis.com/analysis/7091. [Accessed 6 July

Pearson, T. (2014) 'Demonising the "Colectivos": Demonising the Grassroots'. Available from: http://venezuelanalysis.com/analysis/10569. [Accessed April 2

Républica Bolivariana de Venezuela. (2007) 'Líneas generals del plan de desarrollo económico y social de la nación 2007–2013'. *Reforma de la Constitución*. http://www.cenditel.gob.ve/files/u1/linea

Riffiths, T. G. (2013). 'Higher Education for Socialism in Venezuela: Massification, Development and Transformation,' in T. G. Griffiths and Z. Millei (eds), *Logics of Socialist Education: Engaging with Crisis, Insecurity and Uncertainty*, Dordrecht: Springer.

Robertson, E. (2013) 'Venezuela: Workers Control Congress: Neither Capitalists Nor Bureaucrats, All Power to the Working Class', *Links International Journal of Socialist Renewal*. Available from: http://links.org.au/node/3415.

Sheehan, C. (2010) 'Transcript of Cindy Sheehan's Interview with Hugo Chavez'. Available from: http://venezuelanalysis.com/analysis/5233. [Accessed July 30 2015].

Socialist Outlook Editorial (2007) 'Chavez: "I also am a Trotskyist"', *Socialist Outlook*, 11 (Spring). Available from: http://www.isg-fi.org.uk/spip.php?article430.

The Embassy of the Bolivarian Republic of Venezuela in the UK and Ireland (2013). Available from: http://embavenez.co.uk/?q=content/62-venezuelas-2014-budget-allocated-social-investment.

Victor, M. P. (2009) 'From Conquistadores, Dictators and Multinationals to the Bolivarian Revolution, Keynote speech at the Conference on Land and Freedom, of The Caribbean Studies Program, University of Toronto, October 31. Available from: http://www.venezuelanalysis.com/analysis/4979. [Accessed July 30 2015].

Vulliamy, E. (2002) 'Venezuela Coup Linked to Bush Team', *The Observer*, Sunday, 21 April. Available from: http://www.theguardian.com/world/2002/apr/21/usa.venezuela. [Accessed July 30 2015].

World Health Organization (WHO) (2014) 'Washington Consensus' Available from: http://www.who.int/trade/glossary/story094/en/.

Index

ABJOVES Project, 147–8
Actor Network theory, 88, 98
adult education, 47
Agamben, G., 134–5, 142
agency, 99
agrarian reform, 182
algorithmic ideology, 70, 78
algorithms, 62, 66–70, 74
alienation, 21
alternative education, 207–8
anti-Semitism, 13, 23
Anzola, M., 207
Apple, M., 2
Arabs, 133, 135
arbitrary culture, 37, 38
Arendt, H., 1, 5, 13–24, 26
Aruguete, M. S., 158
Astell, M., 115
authority, 14, 17–18, 22, 24
    pedagogical, 31, 33–4
    school, 30–1, 36, 163
Auwarker, A. E., 158
average custodial sentence length
    (ACSL), 138
Ayrton, H., 114
Azzellini, D., 197

Ball, S., 65–6, 163–4
Barad, K., 89, 98, 99, 101, 102–5,
    119–20, 125
Barry, A., 78
Bartoli, M., 41
Bartolovich, C., 210
Beale, D., 115
Becker, Carol, 48
Beer, D., 69, 81, 82
Benn, T., 48
Bernstein, B., 2, 3
best practices, 1
bicultural education, 3
binary mathematics, 63
bio-power, 117
Bishop, R., 3

Black, Asian or Minority Ethnic
    (BAME) groups, 137–8
black feminists, 181–2
Blair, T., 170
Bohr, N., 119
Bolana, L., 188
Bolivarian Republic of Venezuela,
    194–210
Bolivarian Revolution, 5, 8
Bolshevik revolution, 44
Bonal, X., 159
Bourdieu, P., 2, 4, 5, 6, 26–39, 48, 88,
    163
Bowles, S., 1
boys, 7, 111, 114–18, 120
Bravo, D., 201
Brazil, 176
British National Party, 131
Brunkhorst, H., 16
bureaucracy, 19–20, 23
Burrows, R., 81, 82
Butin, D., 88
Butler, J., 117, 130–5, 137, 139, 140,
    142

Cambridge University, 114
Cameron, D., 75
capitalism, 46, 50, 53, 170, 181–2,
    188, 195
Cavendish, M., 115
CCTV cameras, 7
Changing Patterns of Power
    (Popkewitz), 4, 205
Chávez, H., 194–8, 201–2
Chomsky, N., 48
Ciccariello-Maher, G., 197, 201
citizen-as-researcher, 94–8
civil society, 43–4, 46–7, 83
closed circuit television cameras
    (CCTV), 128, 129, 140
Code Club, 71–2, 75, 77, 78, 80, 81
code.org, 75
coding, 6, 39, 53, 61–84

coercion, 1, 44, 47
Colatrella, S., 134
Colombia, 176, 188
Colombian Education Plan, 173
coloniality, 170–2, 178, 181–2
Columbine shooting, 129
commodification, 50
commodities, 50–1
common sense, 51, 170
communal councils, 198–9
communes, 199
computer code, *see* coding
computer science, 68
Computing at School, 73–4, 84
concealed power, 26–39
Connell, R. W., 118
consciousness, 28, 37–8, 45, 51, 53, 170, 179
consent, 47
consumer culture, 51
Conte, I. L., 182–3
context, 32, 33
co-production, 81–2
Cossa, J. A., 4
counter-terrorism discourses, 133, 135–9, 142
critical pedagogy, 3, 53, 54
Critical Race Theory (CRT), 130–4, 140–1
Croce, B., 47
Crow, B., 48
crowdsourcing, 81–2
cultural appropriation, 50
cultural capital, 52, 53, 159
cultural performance, 38, 39
cultural production, 49
cultural reproduction, 2
cultural workers, 49
Culture and Power in the Classroom (Darder), 3
Culture Counts (Bishop and Glynn), 3
culture of fear, 129
culture of poverty, 160
curricula, 49–54

Darder, A., 3
DARPA, 76
decolonial and black feminists, 181–2
Deleuze, G., 7, 124–5

De Lissovoy, N., 3
Derrida, J., 120
Design and Technology (D&T) workshop, 120–4
digital education, 63–4
disciplinary practices, 14, 160–1
discourse, 68, 69, 152–3
discursive practices, 103, 154–62
docile bodies, 137
doctoral training, 96–7
Dodge, M., 80, 82
dominant class, 28, 49
dominant culture, 32, 37, 49, 50
domination, 6, 27–37, 45, 50
Douglas, J., 135, 141
Durkheim, E., 27

early school leavers (ESL), 7, 146–65
    discursive practices regarding, 154–62
    family deficit and, 158–60
    lack of commitment and, 155–8
    policies to combat, 148–53
    psychologisation and pathologisation of, 160–2
economic power, 195
Educaçaodo Campo, 182–7
education
    see also schools
    access to, 114–15, 176
    adult, 47
    alternative, 207–8
    Arendt on, 5, 16–18
    authority and, 17–18
    bicultural, 3
    Bourdieu and Passerson on, 26–39
    commodification of, 2
    as concealed power, 26–39
    digital, 63–4
    domination and, 29–37
    early studies on, 1–5
    empowerment and, 5
    exclusion in, 21
    formal, 39, 182–7, 202–6
    gender and, 111–25
    higher. *see* higher education
    mass society in, 20, 21
    meaning of, 1
    philosophy of, 103

education – *continued*
  policies, 4, 83
  popular, 3
  power and, 13–24, 41–55, 88–9
  self-education, 195, 200–1
  as service, 4
  sociology of, 2, 3, 103, 185
  state control of, 5
  teacher, 4, 173–4, 178–9
  theory, 88–9
  in Venezuela, 200–10
Education Acts, 115
educational institutions, 31, 47, 95
  see also schools
educational system, 31, 35–6, 113
Education and Power (Apple), 2
educators, 21–2, 24, 47, 48, 49, 173
  see also teachers
emancipation, 5, 7, 37, 53–4, 94,
  169–91
empowerment, 3, 5, 7–8, 95, 201–2
Engels, F., 28, 45
engineering, 116–17, 124
Enguita, M., 147
Enterprise Communal Social Property
  (EPSC), 199–200
epistemological emancipation, 177–9
Estrategia de Gestión del Recurso
  Humano en Colombia (EGERH),
  172
ethics, 91–3
exclusion, 21, 124, 175
expertise, 6
experts, 49

factory councils, 6, 46
family deficit, 158–60
Farrokhzad, S., 3
femininity, 111, 117–18, 121–3
feminism, 117–25, 188
Feuerbach, B., 28
Fonseca, da C., 185–6
formal education, 39, 182–7, 202–6
Fortunato, G., 47–8
Foucault, M., 2, 6, 29, 50, 88–106,
  117, 118, 134, 137, 147, 152–7,
  160, 162–3
fraternal patriarchy, 112–14
Freire, P., 2, 52, 53–4, 178

Galloway, G., 209–10
Gay, G., 159
gender, 6–7, 111–25
General Agreement on Trade in
  Services (GATS), 4
general knowledge, 28
Gentile, G., 50, 52
geopolitics, 170–6
German ideology, 28
Gintis, H., 1
Giraldo, 176
girls, 7
  schooling for, 114–25
  self-policing by, 117–18
Giroux, H. A., 47, 48
globalisation, 4, 169, 170–6
Glynn, T., 3
good sense, 51, 170, 179
good vs. evil, 154
governmentality, 6, 90–8, 104, 134,
  142, 171
government of things, 99–102
grammar, 49
grammar schools, 114–15
Gramsci, A., 2, 5, 6, 41–55, 169, 170,
  179–83
Grass, G., 13
Greene, M., 20
Griffiths, T., 203, 205–6, 209
Gros, F., 92
Guattari, F., 7, 124–5
Guevara, C., 50

Habermas, J., 15–16
habitus, 29, 34, 35
hacker culture, 79–80
Halsey, A. H., 2
Harvey, L., 4
Hegel, G. W. F., 28
hegemony, 6, 44–7, 51, 53, 68,
  179–83
higher education
  policies, 4
  in Venezuela, 205–6
Hobbes, T., 14–15, 112–13
homo sacer, 134, 135, 139–42
Hour of Code, 75
Hughes, C., 118
human nature, 38

identities, 14, 132–3
ideology, 47, 52, 68, 69
illiteracy, 202
inclusion, 175
inculcation, 34
Index Ventures, 75–6
indigenous peoples, 3
individualisation, 164
inequalities, 38–9
infocentros, 202
informal movement pedagogies,
    187–91
informed citizenship, 71
institutional racism, 131
intellectuals, 47–9, 179–80, 182
Ives, P., 48

Junemann, C., 65–6

Karabel, J., 2
Kirschenbaum, M., 78
Kitchin, R., 80, 82
Klein, N., 48
Klein, S., 76
knowledge, 2
    creation, 119
    general, 28
    geopolitics of, 170–6
    imposition of, 3
    politics of, 177, 178–9
    as power, 195
    powerful, 53, 54
    production, 6, 162–3
    revolutionary, 180, 200–1
    social construction of, 4, 32,
        178
    special, 28
*Knowledge, Power, and Educational
    Reform* (Moore), 3
Knowledge and Control (Young), 2
knowledge economy, 6, 96–7, 104–5
knowledge workers, 97

labels, 20–1
labour market, 1
labour movement, in Venezuela, 200
Ladson-Billings, G., 131, 133
Laginder, A.-M., 3
La Máscara, 169, 187–91

Landless Rural Workers' Movement
    (MST), 169, 182–7
language, 49–50, 52, 53
Lash, S., 68–9, 79, 84
Latour, B., 88, 89, 98
Lawrence, P., 129
learning, content of, 49–54
learning citizen, 94–8
learning to code, 6, 39, 53, 61–84
legitimacy, 28–9, 32
Lemke, T., 89, 98–102
Levinson, 16, 20
liberation, 2, 37, 38
lifelong learning, 39, 94–8, 104
Light,, 172
Locke, J., 112–13
Lugones, M., 171
Lury, C., 118

Machiavelli, 42, 44, 100
Mackenzie, A., 78
Maduro, N., 195
Mager, A., 69–70
maker movement, 76, 81
Make Things Do Stuff, 72–5, 77, 78,
    80, 81
Mancebo, 176
Manovich, L., 62, 67, 81
Mansell, J., 178
Marchionne, S., 48
Marx, K., 28, 45
masculinity, 111, 117, 118, 124, 181
mass intellectuality, 201–2
mass society, 19, 20, 21
material feminism, 118–25
materialism, 89, 98–105
matter, 102–4, 119, 125
Mauger, G., 27
Mauss, M., 27
media, 47, 48
mental health diagnosis, 161–2
Middle Easterners, 133, 135
minorities, 137–8
modernity, 175, 181
Montaigne, M. De, 21
Moore, R., 3
Morozov, E., 76, 79
MST, *see* Landless Rural Workers'
    Movement (MST)

Murphy, P., 120
Muslims, 7, 131, 135, 137, 139–40, 142

natality, 14–17
Naughton, J., 70–1, 73, 76
Nazis, 134
neoliberalism, 2–3, 8, 88, 169, 170–6, 196
Neo-Nazis, 131
Nesta (National Endowment for Science, Technology and the Arts), 61, 63–6, 72, 73, 74, 77, 79, 81, 83
network governance, 65–6
new material feminism, 118–25
new materialism, 98–102
Next Gen, 74
9/11 attacks, 131
Nominet Trust, 61, 63–6, 72–5, 77, 79, 81, 83
norms/normalisation, 160–2
Novelli, M., 174

Olssen, M., 89
Open Marxism, 195
oppression, 27, 175
Organic Act for the Improvement of the Quality of Education (LOMCE), 148–53
organic intellectuals, 48–9, 179–80, 182
Oxford University, 114
Oztas, C., 131, 133

Panopticon, 137
Parsons, M. D., 4
Participatory Action Research (PAR), 205
Party of the Venezuelan Revolution (PRV), 201
Passerson, J.-C., 2, 4, 5, 6, 26–39, 163
Pateman, C., 111, 112–14
paternal patriarchy, 113–14
patriarchy, 111–25, 181, 188
Pearson, T., 204–5
pedagogic action, 31–3
pedagogical action, 36–8
pedagogical authority, 33–4

pedagogical practices, 7–8, 29, 169, 177
pedagogic authority, 31
pedagogic work, 31, 34–5
pedagogies, 6
    critical, 53, 54
    Freirean, 53–4
    informal movement, 187–91
    programming, 70–7
Pedagogy of the Oppressed (Freire), 2
photography, 139
Pinilla, 172
plurality, 19–23
policies, 4
    to combat early school leaving, 148–53
policy network analysis, 63–6
polis, 15–16, 18
political power, 195
political society, 43, 47
politics, 4, 177, 178–9
    of Bolivarian revolution, 196–200
Popkewitz, T. S., 4
popular culture, 37, 47, 51, 82
Popular Education, Power and Democracy (Laginder et al.), 3
popular education, 3
posthumanism, 99, 101
post-structuralism, 117–18
power
    Arendt on, 14–17
    Bourdieu and Passerson on, 26–39
    concealed, 26–39
    as concealed domination, 6
    as domination, 29–37
    early studies on, 1–5
    economic, 195
    education and, 13–24, 41–55, 88–9
    Foucault on, 6, 90–4, 99–105, 118, 152–3
    gender and, 111–25
    governmentality and, 90–4
    Gramsci on, 6, 42–5
    meaning of, 1
    oppressive, 27
    patriarchal, 112–14
    policy networks and, 63–6
    political, 195
    in public realm, 15–16

power – *continued*
  in schools, 13–14, 16–23
  social inequality and, 3, 4
  sociological debate on, 27–9
  symbolic, 30
  of teachers, 7
  truth and, 118
  in Venezuela, 194–210
  violence and, 5, 14–17, 22–4, 91
*Power, Crisis, an d Education for
    Liberation* (De Lissovoy), 3
power alienation, 21
Power and Ideology in Education
    (Karabel and Halsey), 2
Power and Politics (Parsons), 4
powerful knowledge, 53, 54
powerlessness, 20–1
power relations, 28, 30, 32, 33, 36–9,
    91, 96, 153, 162–3
programmers, 77–83
programming pedagogies, 70–7
programming power, 66–70
programming skills, 6, 39, 53, 61–84
proletarian culture, 49
prosumers, 77–83
public intellectuals, 47–8
public pedagogy, 47
public realm, 15–16, 18, 19
Purvis, J., 115

race
  Critical Race Theory, 130–4, 140–1
  surveillance and, 129–30, 135–9
  war on terror and, 131
racism, 131
Ragnedda, M., 129
rationality, 181
regimes of truth, 147, 148–53
regional identity, 51
regulation, 117
repression, 44–5, 47
research, 6, 88–106
resistance, 3, 90–1
responsibilisation, 155
Restrepo, P., 188–9, 190
revolution, 50
revolutionary knowledge, 180, 200–1
Revolutionary Reading Plan, 201–2
Rist, R., 154

Robertson, E., 4
Rose, N., 171
Rosen, L., 3
Rousseau, 112–13
Royal Society, 114
ruling class, 45
Rumberger, R., 147
Rushkoff, D., 71
Russian revolution, 44

Said, E., 48
Salzburg Principles and
    Recommendation, 96
Sartre, J.-P., 210
school authority, 30–1, 36, 163
schooling, 35–6, 39, 52
Schooling in Capitalist America
    (Bowles and Gintis), 1
school policies, 4
schools
  alternative, 207–8
  domination and, 29–37
  early school leavers, 7, 146–65
  gender and, 7, 114–25
  hostility in, 13
  power and, 13–14, 19–23
  power relations in, 28, 30, 32, 33,
    36–7, 38–9
  repression in, 44–5
  surveillance in, 7, 128–43
  teaching i n, 31–3
  violence in, 14, 18, 23–4
school shootings, 129
science education, 116–17, 124
science labs, 7
self-education, 195, 200–1
self-government, 95
Selwyn, N., 62
Silva, R., 75
Simons, M., 94–5
socia institutions, 113–14
social class, 154–5
social context, 32, 33
social contract theory, 112–14
social good, 83
social hierarchies, 6, 7, 26, 32, 34–9
social inequality, 3, 4, 6–7
socialism, 196–7
socialist state, 46

social media, 71, 81, 82, 84
social movements, 43–4, 169, 177
social norms, 160–1
social relations, 42, 45–6
societal change, 5, 7–8
socio-economic status, 154–5
sociology, 28
sociomaterialism, 88
software, 6, 53, 61–84
solutionism, 62, 79–80
South America
    social movements in, 169, 177
    Washington Consensus and, 196
sovereignty, 7, 100–1, 128, 134–5,
    143
Spain, early school leaving in,
    146–65
Spartacus League, 43
special knowledge, 28
spectatorship, 18
state
    capitalist, 46
    control of education by, 5, 47
state of exception, 134–5, 141–3
STEM subjects, 116–17
Stensaker, B., 4
stereotypes, 20–1
students
    as consumers, 174–5
    early school leavers, 146–65
    family deficit and, 158–60
    good vs. bad, 156–7, 163
    lack of commitment by, 155–8
    middle-class, 154, 159
    social class of, 154–5
    surveillance of, 7, 128–43
    teachers' expectations of, 154
subalterns, 48, 170
subjectification, 117–18, 174–5
subjectivity, 90–4, 96, 104
success, 175
surveillance, 128–43
    race and, 129–30, 135–9
    technologies, 7, 128–9, 138
    war on terror and, 128–30
symbolic power, 30
symbolic violence, 4, 6, 26–39
    critique of concept, 37–8
    domination and, 29–37

sociological debate on power and,
    27–9
systems thinking, 62

teacher education, 4, 173–4, 178–9
teachers, 38
    authority of, 22, 33–4, 36
    discursive practices of, 154–62
    expectations of, 154
    gendered discourses by, 116
    power of, 7
    role of, 173
    as transformative intellectuals, 3
teaching, 34–5, 52, 54
technology education, 116–17,
    120–3
territorialization, 7
terrorism, 128–30, 131, 136
theatre of the oppressed, 187–91
Thomas, K., 111
traditional intellectuals, 48
transformation, 47
trust, 19–23
truth, 93, 118, 147

UK National Curriculum, 6, 61, 73,
    75–6
unconsciousness, 29
university, 105
Uribe, A., 170, 172
user-centered design, 81

Venezuela, 194–210
    communal councils, 198–9
    communes, 199
    education in, 200–10
    politics, 196–200
    workplace democracy, 199–200
Venger, A., 4
violence
    power and, 5, 14–17, 22–4, 91
    in schools, 14, 18, 23–4
    symbolic, 4, 6, 26–39
war on terror, 7, 128–31, 134–5, 137,
    139–40, 142
Washington Consensus, 196
Weber, M., 1, 28–9, 33
white supremacy, 130–4, 139–42

Williams, J., 203, 205–6, 209
Williamson, B., 62
Wollstonecraft, Mary, 115
women's colleges, 114
working class, 46, 115
work of schooling, 31
workplace democracy, 199–200
worlding, 120

World Trade Organisation (WTO), 4

Year of Code, 75–6, 77, 78, 80
Youdell, D., 4
Young, M., 2, 23, 38, 49, 52, 53

Zinn, H., 48
Žižek, S., 48

Printed and bound in Great Britain by
CPI Group (UK) Ltd, Croydon, CR0 4YY